# The New York Times

## CLEVER CROSSWORDS

# The New York Times

## CLEVER CROSSWORDS
### 150 Easy to Hard Puzzles

Edited by Will Shortz

ST. MARTIN'S GRIFFIN NEW YORK

THE NEW YORK TIMES CLEVER CROSSWORDS.

Printed in the United States of America. For information,
address St. Martin's Press,
175 Fifth Avenue, New York, N.Y. 10010.

www.stmartins.com



ISBN 978-0-312-65425-2

10 9 8 7 6 5 4 3

# DIFFICULTY KEY

Easy:

Medium: 

Hard:   

# The New York Times

## CLEVER CROSSWORDS

RBAS? RHI?

# 1

## ACROSS

1 Smart ___ (wise guy)
5 Persian tongue
10 Roadies carry them
14 Sandwich spread
15 Sandwich spreads
16 Ark builder
17 Bakery fixture
18 Nickname for Andrew Jackson
20 Island east of Australia
22 Says hello to
23 Treasure chest
27 Trap
28 Mao ___-tung
31 The "R" in RCA
32 Shorebird
33 Depressed urban area
35 Former vice president Quayle
36 Word that can precede the starts of 18-, 20-, 53- and 58-Across
39 Smart ___ (wise guy)
42 Any member of a classic punk rock band
43 Morales of "La Bamba"
47 ___ New Guinea
49 Brian of Roxy Music
50 What the nose picks up
51 Pharaoh's realm
52 Dreary
53 Dangerous thing to be living on
58 First prize at a fair
61 Force felt on the earth, informally
62 Civil rights pioneer Parks
63 Cockpit occupant
64 Zippo
65 Aid and ___
66 Make ___ (do some business)
67 Carrier to Tel Aviv

## DOWN

1 Surrounded by
2 Shirley's friend in 1970s–'80s TV
3 Goggles and glasses
4 People's worries
5 Jesters
6 It means everyone to Hans
7 Comedian Foxx
8 TriBeCa neighbor
9 "Beauty ___ the eye . . ."
10 Turkey's capital
11 Neigh : horse :: ___ : cow
12 Number on a golf course
13 Wallflower-ish
19 Lemonlike fruit
21 Dined
24 Like 1, 3, 5, 7, etc.
25 By way of
26 Long stretch of time
28 Parts of a bride's attire, for this puzzle
29 ___ Hall Pirates (1953 N.I.T. champs)
30 Prefix with -centric
33 "Today" rival, for short
34 1-1 or 2-2, e.g.
37 Daniel Webster, for one
38 Opal or topaz
39 Gorilla
40 What mattresses do over time
41 007, for one
44 Original
45 Oakland's county
46 Law-breaking
48 Optimistic
50 Caesar whose forum was TV
52 Al ___ (cooked, yet firm)
54 Kelly of morning TV
55 Sluggers' figs.
56 Syllables before "di" or "da" in a Beatles song
57 Winter coat material
58 Push-up provider
59 High tennis shot
60 Have no ___ for

*by Steve Dobis*

# 2

## ACROSS

1 1996 candidate Dole
4 "10 ___ or less" (checkout line sign that grates on grammarians)
9 The real ___
14 When a plane is due in, for short
15 Nerve
16 [Crossing my fingers]
17 ___ center (community facility)
18 Unrealized gain on an investment
20 Suffix with cyclo- or Jumbo
22 Braga a k a the Brazilian Bombshell
23 "Bah, humbug!"
24 Merely suggest
26 SSW's opposite
28 Letters on an ambulance
29 Detective, in slang
32 Give up, as rights
34 Evergreen
36 Fancy
40 "That's ___ haven't heard!"
42 "Jaws" menace
43 Wished
44 Good luck charms
47 Charles Dickens pseudonym
48 Kuwaiti leader
49 Kettledrum
51 Buddy
53 Mesh
55 Facet
58 Guthrie with a guitar
60 Pat of "Wheel of Fortune"
63 Mountain lift
64 They measure the tonnage of trucks
67 Singer Yoko
68 W.W. II bomber ___ Gay
69 Outdo
70 Giant great Mel
71 Copenhageners, e.g.
72 Tending to ooze
73 Flattens in the ring, for short

## DOWN

1 Train sleeping spot
2 Former "S.N.L." comic Cheri
3 1676 Virginia uprising
4 Little devil
5 Woman presiding at a banquet
6 Giant fair
7 Appearance
8 Small finch
9 Former Russian space station
10 Take an ax to
11 Photo-filled reading matter in the living room
12 Poppy product
13 Reported Himalayan sightings
19 Cosmetic applied with a damp sponge
21 To the ___ degree
25 What to say to a doctor with a tongue depressor
27 Snakelike fish
30 Terse critiques
31 Path down to a mine
33 Talk over?
34 In favor of
35 Once ___ blue moon
37 Costing nothing, in Cologne
38 Wedding vow
39 ___ Percé tribe
41 Company called "Big Blue"
45 "Am ___ your way?"
46 Atlanta-based sta.
50 Well-put
51 Manhandled
52 Indoor game site
54 Tex-Mex sandwiches
56 Poetic chapter for Ezra Pound
57 Gaits between walks and canters
59 Look at amorously
61 Tarzan's woman
62 On the sheltered side
65 Contains
66 Word repeated in Mad magazine's "___ vs. ___"

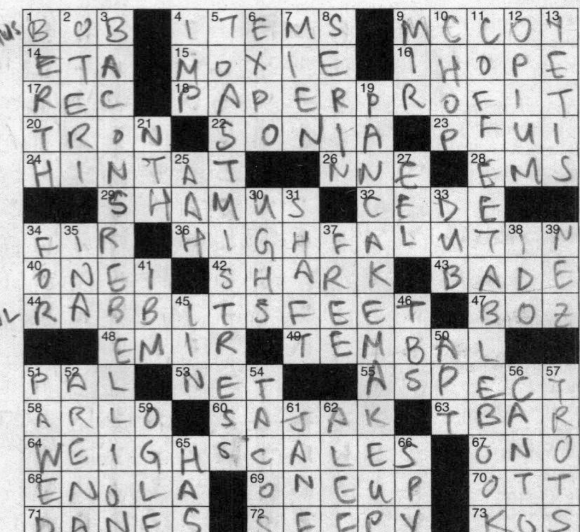

*by Brendan Emmett Quigley*

**ACROSS**

**1** Capitalized, as a noun
**7** Tapioca source
**14** Raw material for a steel factory
**15** Draws in
**16** Home of the U.S. Air Force Academy
**18** Adam and ___
**19** Chimney grime
**20** Fit ___ (be perfect on)
**21** State that was once a republic
**24** Letters after epsilons
**27** Vampire slayer of film and TV
**33** Brit's goodbye
**36** Nephews' counterparts
**37** Once around the track
**38** Service charge
**39** Santa ___ winds
**40** Stetson or sombrero
**41** Comes into play
**43** Writers of i.o.u.'s
**45** City in 21-Across
**48** Big name in video arcades
**49** Literature Nobelist William Butler ___
**53** Chester Arthur's middle name
**56** "Mad Money" network
**59** Slime
**60** Comedic inspiration for Robin Williams
**65** Leave high and dry
**66** Eroded
**67** Take another sip of
**68** Bread bakers' buys

**DOWN**

**1** Show to be true
**2** Watch with a flexible wristband
**3** John Lennon's middle name
**4** ___ favor (Spanish "please")
**5** Big slices of history
**6** Make over
**7** Social divisions in India
**8** Swiss peak
**9** Camera type, for short
**10** "I have no problem with that"
**11** River of Florence
**12** Bright northern star
**13** Aide: Abbr.
**14** Rapper/actor on "Law & Order: SVU"
**17** Seeping
**22** Honest ___ (presidential moniker)
**23** Overabundance
**25** Path for a mole
**26** In a cordial way
**28** Big Spanish celebration
**29** Enemy
**30** Sound heard in a canyon
**31** Front's opposite
**32** Old trans-Atlantic jets, for short
**33** Animal's nail
**34** Mata ___ (W.W. I spy)
**35** Of sweeping proportions
**39** Tooth doctors' org.
**42** Musical group with its own 1977–81 TV show
**44** Mao ___-tung
**46** Esoteric
**47** Huckleberry ___
**50** Representative
**51** Law school course
**52** Middling
**53** Not quite shut
**54** Ear part
**55** Sci. course for a doctor-to-be
**57** Street through Times Sq.
**58** Give as an example
**61** Six-point scores, for short
**62** Just off the grill
**63** Teachers' union, in brief
**64** "___ the season to be jolly"

*by Stanley Newman*

# 4

**ACROSS**

**1** Sank, as a putt
**6** What bird wings do
**10** Usually deleted e-mail
**14** Item stuffed with pimento
**15** Suffix with zillion
**16** Living ___ (what an employer is asked to pay)
**17** Two steeds?
**19** Pi r squared, for a circle
**20** Somewhat
**21** One signing with a landlord
**23** Groove
**24** Industrialist J. Paul ___
**25** Pants ending just below the knees
**29** Small whiskey glass
**32** Hang around for
**33** $$$
**34** Boat propeller
**37** "Cheers" barfly
**38** Isolated hill
**39** "___ cow!"
**40** In the style of
**41** Hearty enjoyment
**42** Small error
**43** Poor, depressed neighborhood
**45** Rodeo ropes
**46** Hank whose homerun record was surpassed by Barry Bonds
**48** ___ de toilette
**49** Intelligence
**51** Move to another country
**56** Cuts off, as branches
**57** Two water slides?
**59** Dull hurt
**60** Bug-eyed
**61** Sewing machine inventor Howe
**62** Like a buttinsky
**63** Deep-six
**64** Harking back to an earlier style

**DOWN**

**1** Arizona tribe
**2** "The Good Earth" heroine
**3** Italian currency before the euro
**4** Actresses Mendes and Longoria
**5** Point off, as for bad behavior
**6** In legend he sold his soul to the devil
**7** Queue
**8** The "A" in MoMA
**9** Cockroach or termite
**10** Al Jolson classic
**11** Two scout groups?
**12** Player's rep
**13** Full of substance
**18** Cross to bear
**22** Like omelets
**25** Biblical water-to-wine site
**26** Missing roll call, say
**27** Two charts?
**28** Salt's place on a margarita glass
**29** Word-guessing game
**30** Wild about
**31** "Wow, I didn't know that!"
**33** Event not to be missed
**35** "Not to mention . . ."
**36** Dark loaves
**38** "However . . ."
**39** Is afflicted with
**41** Mannerly guy
**42** Lopsided win, in slang
**44** Rocking toy, in tot-speak
**45** Of the flock
**46** Lion in "The Chronicles of Narnia"
**47** Oil company acquired by BP
**48** Online publications, briefly
**50** Small argument
**51** Greek Cupid
**52** Govern
**53** Going ___ tooth and nail
**54** Go like hell
**55** Old U.S. gas brand
**58** "Fourscore and seven years ___ . . ."

*by Fred Piscop*

# 5

**ACROSS**

**1** J.F.K.'s predecessor
**4** Thesaurus creator
**9** Roil, as the waters
**14** Film critic Reed
**15** Embarrass
**16** Licorice flavoring
**17** All around, as on a trip
**20** Common cold cause
**21** Spanish bulls
**22** Suffix with disk
**23** Young and feminine
**26** Money on a poker table
**29** "Hel-l-lp!"
**30** Dashing actor Flynn
**31** Ho-hum sort
**32** "Remember the ___!"
**33** Horse color
**35** TV show with many doors
**38** Last words of "Green Eggs and Ham"
**39** Get by logic
**40** "___ a fool to . . ."
**41** Passover meal
**42** Caboodle's partner
**45** Sleepless princess' bane
**46** Heat detector, e.g.
**48** Walk a hole in the carpet, maybe
**49** River of Arles
**51** Richard's partner in the Carpenters
**52** Move into first place in a race
**57** Pillowcase accompanier
**58** Celebrate boisterously
**59** Sense of self-importance
**60** Rice field
**61** Rascal
**62** Fellows

**DOWN**

**1** Herds
**2** Danny of "Throw Momma From the Train"
**3** Applies, as pressure
**4** Stadium cheers
**5** Kabuki sash
**6** Guy's date
**7** Night school subj.
**8** Buddy Holly's "___ Be the Day"
**9** "The Treasure of the Sierra ___"
**10** Reverse, as an action
**11** Scattering of an ethnic group
**12** Internet connection faster than dial-up
**13** "___-haw!" (cry of delight)
**18** Street, in Paris
**19** "There is ___ in 'team'"
**23** Former Texas senator Phil
**24** "___ la Douce"
**25** First-year players
**27** Pitcher Hershiser
**28** ___ Aviv
**30** "Born Free" lioness
**31** Title before Rabbit or Fox
**32** End in ___ (come out even)
**33** More secure
**34** German/Polish border river
**35** Stow, as cargo . . . or an anagram of the last word of 17-, 35- or 52-Across
**36** Started out (on), as a journey
**37** Prefix with skeleton
**38** Tiniest drink
**41** Contemptuous looks
**42** N.B.A.'s ___ Abdul-Jabbar
**43** Period of advancing glaciers
**44** Sinew
**46** Like Santa's suit after going through the chimney
**47** Letter holder: Abbr.
**48** Chum
**50** Follow, as advice
**51** Seaweed used as food
**52** Recipe amt.
**53** "That's brilliant!"
**54** ___ center (community facility)
**55** Energy inits. in the South
**56** Bottom line?

*by Andrea Carla Michaels*

# 6

## ACROSS

1 Wash very hard
6 "The racer's edge"
9 Chart anew
14 Hot love interest
15 ___-la-la
16 Former Mrs. Trump
17 Elvis Presley feature
19 Mamie Eisenhower feature
20 Tooth specialist's deg.
21 At the peak of maturity, as an apple
23 Shoulder muscle, informally
24 Author Ferber
25 Formidable opponents
27 Scads
30 Clad
32 Insolent
34 Tach readings
35 Drinker's road offense, for short
38 Fixed as a target . . . or a hint to four pairs of intersecting answers in this puzzle
42 Commercials
43 Appear to be
44 Its capital is Sana
45 Sugary drink
48 Apartment dweller's payment
49 Clothing
52 Move, in Realtor-speak
54 Opposite of freeze
55 Spanish devil
57 T in a fraternity
60 Willie Nelson feature
62 Betty Boop and Superman features
64 France's longest river
65 Asian New Year
66 Weapon in Clue
67 Step into
68 Grp. that opposed the Vietnam War
69 Not ___ (middling)

## DOWN

1 Dirty Harry's employer: Abbr.
2 Dirt clump
3 Ewes' mates
4 Caller of strikes and balls, for short
5 Abraham Lincoln feature
6 Pull into
7 T on a test
8 Cousins of carrots
9 Tease
10 Got around
11 Jon Bon Jovi and Tina Turner features
12 It's measured in degrees
13 They may be sordid
18 Actress Merrill
22 Contract provisions
24 Impress, as in the memory
26 Like a net
27 Part of Istanbul is in it
28 Real estate
29 What tagging a runner and catching a fly ball result in
31 Give a shellacking
33 "___ no?"
35 Coin with F.D.R.'s profile
36 Bird that perches with its tail erect
37 George Harrison's "___ It a Pity"
39 Surrendered
40 They see things as they are
41 Prefix with dynamic
45 Lampoon
46 Circles, as the earth
47 Throw things at
49 Mosey along
50 Juan of Argentina
51 Pippi Longstocking feature
53 Rapunzel feature
56 Parroted
57 Chi-town paper, with "the"
58 ___ Romeo
59 Preowned
61 Architect Mies van ___ Rohe
63 Game with Skip and Draw 2 cards

*by John Dunn*

# 7

## ACROSS

**1** Going for broke, as a poker player
**6** Goatee, for one
**11** Corp.'s head money person
**14** Sarge's superior
**15** ___-Detoo of "Star Wars"
**16** Flight board abbr.
**17** Campus/off-campus community, collectively
**19** Bone that's part of a "cage"
**20** iPhone downloads
**21** Composer Stravinsky
**22** Peru's peaks
**24** Majority Muslim in Iran
**26** Declaration that may be followed by "So sue me"
**27** Confederate flag
**31** Roasting rods
**34** Med. group
**35** Place for ChapStick
**36** Charged particle
**37** John Lennon's lady
**41** Environmentalist's prefix
**42** "Believe It or ___!"
**43** Daisy ___ of "Li'l Abner"
**44** Hat for a military specialist
**46** Extreme pessimism
**51** Job for a roadside assistance worker
**52** Tater Tots maker
**55** No longer vivid
**56** ___ bene
**58** Oompah band instrument
**60** Lincoln, the Rail-Splitter
**61** Damage from ordinary use
**64** ___ de France
**65** Where a wedding march ends
**66** River mouth feature
**67** Dem.'s foe
**68** Triangular road sign
**69** 1950s Ford flop

## DOWN

**1** Resort near Snowbird
**2** Figure skating figures
**3** Boast of some shampoos
**4** "No use arguing with me"
**5** PBS funder
**6** Nag to death
**7** As a result
**8** Suffix with origin
**9** Part of an airplane seat assignment
**10** Disney's ___ Duck
**11** Seller of coupes and sedans
**12** Chinese side dish
**13** Heavenly bodies
**18** Old-time actress Talbot or Naldi
**23** Penpoint
**25** Teeny, informally
**26** Listen ___ (hear via eavesdropping)
**28** Protected, as the feet
**29** "I love," in Latin
**30** Parking space
**31** Perform on "American Idol," e.g.
**32** Place to "rack 'em up"
**33** Unable to dig oneself out
**38** Muscat's land
**39** It's north of Okla.
**40** Melancholy instrument
**45** Sent out, as rays
**47** Fall behind financially
**48** Chicago alternative to O'Hare
**49** Senile sort
**50** Algerian port
**53** Face-offs with guns or swords
**54** Lessen
**55** Without a cloud in the sky
**56** ___ the Great of children's literature
**57** Grueling grilling
**59** Asia's shrunken ___ Sea
**62** "The Book of ___" (2010 film)
**63** Ike's monogram

*by Nancy Salomon*

# 8

**ACROSS**

**1** As a result
**5** Handed (out)
**10** Furry creature allied with Luke Skywalker and the Jedi knights
**14** ___ of students
**15** Deadly virus
**16** Caster of spells
**17** "My deepest apologies"
**20** They go into overtime
**21** Coffee orders with foamy tops
**22** Actress Gardner and others
**23** Deceptive talk, in slang
**24** Soup ingredient from a pod
**27** Worker's pay
**28** Car navigational aid, for short
**31** Had home cooking
**32** Place for the words "Miss USA"
**33** Margarita garnish
**34** "No idea"
**37** Actor's pursuit
**38** Elvis ___ Presley
**39** Emmy category
**40** Opposite of NNW
**41** Federal agent investigating taxes, informally
**42** Pop maker in a nursery rhyme
**43** Witches' ___
**44** Sound gravelly
**45** Nixed by Nixon, e.g.
**48** Diversions . . . as hinted at by the ends of 17-, 34- and 52-Across
**52** "Let's take that gamble"
**54** And others: Abbr.
**55** "Live Free ___" (New Hampshire motto)
**56** Quadri- times two
**57** "Star ___," biggest movie of 1977
**58** Mexican dollars
**59** Having everything in its place

**DOWN**

**1** Cut and paste, say
**2** Notes after do
**3** Golden ___ Bridge
**4** So-called universal donor blood
**5** Skin-related
**6** Theater awards
**7** Arcing shots
**8** 90-degree turn
**9** Vampire's undoing
**10** Act with great feeling
**11** Witch's blemish
**12** Meanie
**13** Frequently misplaced items
**18** Large gully
**19** Put money in the bank
**23** Golden Fleece pursuer
**24** Hideouts
**25** Set of guiding beliefs
**26** Author Zora ___ Hurston
**27** Car with a big carrying capacity, informally
**28** Lavish parties
**29** Feather in one's cap
**30** Super bargain
**32** Scarecrow stuffing
**33** Recycled metal
**35** Try to impress in a conversation, say
**36** "___ Fideles"
**41** BlackBerry rival
**42** Bathes
**43** Plays tenpins
**44** 3:5, e.g.
**45** It's afforded by a scenic overlook
**46** Jazzy James
**47** Peter the Great, for one
**48** Highest degrees
**49** They're often double-clicked
**50** "Cómo ___ usted?"
**51** 32-card game
**53** III in modern Rome

*by Ian Livengood*

## ACROSS

1 Noisy bird
6 "___ the night before . . ."
10 Exhilaration
14 Ninth planet no more
15 Days of King Arthur's Round Table, e.g.
16 Any brother in "Animal Crackers"
17 Broadway lyricist/composer who wrote "I Can Get It for You Wholesale"
19 Amo, amas, ___
20 Opposite of melted
21 Make ___ for (advocate)
22 California wine county
26 Whoop
28 Buddhist sect
29 Gas log fuel
31 Certify (to)
33 Virginia-born Pulitzer Prize novelist of 1942
36 Actress Cannon
37 Three ___ match
38 "Anybody home? . . . home? . . . home? . . ."
42 "God Bless America" composer
47 Drink that might come with a mint leaf
50 Japanese site of the 1972 Winter Olympics
51 Lon ___ of Cambodia
52 Greek portico
55 "You said it, ___!"
56 Elite roster
58 Cook, as steaks in an oven
60 Indy 500, e.g.
61 "The Call of the Wild" author
66 Chief Norse god
67 The "A" in U.S.A.: Abbr.
68 Seeing Eye dog, e.g.
69 Light bulb unit
70 Nothing, in Juárez
71 Pegasus, e.g.

## DOWN

1 Speedometer reading: Abbr.
2 ___ carte
3 Dog prone to biting
4 From ___ Z
5 One who changes form during a full moon
6 Beginner
7 Mentally unclear
8 French military force
9 Go out with
10 Auto financing inits.
11 Childbirth training method
12 Undoes pencil marks
13 Scope
18 Sturm und ___
21 Kind of sax
22 Hurried
23 Paris suburb
24 Theme song of bandleader Vincent Lopez
25 Gift-giver's urging
27 Fall behind
30 "The Time Machine" people
32 Dweebs
34 The Beach Boys' "Barbara ___"
35 Is low around the waist, as pants
39 Blood circulation problem
40 Put on the payroll
41 ___ off (light switch options)
43 Remainder
44 Industrial container
45 Pesto seasoning
46 Ends of some novels
47 Lined up
48 Piña ___
49 Bring out
53 First president born in Hawaii
54 Followed a curved path
57 E-mail folder
59 Gumbo pod
61 First mo.
62 Hickory ___
63 What immortals never do
64 Shelley's "___ to the West Wind"
65 ___ Flanders of "The Simpsons"

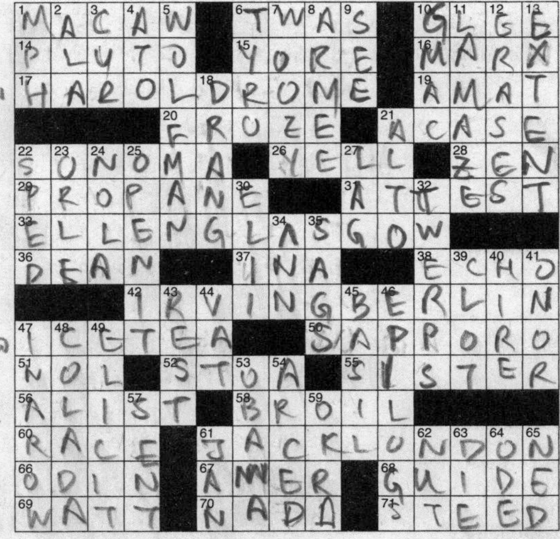

by Randy Sowell

# 10

## ACROSS

1 Navajo's neighbor in Arizona
5 Edinburg native
9 Defect
13 Racetrack shapes
15 Many millennia
16 Parks who received the Presidential Medal of Freedom
17 Tendon
18 Common advice to travelers
20 Terminus
21 Seed with a licoricelike flavor
23 Beginning
24 Race that finishes in a tie
26 Warm embrace
27 Worms, to a fisherman
28 Early Fords that "put America on wheels"
32 Say "C-A-T" or "D-O-G," e.g.
34 Boathouse gear
36 "___ don't say!"
37 Doing something risky . . . or a hint to the last words of 18-, 24-, 49- and 58- Across
41 Avis or Alamo offering
42 Misfortunes
43 Uncles' mates
44 Being risked, as in a bet
47 Cassini of fashion
48 Cubes from the freezer
49 Bygone love interest
53 Digging tool
56 Weak-___ (easily intimidated)
57 Candlemaking supply
58 "Omigosh!"
60 Oven brand
62 Language of Pakistan
63 What Yale became in 1969
64 Hayseed
65 Vault (over)
66 "The ___ the limit"
67 Crème de la crème

## DOWN

1 Cleaned with water, as a sidewalk
2 Sheeplike
3 Adorable zoo critters from China
4 Suffix with percent
5 Tone of many old photos
6 Where a hurricane makes landfall
7 ___ in a blue moon
8 "For shame!"
9 Outer edge
10 Hearth contents
11 U.S. tennis legend on a 37¢ stamp
12 The "W" of kWh
14 Widespread language of East Africa
19 Earsplitting
22 Ping-Pong table divider
25 Tyne of "Cagney & Lacey"
26 Party giver
28 CT scan alternatives
29 Suffering from insomnia
30 Wrong that's adjudicated in court
31 Takes to court
32 Org. for cat and dog lovers
33 Builder's map
34 Look at lustfully
35 Hole-making tool
38 Athletics brand with a swoosh
39 9:00 a.m. to 12:30 p.m., say, for a worker
40 Gasoline or peat
45 Neaten
46 Unreturned tennis serves
47 Keats's "___ to Psyche"
49 Not sharp or flat
50 Textile city of north-central England
51 Grooms comb them
52 Praise mightily
53 Place for a bar mitzvah service
54 Skin opening
55 Alan of "M*A*S*H"
56 Nutcase
59 Introducers of a show's acts, e.g.
61 "The Godfather" crowd, with "the"

by Lynn Lempel

# 11

**ACROSS**

**1** Vision that isn't real
**6** Areas of urban decay
**11** Country singer Ritter
**14** Ahead of time
**15** Vietnam's capital
**16** Vietnam ___
**17** A-team
**19** Provision for old age, in brief
**20** Footballers' measures: Abbr.
**21** Pay attention to
**22** Excellent, in slang
**24** Abruptly dump, as a lover
**25** Curly-haired dogs
**26** Composer's work for a film
**30** Caribbean resort island
**31** "Sesame Street" airer
**32** Realtor's favorite sign
**36** Five-digit postal number, informally
**37** Slow-moving primates
**41** ___ de Janeiro
**42** Canadian gas brand
**44** Former Mideast inits.
**45** "Come on!" and "Go!"
**47** Portuguese, for Brazilians, e.g.
**51** Waltz composer
**54** Love god
**55** Fireplace floor
**56** Spew
**57** Drunk's road offense, for short
**60** "Star Trek" rank: Abbr.
**61** Really steamed . . . or what the ends of 17-, 26- and 47-Across are?
**64** Conk
**65** Map close-up
**66** "Boléro" composer
**67** "___ questions?"
**68** Show just a little bit of leg, say
**69** Winding

**DOWN**

**1** Go against, as someone's will
**2** Antibug spray
**3** Makes a boo-boo
**4** Gore and Green
**5** Like dragons and centaurs
**6** Yiddish for "small town"
**7** Cooking fat
**8** Prefix with cycle
**9** Kipling's Rikki-Tikki-Tavi, for one
**10** Milan mister
**11** Band majorette's move
**12** Country star Steve
**13** Pictures at a dentist's
**18** Actress Ward
**23** Fruity drinks
**24** Triangular sail
**25** Banned pollutants, briefly
**26** Labyrinth
**27** Literary Leon
**28** Dines
**29** Church feature seen from a distance
**33** Not a copy: Abbr.
**34** In ___ of (replacing)
**35** One teaspoonful or two caplets, maybe
**38** Surpass
**39** Stadium cheers
**40** Relatives of mopeds
**43** "The Rubáiyát" poet ___ Khayyám
**46** E.R. or O.R. workers
**48** Barbie doll purchase
**49** What a couch potato probably holds
**50** Oakland paper, informally
**51** Biblical queendom
**52** It's inserted in a mortise
**53** Hoarse
**56** Hot times on the Riviera
**57** One who might receive roses at the end of a performance
**58** Timespan for The Economist
**59** How thumbs are twiddled
**62** Airport worker's org.
**63** Light brown

*by Susan Gelfand*

# 12

## ACROSS

**1** 2006 boorish film character from Kazakhstan
**6** Castle-defending ditches
**11** David Letterman's network
**14** Smells
**15** Suffer ignominious defeat, in slang
**16** Feedbag tidbit
**17** Second- or third-string player
**19** Actress Hagen
**20** Cyclotron particles
**21** Interest-grabbing
**23** "Apologies"
**27** "As old as the hills" and others
**28** What wheels do on an axis
**29** Talk to flirtatiously
**30** Screwballs
**31** "God ___ America"
**32** Photo ___ (when pictures may be taken)
**35** Son of Seth
**36** Audio censor's sound
**37** Molecule component
**38** Broadband connection inits.
**39** Lewis's partner in an expedition
**40** Stiller and ___ (comedy duo)
**41** One-horse town
**43** Explorer Hernando
**44** One showing diners to their tables
**46** Indian baby on a back
**47** Spider's cocoon, e.g.
**48** Suspect, to a cop
**49** "Norma ___"
**50** Presider at a meeting
**56** Stock debut, for short
**57** Newsstand
**58** Decorative fabric
**59** Highest non-face card
**60** Spread, as the legs
**61** Assail

## DOWN

**1** Dylan or Dole
**2** Praiseful poem
**3** Director Howard
**4** Lob's path
**5** Gift shop apparel
**6** George who was the first president of the A.F.L.-C.I.O.
**7** Items fitting in rowlocks
**8** Place to enter a PIN
**9** Man's jewelry item
**10** Narrow passageways
**11** Boob tube lover
**12** Wash oneself
**13** Remains
**18** Had on
**22** Fort Worth sch.
**23** Annoyed
**24** Time periods lasting about 29 1/2 days
**25** Police informant
**26** Acorn producers
**27** Where rouge goes
**29** Office worker
**31** Lacking individuality
**33** Skin openings
**34** Some air pollution
**36** Kind of stock
**37** Prefix with dynamic
**39** Music store fixtures
**40** Tots
**42** Tie-breaking play periods: Abbr.
**43** Complain
**44** ___ badge
**45** Open-mouthed
**46** Cheerful
**48** Leaning Tower site
**51** Yahoo! competitor
**52** ___ v. Wade
**53** Use the start of 17- or 50-Across or 11- or 25-Down?
**54** Suffix with schnozz
**55** What 51-Down connects to, with "the"

*by Randy Sowell*

## ACROSS

**1** Mount ___, Ten Commandments locale
**6** Normandy invasion town
**10** Sweat opening
**14** Writer Nin
**15** Cupid
**16** Genesis son
**17** Antiterrorism legislation of 2001
**19** Gun blast
**20** Proverbial saver of nine, with "a"
**22** Snake or alligator
**25** Playful knuckle-rub
**26** Eggs ___ easy
**27** Suck-up
**30** Pants part
**31** Kentucky's ___ College
**33** Try to strike
**35** "My Cousin Vinny" Oscar winner
**39** Word with Asia or Ursa
**40** Ultimately become
**43** Necessity: Abbr.
**46** "Keep it simple, ___"
**49** Earthen pot
**50** Bet on a one-two finish
**52** Dreamlike
**54** Classic battles between the Giants and Dodgers, e.g.
**57** "Beetle Bailey" bulldog
**58** 1986 world champion American figure skater
**62** Pants part
**63** "The Last Tycoon" director Kazan
**64** "I was at a movie theater when it happened," e.g.
**65** Highlands Gaelic
**66** What gears do
**67** Tyson or Holyfield

## DOWN

**1** Maple syrup source
**2** Bull ___ china shop
**3** Turner who led a revolt
**4** Wind tunnel wind
**5** "Lord, ___?" (Last Supper query)
**6** Certain sofa
**7** ___ II razor
**8** ___ Ness monster
**9** Recurring melodic phrase
**10** Green Italian sauce
**11** Like angels we have heard?
**12** Dormmate
**13** Think the world of
**18** Greasy
**21** Unbranded
**22** Steal from
**23** December 24, e.g.
**24** Salon job
**28** On the ball or on the dot
**29** Sch. in Cambridge, Mass.
**32** Record label for the Kinks and the Grateful Dead
**34** Pavarotti performance
**36** Working together
**37** Trivial amount
**38** Not doing anything
**41** Diminutive suffix
**42** Buddy
**43** Tranquillity
**44** New Hampshire prep school
**45** Airline with a kangaroo logo
**47** Book after Song of Solomon
**48** It'll bring a tear to your eye
**51** Equivalent of 10 sawbucks
**53** Place to "dry out"
**55** The "T" of TV
**56** Diamond stats
**59** Blend
**60** President Lincoln
**61** Madam's partner

*by Bob Klahn*

## 14

### ACROSS

1 New ___, India
6 Massachusetts vacation spot, with "the"
10 "Yeah, sure!"
14 Like the outfield walls at Wrigley Field
15 Downwind, to a sailor
16 Musical finale
17 Red Sox stadium
19 Frozen waffle brand
20 Actor Omar
21 Precious Chinese carvings
22 Look through the cross hairs
25 ". . . ___ quit!"
26 Alpha's opposite
28 New York City's ___ Island
30 Makes believe
33 Peels, as an apple
34 Copper/zinc alloy
35 Cockney's residence
36 "Anything ___?"
37 "To Autumn" poet
38 Roman poet who wrote the "Metamorphoses"
39 Fed. biomedical research agency
40 "O Come, ___ Faithful"
41 Packing string
42 Watergate and Irangate
44 Bitterness
45 Everest or Kilimanjaro
46 Diving seabird
47 College credit units: Abbr.
48 Classic Alan Ladd western
50 Lacking any guarantee of being paid
53 Score the 3 in a 4-3 game
54 Seaside community NE of Boston
58 Natural balm
59 Actress Rowlands
60 House of Henry VII and Henry VIII
61 Fairy's stick
62 Stepped (on)
63 "Tosca" or "Thaïs"

### DOWN

1 "What's the ___?" ("So what?")
2 Holiday preceder
3 China's ___ Yutang
4 Cuts with an ax
5 Potatoes from the Northwest
6 Blue Grotto's island
7 Jai ___
8 Make holes in, as for ease of tearing
9 Hair-raising cry
10 Period ending about 9000 B.C.
11 Peter who directed "The Last Picture Show"
12 Periphery
13 New Mexico city or county
18 A knitter might have a ball with it
21 "Cool your ___!"
22 Forest quakers
23 Like right-slanting type
24 "The Goodbye Girl" actress
27 Cafeteria, to a soldier
29 Football kicker's aid
30 Says grace, e.g.
31 Key of Beethoven's Ninth
32 Passover meals
34 Carillon site
37 Group investigated in "Mississippi Burning"
38 Have title to
40 Together, in music
41 Likes immediately
43 "Thanks, but I'm O.K."
44 Coach Adolph in the Basketball Hall of Fame
46 Comparable to a wet hen?
48 Picnic side dish
49 Spanish greeting
51 One billionth: Prefix
52 Medium bra size
54 "___ Pepper's Lonely Hearts Club Band"
55 "To Autumn," e.g.
56 Rocky peak
57 ___ la la

*by Ed Early*

## ACROSS

**1** C.S.A. soldier
**4** Unconscious states
**9** Sounds of bells or laughter
**14** Grp. putting on shows for the troops
**15** Journalist ___ Rogers St. Johns
**16** Whodunit award
**17** Rev. ___ (Bible ver.)
**18** Like "Have a nice day"
**19** Denizens of 45-Down
**20** 1934 title role for Ginger Rogers
**23** 8 1/2" × 14" paper size
**24** "Yes, madame"
**25** With 56-Across, Saint of Hollywood
**27** The Depression and the Cold War, for two
**28** "This is only ___"
**31** Bank acct. guarantor
**32** "That's one small step for ___ . . ."
**33** Candidate lists
**35** 1934 title role for Jeanette MacDonald
**39** Emperor killed on the Ides of March
**40** Fail to include
**41** "Darn," more formally
**42** Imam's faith
**44** Bills and coins
**48** Nonvegetarian sandwich, for short
**49** Biol. or chem.
**50** Slow, in music
**51** 1975 title role for Lynn Redgrave
**56** See 25-Across
**57** Base-clearing hit
**58** Urban address abbr.
**59** Uniquely
**60** "Sesame Street" grouch
**61** Brazilian hot spot
**62** Stinky stream
**63** Writer Zora ___ Hurston
**64** New England's Cape ___

## DOWN

**1** What leaves do in the wind
**2** Purim heroine
**3** Barrio grocery
**4** Plotters' plot
**5** Jazzy Anita
**6** Darn
**7** Jai ___
**8** Series of shots, as from warships
**9** Lab's ___ dish
**10** The "E" of N.E.A.: Abbr.
**11** Accepted, as terms
**12** Placid vacation vista
**13** Soon-to-be grads: Abbr.
**21** Phase hotter than liquid
**22** Defeat by a stroke?
**26** Window units, briefly
**28** Song that begins "My country, 'tis of thee"
**29** Part of a cigarette rating
**30** Sign up
**31** Furbys or yo-yos, once
**32** Doc grp.
**34** On fire
**35** Sailor's yarn
**36** Charles de Gaulle : Paris :: ___ : London
**37** Twisty curve
**38** Singer Sumac
**39** What a hack drives
**43** Drain furtively, maybe
**44** Corp. biggie
**45** Capital ESE of Istanbul
**46** Enter
**47** Dr. Seuss elephant
**49** Like pantyhose
**50** Peter of "M"
**52** "___ kleine Nachtmusik"
**53** Ask, as questions
**54** Gym locale, for short
**55** Get better
**56** "No ___!" ("Stop!," in Spanish)

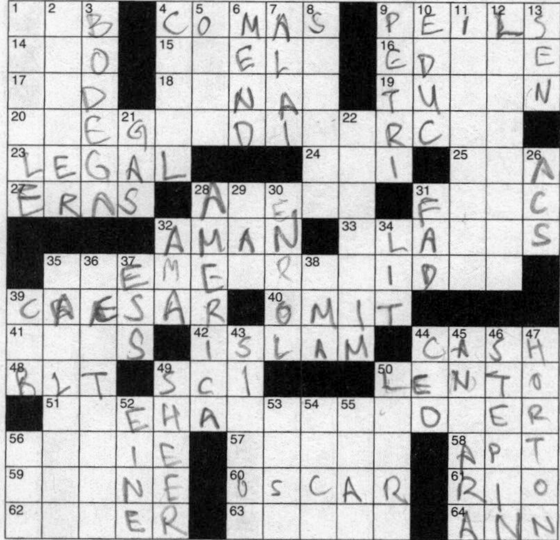

by Gilbert H. Ludwig

# 16

## ACROSS

**1** With 21-Across, begin from scratch
**6** Heart of the matter
**10** Hair untangler
**14** Tithing portion
**15** Great Lake touching four states
**16** Cry to a matey
**17** Zealous
**18** Tailless cat
**19** Emulate a mob
**20** WNW's opposite
**21** See 1-Across
**24** Hot dog topping
**26** Number of a magazine
**27** Where to store a lawn mower
**29** Entirely
**33** Christmas ___ (holiday stamp)
**36** Woodsy
**40** Coffee, in slang
**41** Move into the limelight
**44** "___ was saying . . ."
**45** Once did
**46** Givers and receivers of alimony
**47** Element of a doctrine
**49** Sign from above
**51** Recreation center posting
**55** "Really!"
**59** With 73-Across, be beaten by the rest of the field
**63** Dump cleanup grp.
**64** Gunk
**65** It's "catchy"
**66** Lets or sublets
**68** Fail to mention
**69** Something to whistle
**70** Peeved, after "in"
**71** 7–6, 2–6, 6–4, e.g.
**72** ___-specific (like the answers at 1-, 41- and 73-Across)
**73** See 59-Across

## DOWN

**1** Have the wheel of a car
**2** Tempt
**3** Extremely well-behaved child
**4** 66 on a map, e.g.: Abbr.
**5** Defeat soundly
**6** Onyx and opal
**7** Baghdad native
**8** Nasal congestion locale
**9** Sam Houston served as its president, senator and governor
**10** Lurch from side to side
**11** One of the states touched by 15-Across
**12** Apollo 11 destination
**13** Computer unit
**22** Dissertations
**23** Aztec or Mayan cities, today
**25** ___ of Wight
**28** Unit of force
**30** Cleanser whose name comes from Greek myth
**31** High-priced seating area
**32** Performers Peggy and Pinky
**33** Goals or assists
**34** Simplicity
**35** Related (to)
**37** Bygone Ford
**38** Nix, presidentially
**39** Kitchen emanations
**42** Such a jokester
**43** Be inclined (to)
**48** Totally loses one's cool
**50** Nab in a sting operation
**52** Tilts
**53** Ho-hum feeling
**54** Tilt
**56** Dye in temporary tattoos
**57** ___ nerve
**58** Fritter away
**59** What modest people lack
**60** City south of the Bering Land Bridge National Preserve
**61** "Go ahead!"
**62** Writer James
**67** Course for a future U.S. citizen, maybe: Abbr.

*by Roger Baiocchi*

## ACROSS

**1** Christmas drink
**4** Little bit, as of color
**7** ___ de plume
**10** T.L.C. giver
**13** 1945 battle site with a flag-raising
**15** Like waves on a shore
**17** One offering kudos
**18** Mountain climbers' tools
**19** Books for jotting down appointments
**21** Lendee's note
**22** Pretentious
**23** Hospital imaging devices
**31** Author Wharton
**32** Not rot
**33** Hip-hop greetings
**36** Cruise around the Web
**39** Award won by Roger Clemens seven times
**41** General on Chinese menus
**42** Word before ring or swing
**44** Miniature hooter
**45** Burping and slurping in public
**48** Moments, in brief
**52** ___ Lingus
**53** Places for antiwar slogans
**61** Case for an otologist
**62** Say "Sure, why not?"
**64** Invites to a movie, say
**65** Ralph who wrote "Invisible Man"
**66** Florida island
**67** Opposite of SSW
**68** Nutritional stat.
**69** ___ Dhabi, Persian Gulf port

## DOWN

**1** Biomedical research org.
**2** "Man, that hurts!"
**3** All used up
**4** Dagger
**5** Earhart who was the first aviatrix to fly solo across the Atlantic
**6** Subatomic particle made of three quarks
**7** Young of Crosby, Stills, Nash & Young
**8** Killer whale
**9** Big name in faucets
**10** The 7-Up in a 7 and 7
**11** Conspicuous
**12** Like dorm rooms, often
**14** Quarterback Namath
**16** Yemen's capital
**20** The Sex Pistols' genre
**23** ¢
**24** Juice drinks
**25** Marshal ___, Yugoslavian hero
**26** Ave. crossers
**27** ___ change
**28** The Common Market: Abbr.
**29** Playa del ___, Calif.
**30** Watch through binoculars, say
**33** Christmas
**34** Lollapalooza
**35** Bilko and Pepper: Abbr.
**37** A. A. Milne baby
**38** Rock's ___ Fighters
**40** Have the rights to
**43** Lacking color
**46** Scanty
**47** Gov. Schwarzenegger
**48** Command to Fido
**49** Wipe out
**50** Like the taste of some bad wine
**51** Subway stops: Abbr.
**54** Supply-and-demand subj.
**55** Ostracize
**56** French bean?
**57** "The Lion King" daughter
**58** Priest who raised Samuel
**59** Sub ___ (secretly)
**60** One looking down on the "little people"
**63** Wildebeest

*by Oliver Hill*

# 18

**ACROSS**

**1** Feeling bloated
**6** Eyeliner boo-boo
**11** "Don't tase me, ___!"
**14** Make amends (for)
**15** Bizarre
**16** Experiment site
**17** Psychologically manipulated
**19** I
**20** Lawman Wyatt
**21** "The Andy Griffith Show" boy
**22** Cowboy's greeting
**24** End of a student's e-mail address
**26** Town shouters
**28** Place to play twenty-one
**31** Jewish mystical doctrine
**34** Formulaic
**37** "Long ago and ___ away . . ."
**38** Furnace output
**39** Western treaty grp.
**40** Car with a logo of four rings
**41** Lubricate
**42** Put-upon
**46** Out, as a library book
**48** Smooth and lustrous
**49** At an angle
**52** Galas
**53** Norwegian coastal feature
**55** Car that comes with a driver
**57** Opera set along the Nile
**61** ___ Vegas
**62** Like players in pin-the-tail-on-the-donkey
**65** Likely
**66** Helpers
**67** Rationed (out)
**68** Crosses out
**69** Silly birds
**70** Escalator parts

**DOWN**

**1** Comic Kaplan
**2** Gillette razor
**3** Go out of sight, as gas prices
**4** Criticizes, perhaps unfairly
**5** Craving
**6** Ivory or Coast
**7** "If ___ be the food of love, play on": Shak.
**8** Onetime dental anesthetic
**9** "___ you sleeping?"
**10** Fiery-tempered sort, they say
**11** Loses it
**12** Ayn who wrote "Atlas Shrugged"
**13** Follow orders
**18** Cause for stitches
**23** Globe
**25** Racket
**27** "Rocks"
**28** Make aware
**29** No matter what
**30** Stench
**32** Weighed down
**33** Desertlike
**34** When repeated, a toy train
**35** Way cool
**36** AOL and others, in brief
**40** Demands much (of)
**42** Pocketbook
**43** Termite look-alike
**44** Free from
**45** "Xanadu" grp.
**47** Rower's need
**50** Omit in pronunciation
**51** Eats by candlelight, say
**53** Source of linen
**54** Mock
**56** Retailer's goods: Abbr.
**58** Unemployed
**59** Bottomless
**60** Tosses in
**63** "This puzzle is really, really hard," e.g.
**64** Takes too much, for short

*by Thomas Heilman*

# 19

## ACROSS

**1** Univ. military program
**5** Samsung and Sony products
**8** In unison
**13** Type that leans: Abbr.
**14** Hurry
**15** High point of a story
**16** *1981 film starring William Hurt and Kathleen Turner
**18** If all goes exactly according to plan
**19** Peter Pan lost his
**20** Thomas ___ Edison
**22** Fed. auditing agency
**23** List ender: Abbr.
**25** *Hoopster's complete miss
**27** A/C meas.
**30** Night before a holiday
**31** Encl. with a manuscript
**32** *Z, alphabetically
**35** "Livin' La ___ Loca"
**39** Former Montreal team
**40** Sea, to Debussy
**41** Like Robin Hood's men
**42** Trace of smoke
**43** *Painted highway divider
**45** Amo, ___, amat
**47** Collection of scenes
**48** Call for help
**49** *Touchdown site
**52** Sticky stuff
**54** Here–there link
**55** Eye part
**57** Setting for many a fairy tale
**61** Title girl in a 1983 Kool & the Gang hit
**63** Jerry Garcia fan . . . or what each part of the answers to the starred clues can take
**65** Sedated, perhaps
**66** Follower of Mar.
**67** Adolescent outbreak
**68** Poet William Butler ___
**69** Moms
**70** "Say ___" (pourer's request)

## DOWN

**1** Barbecue dish
**2** From a different perspective, in chat room lingo
**3** "Look what I did!"
**4** Outlaw partner of Bonnie
**5** Motion made by fans in a stadium
**6** By way of
**7** ___ good example
**8** Hitching posts?
**9** Bro or sis
**10** The end, to Euripides
**11** Vocally twangy
**12** Shower with praise
**15** Expensive topping served with a tiny spoon
**17** Monopoly purchases
**21** Team game with infrared-sensitive targets
**24** "I'll try to think of something . . ."
**26** Cut at an angle
**27** Missed, as a chance
**28** Ride that's hailed
**29** Mail carrier's grp.
**33** November birthstone
**34** Countdown start
**36** Bearded flower
**37** Early 007 foe
**38** Affirmative votes
**41** "The Wind in the Willows" amphibian
**43** Sail material
**44** High-m.p.g. vehicles
**46** Hershey's bar with coconut
**49** Take pleasure in
**50** Nary a soul
**51** Euripides' genre
**53** "Shucks!"
**56** Funnyman Sandler
**58** Engineers' school, briefly
**59** Lois of the "Daily Planet"
**60** Place of bliss
**62** Take-home pay
**64** Org. monitoring industrial wastes

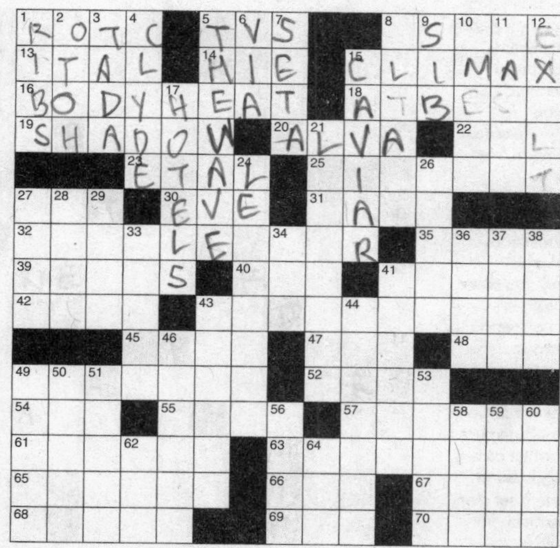

*by Paula Gamache*

# 20

**ACROSS**

**1** Opposed to
**5** Leg part below the knee
**9** Come from ___
**13** Have as a definition
**14** Tour of duty
**15** Singsong syllables
**16** Be very potent
**18** Londoner, e.g., for short
**19** "Seats sold out" sign
**20** Singer Ronstadt
**21** "Pet" annoyance
**22** Social hierarchy
**24** Shout before "Open up!"
**27** Toronto's prov.
**28** Neighbor of Yemen
**29** Capital of Bolivia
**32** Engine additive brand
**35** Very best puppy or kitten
**39** Pig's place
**40** Moth-repellent wood
**41** Lower-priced spread
**42** RR stop
**43** Burr and Copland
**45** Miscellaneous coins
**51** Dark
**52** "Steppenwolf" writer Hermann
**53** Fuss
**56** Squad
**57** Got ready to kiss
**59** Tent floor, maybe
**60** Lucy's pal on "I Love Lucy"
**61** Go ballistic
**62** Kill
**63** Requirement
**64** Ed with the 1967 hit "My Cup Runneth Over"

**DOWN**

**1** Concert equipment
**2** Within easy reach
**3** Stuffed tortilla
**4** What a quill may be dipped in
**5** Reeked
**6** Language of India
**7** Of an old Andean empire
**8** To the ___ degree
**9** Physicist Einstein
**10** Got along
**11** Dead's opposite
**12** "Consumer Reports" employee
**14** Zest
**17** Baldwin of "30 Rock"
**21** Kind of scheme that's fraudulent
**22** Like the sky at dawn or sunset
**23** Aim
**24** Boston ___
**25** Leave out
**26** Like some delicate lingerie
**29** Inc., in England
**30** "I get it!"
**31** The "p" in m.p.g.
**32** Normandy town in W.W. II fighting
**33** College freshman, usually
**34** Experts
**36** Eight-piece band
**37** Accomplishment
**38** Ripped
**42** Meager
**43** Photographer Adams
**44** Ripening agent
**45** Strokes on the green
**46** Hollywood's Ryan or Tatum
**47** Barton of the Red Cross
**48** Water park slide
**49** "Men in Trees" actress Anne
**50** Inquired
**53** Father of Cain and Abel
**54** Hill you might drive a buggy over
**55** Chooses, with "for"
**57** Quill, sometimes
**58** Eisenhower years, e.g.

*by Andrea Carla Michaels and Michael Blake*

**ACROSS**

**1** Camera openings
**10** Wooden shoe
**15** Patron of the hearts?
**16** Weather of a region
**17** Fidgety
**18** "What's it all about, ___?"
**19** Too much of e-mail
**20** They lift kites
**22** Bouquet holder
**25** Half of the tai chi symbol
**26** And other women: Lat.
**30** Day's end, to a poet
**31** Grappling site
**34** "Come and get it" signals in the Army
**36** Candied, as fruits
**38** Org. that approves trailers
**39** Is a Maître d' for, say
**41** Hibernia
**42** Busybody
**44** Service leaders in the service
**46** See 59-Down
**47** "Ready or ___ . . ."
**49** Like most promgoers
**50** Wildebeest
**51** Grant
**52** Song whose title is repeated before and after "gentille" in its first line
**56** John who wrote "My First Summer in the Sierra"
**60** Sainted 11th-century pope
**61** References
**65** Having plenty to spare
**66** Den mothers
**67** Wedding invitation encls.
**68** Geographical features . . . or what the circled squares in this puzzle represent

**DOWN**

**1** Dollar competitor
**2** Sensory appendage
**3** First name of the First Lady of Song
**4** 500 sheets
**5** Blast producer
**6** Colorado tribe
**7** Narrow inlet
**8** Come after
**9** Trickle (through)
**10** Halloween activity
**11** Edgar ___ Poe
**12** "Back to the Future" bully
**13** Not mention
**14** Caddie's bagful
**21** Tint
**22** Trader ___ (restaurant eponym)
**23** Some batteries
**24** Grade of beef
**26** Outstanding Miniseries and Outstanding Drama Series
**27** Conical dwelling
**28** Yoga position
**29** Exam with sections known as "arguments," for short
**30** Brideshead, for one
**31** Mrs. Arnold Schwarzenegger
**32** Getting an A+ on
**33** Uptight
**35** "Well, ___-di-dah!"
**37** Meager
**40** Hightailed it
**43** Extensions
**45** Founding father Richard Henry ___
**48** No longer fashionable
**50** Slyness
**51** Salsa singer Cruz
**52** "Lackaday!"
**53** Champagne Tony of golf
**54** "Well, that was stupid of me!"
**55** Like most N.B.A. players
**56** Prefix with -zoic
**57** CCCP, in English
**58** Line-___ veto
**59** With 46-Across, Antarctic waters
**62** Cambodia's ___ Nol
**63** "Tristan ___ Isolde"
**64** 3, on a telephone

by Joanne Sullivan

# 22

## ACROSS

1 *"In like a ___ . . ."
5 Voice below soprano
9 Goat-men in a Rubens painting
14 Capital once called Christiania
15 *Kook
16 Welles of film
17 Lone Star State sch.
18 *Godsend
19 Go from ___ worse
20 Choreographer Twyla
22 Greek gathering spot
24 *Doofus
25 Married woman, in Madrid
27 Author Silverstein
29 *Dud
31 Wood finish
34 Pub crawler
37 Minimal amount
39 Andean animal
40 Period described by the clues and answers to 1- and 72-Across (which are the start and end of a word ladder formed by the answers to the 10 asterisked clues)
43 Actor Williams of "Happy Days"
44 Gala night duds
45 Govt. ID
46 Handy man?
48 *Jim's gift in "The Gift of the Magi"
50 Looped handle, in archaeology
51 Look over
55 *Provide for free
57 ___ Brasi, enforcer in "The Godfather"
61 Cathedral areas
62 Absorbed the loss
64 *Sleepaway, e.g.
66 Sunday best, e.g.
67 Sea eagles
68 *Tiffany treasure
69 "Casablanca" heroine
70 "I beg to differ!"
71 Parts of una década
72 *". . . out like a ___"

## DOWN

1 Lummoxes
2 "This ___ life!"
3 Ingredient in some potato chips
4 "Easy!"
5 Priest's robe
6 Going places?
7 Trolley warning
8 ___ occasion (never)
9 Dalla's gift in "The Gift of the Magi"
10 Title heroine of a Strauss opera
11 Mint green?
12 Say ___ (reject)
13 Name-dropper, perhaps
21 Draws out
23 Pale wood
26 Grace period?
28 Steering committee?
30 Nuts
31 Betraying no emotion
32 Gremlins and Hornets of old autodom
33 Songwriter Sammy
34 Partnerless, as at a party
35 "This can't be!"
36 Provider of a dead giveaway?
38 ___ Na Na
41 Sweet, gooey sandwiches
42 Dud
47 "Fly the friendly skies" co.
49 São Paulo's land, to natives
52 Throat dangler
53 Great shakes?
54 Sign abbr. meaning "founded in"
55 "It's News to Me" columnist Herb
56 Others: Sp.
58 The Bruins of the N.C.A.A.
59 James of "Thief"
60 Bullets
63 General on a Chinese menu
65 Second afterthought in a letter: Abbr.

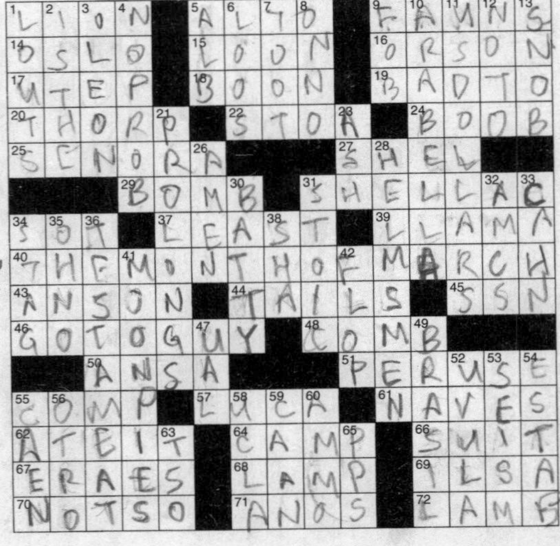

*by Elizabeth C. Gorski*

## ACROSS

1 Telltale sign
7 Stick in one's ___
11 Paid no attention to
13 Protection
15 With 23-Across, famous "opening" line
17 Heavy coats
18 Respectful acts
19 Rapper ___ Rida
20 Says "Nice Job!" to
23 See 15-Across
28 "Given the situation . . ."
29 Alberto VO5 product
30 With 35-Across, source of 15-/23-Across
32 Support for an ear of corn
34 "Olympia" artist
35 See 30-Across
37 Belief system
38 Like 10, but not X
40 15-/23-Across location
46 "England hath long been mad, and scarr'd ___": Richmond in "King Richard III"
47 Lost soldier, briefly
48 Hall providing entertainment
51 "Dear" columnist
52 Creator of 30-/35-Across
56 Family name in early violin-making
57 "Our Miss Brooks" star of 1950s TV
58 Like two peas in ___
59 Emphasize

## DOWN

1 Tiny biological channel, as in the kidney
2 Aligned
3 Waterman products
4 Weird
5 ___ dog (Chinese breed)
6 Playfulness
7 Not so stormy
8 Go over and over, as arguments
9 Spellbound
10 Cinematic scene-changer
11 Chewy confection
12 Captain Cook landfall of April 1769
14 His or her: Fr.
16 Comes up short, say
20 Suggest
21 Restraint
22 Amount of money that can be raised?
24 "What will you ___?"
25 "Zounds!"
26 Depend (on)
27 Yellowstone roamer
30 –
31 "I didn't know I had it ___!"
32 Knucklehead ___, Paul Winchell dummy of old TV
33 Lab ___
34 Alex Doonesbury's school, for short
35 Lawyer's assignment
36 Silver coin of ancient Greece
38 Open-air lobbies
39 Fix, as a boot
41 ___ blaster
42 Classic tale in dactylic hexameter
43 Some Iraq war reporters
44 Cuba ___ (rum highballs)
45 Store, as supplies
48 Org. that promotes sugarless gum
49 Blue-skinned deity
50 Jacket fastener
51 Suffix with Frigid-
53 Hosp. hookups
54 Acquire
55 Raucous laugh syllable

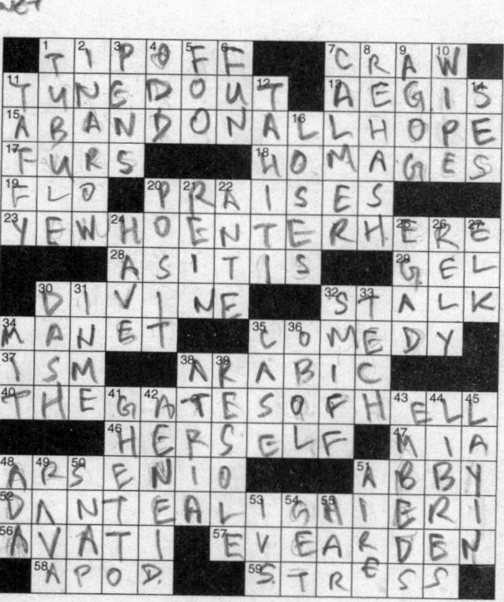

*by Jeffrey Wechsler*

# 24 ★

## ACROSS

1 One "in the woods"
5 Troop group: Abbr.
8 Tiny light that's here and gone
12 Classic door-to-door marketer
13 Manufactured
15 Radames's love, in opera
16 Something that swings
17 Keyboard key
18 Manual reader
19 Show ___
20 Stand-up comic's material
21 Film bomb of 1987
23 "You can't make me!"
25 Sch. with home games at Pauley Pavilion
26 Speediness
27 Kwame ___, advocate of pan-Africanism and the first P.M. of Ghana
31 Stewed to the gills
33 Pronto
34 Half-off event
35 Lucy of "Kill Bill"
36 Period of low activity
39 Bamboozle
40 Sell
42 Buff thing
43 Figure-skating figures
45 Dressed to the nines
47 Computer data acronym
48 Makes public
49 Gasoline additive
52 What 3-, 13-, 14- and 28-Down may be
55 Soft white cheese
56 Program file-name extension
57 Puppy's plaint
58 Farm letters?
60 Votin' no on
61 Poet laureate Dove
62 Ryan in Cooperstown
63 Newsman Roger
64 Pizazz
65 The Cards, on scoreboards
66 Low ratings

## DOWN

1 Disney fawn
2 To have, to Henri
3 Tippler
4 Remnant
5 ___ jumping
6 Plops down
7 Ballantine product
8 German design school founded in 1919
9 Grocery shopper's aid
10 It's a thought
11 Catherine ___, last wife of Henry VIII
13 Donkey, for one
14 "How many months have 28 days?," e.g.
20 Zest
22 Professional's camera, for short
24 Too heavy
25 Cancel
28 Rat-a-tat-tat weapon
29 ___ very much
30 Chickens that come home to roost
31 Hollywood or Sunset: Abbr.
32 Place
33 Third degree?
37 Dandy sorts
38 Nouveau ___
41 Expressionless
44 Scala of "The Guns of Navarone"
46 Fizzle
47 Formerly common rooftop sight
50 Water or rust
51 Makes advances?
52 Instrument in ancient Greek art
53 Trompe l'___
54 Utah ski resort
55 Big swig
59 Cyclades island
60 ___, amas, amat . . .

*by Paula Gamache*

## ACROSS

**1** Vapors
**6** Trades
**11** Alternative to La Guardia or Newark, in brief
**14** Travis who sang "T-R-O-U-B-L-E"
**15** Picasso or Casals
**16** Peyton Manning's brother
**17** Try a North Atlantic fish for the first time?
**19** Jamaican term of address
**20** Afternoon hour
**21** Rhino relatives with long snouts
**23** "I'll alert ___": Hobson, in "Arthur" (with 25-Across)
**25** See 23-Across
**28** French girlfriend
**29** Bind with a belt
**31** Ekco or Farberware?
**34** Notions, in Nantes
**36** Old photo color
**37** Part of F.B.I.
**40** Turning down
**44** Like a visit from Benedict XVI, e.g.
**46** Middle of the abdomen
**47** Registers for a meditation class?
**52** Big rig
**53** Its capitals is Muscat
**54** Defendants enter them
**56** Hunk
**57** Airplane seating request
**60** Houston baseballer
**62** They're checked at checkpoints, briefly
**63** Store photographer?
**68** Code-breaking org.
**69** "Hill Street Blues" actress Veronica
**70** Augusta's home
**71** Fast sports cars
**72** Cornered
**73** ___-Detoo . . . or, when read in three parts, a hint to 17-, 31-, 47- and 63-Across

## DOWN

**1** Co. with a blooming business?
**2** Spoon-bending Geller
**3** 1960s sitcom with a talking palomino
**4** Engrave glass with acid
**5** Nor'easter, for one
**6** Big name in small swimwear
**7** Hell, to General Sherman
**8** "Dancing With the Stars" network
**9** Secret plan
**10** Scotch's partner
**11** Aunt known for her pancakes
**12** Old European gold coin
**13** Sex authority Alfred
**18** Prez's #2
**22** Melonlike tropical fruits
**23** Letters said with a shout
**24** Camouflage
**26** The "I" in 23-Down
**27** Got a perfect score on
**30** Where to find the diving board
**32** Unlock, in poetry
**33** Wisc. neighbor
**35** Ladies of Spain: Abbr.
**38** Storekeeper on "The Simpsons"
**39** Dweller above the Arctic Circle
**41** "Eureka!"
**42** Nautilus captain
**43** Insincerely eloquent
**45** I.M. snicker
**47** A.A.A. activity
**48** Surrounded by
**49** "The Wizard of Oz" setting
**50** Paltry
**51** Miss America accessory
**55** Leaf opening
**58** Workers' protection agcy.
**59** "Say again?"
**61** Lion's warning
**64** Govt. book balancer
**65** Podded plant
**66** British musician Brian
**67** ___ Speedwagon

*by Kurt Krauss*

## ACROSS

1 Explorers on a hwy., e.g.
5 ___ soup (starter at a Japanese restaurant)
9 Cops, in slang . . . or a hint to this puzzle's theme
14 Made quickly, as a meal
16 Indo-European
17 Up-to-date
18 Singer Bonnie
19 Gas bill unit
20 Gershwin's "Concerto ___"
22 Medical research agcy.
23 Brut or Paco Rabanne
28 Physical reactions?
31 Pro wrestling move
32 Informal British term of address
33 Schreiber of "X-Men Origins: Wolverine"
35 New Haven collegians
37 Gold-medal gymnast Comaneci
41 Browning opening line preceding "Now that April's there"
44 1900 Puccini premiere
45 Look
46 Site of Zeno's teaching
47 Civil War prez
49 Natasha's refusal
51 Whichever
52 Be indebted to the I.R.S.
57 Jap. computer giant
58 Took home the gold
59 Spirit of a group
63 "Welcome to Maui!"
65 Willa Cather novel
69 "So what else ___?"
70 Computer setup to facilitate instant messaging
71 Mary's upstairs neighbor, in 1970s TV
72 Floored it
73 Lover boy?

## DOWN

1 Sultan of ___ (Babe Ruth)
2 "No way, no how"
3 Gambling or drinking
4 Fungus production
5 Sea, to Cousteau
6 Civil rights advocate ___ B. Wells
7 Light from above
8 Eye-related
9 Widespread
10 Nest egg for old age, in brief
11 Competing
12 Have dinner at home
13 Words before rocks, ropes or run
15 Alternative to Nikes
21 Eggy drink
24 Beekeeper of filmdom
25 Some Surrealist paintings
26 Distinguished
27 Egg shapes
28 Gazillions
29 Bygone cracker brand
30 Squash match units
34 Lexicon contents, for short
36 "Adios!"
38 Facts and figures
39 Privy to
40 The Beatles' "___ in the Life"
42 Gilda Radner character
43 Ariz. neighbor
48 Prefix with friendly
50 Wee
52 Broadcasting now
53 Like the name "Bryn Mawr"
54 ___ Lodge
55 Door handles
56 Inscribed pillar
60 Prince, e.g.
61 Roughly
62 Former fast jets
64 "I knew a man Bojangles and ___ dance for you . . ."
66 Young dog
67 Chemical suffix
68 Like 1, 3, 5, 7 . . .

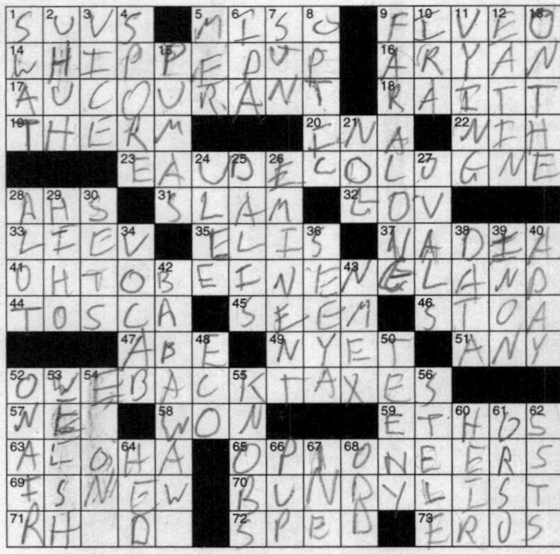

by Elizabeth C. Gorski

## ACROSS

**1** Establishments with mirrored balls
**7** Snacked
**10** In a state of 10-Down
**14** Involve
**15** South of South America
**16** Help the dishwasher, perhaps
**17** In a precise manner
**18** It's directly below V-B-N-M
**20** Turn in many a children's game
**21** Relative of a raccoon
**22** Bark beetle's habitat
**23** Highway safety marker
**27** Caballer's need
**28** No ___ sight
**32** Away from home
**35** Unwelcome financial exams
**39** French river or department
**40** Punch in the mouth, slangily
**43** Westernmost of the Aleutians
**44** Alice's best friend on "The Honeymooners"
**45** Honor society letter
**46** "___ never believe this!"
**48** "___ first you don't succeed . . ."
**50** Homecoming display
**56** Pompous fool
**59** Cut down
**60** Cuts down
**62** Cold treat that can precede the last word of 18-, 23-, 40- or 50-Across
**64** Menu selection
**66** Not dry
**67** Full house sign
**68** Pig, when rummaging for truffles
**69** Diva's delivery
**70** Newspaper staffers, in brief
**71** Fleet of warships

## DOWN

**1** Rooms with recliners
**2** All thumbs
**3** Flight segment
**4** Forty winks
**5** Olive product
**6** Tricky
**7** Part of P.G.A.: Abbr.
**8** Rapper ___ Shakur
**9** Sister of Clio
**10** Feeling when you're 10-Across
**11** Taunt
**12** Birthstone for most Libras
**13** Start, as of an idea
**19** French filmdom
**21** Remnant of a burned coal
**24** Verbal brickbats
**25** Tennis "misstep"
**26** Plenty, to a poet
**29** Icicle feature
**30** Narrow winning margin
**31** Classic soda pop
**32** Give the go-ahead
**33** "Do ___ others . . ."
**34** South African Peace Nobelist, 1984
**36** "It ___" (reply to "Who's there?")
**37** Prepared for takeoff
**38** [Well, see if I care!]
**41** Late actor Robert of "I Spy"
**42** Give out cards
**47** Bert of "The Wizard of Oz"
**49** Indian percussion
**51** Witherspoon of "Legally Blonde"
**52** Cy Young, e.g.
**53** Visual sales pitches
**54** Line from the heart
**55** Tammany Hall "boss"
**56** Elton John/Tim Rice musical
**57** Mark for life
**58** Place for a cab
**61** It's repeated after "Que" in song
**63** Tax preparer, for short
**64** Diamond stat
**65** Neither's partner

*by Sarah Keller*

# 28 

## ACROSS

**1** Biblical strongman
**7** Two cents' worth
**10** Anti-D.U.I. org.
**14** Climber's chopper
**15** Sports org. with a tour
**16** Skin care brand
**17** Place to freshen up
**19** Rock legend Hendrix
**20** Display of grandeur
**21** French-speaking African nation
**22** Sport involving a chute
**25** "Unforgettable" duettist Cole
**31** Caen's river
**32** Like clocks with hands
**33** Tot's repeated questions
**34** ID with two hyphens
**37** Britney Spears's debut hit
**40** Early Beatle Sutcliffe
**41** Fully convinced
**42** Joins
**43** Hatcher with a Golden Globe
**44** Disassembles, as a model airplane
**45** Elite military group
**49** On one's toes
**50** Treatment with carbon dioxide
**57** Prefix with star or bucks
**58** Classic Miles Davis album . . . or a hint to the start of 17-, 22-, 37- or 45-Across
**60** "___ Almighty" (Steve Carell movie)
**61** Tattooist's supply
**62** Characteristics
**63** Bumper blemish
**64** "Pick a card, ___ card"
**65** Most achy

## DOWN

**1** Nurses, at the bar
**2** Rent-___ (private security guard)
**3** Whimper like a baby
**4** One-named Nigerian songstress
**5** Paul Bunyan's Babe and others
**6** Dorky sort
**7** Hybrid utensil
**8** Way back when
**9** Sweet potato
**10** Desert with Joshua trees
**11** Suspect's story
**12** Friend of Pythias
**13** Flopping at a comedy club
**18** Ascended
**21** Root used in some energy drinks
**23** Start of a pirate's chant
**24** Practice go-round
**25** Catches, as a perp
**26** Med school subj.
**27** Forbidden-sounding perfume
**28** Prince ___ Khan
**29** Least strict
**30** Pay no heed to
**33** Subj. of a U.N. inspection, maybe
**34** In ___ (as placed)
**35** "Peter Pan" pirate
**36** Loch ___ monster
**38** Director Kazan
**39** Up to, in ads
**43** Iron-fisted boss
**44** ___ car dealer
**45** Identified
**46** Tylenol alternative
**47** Lacking meat, eggs, dairy, etc.
**48** Like Abe Lincoln, physiologically
**51** Goes bad
**52** Early Jesse Jackson hairdo
**53** Way up the slope
**54** Netman Nastase
**55** Contract loopholes, e.g.
**56** Digs of twigs
**58** Spectra automaker
**59** B&B, e.g.

*by Alex Boisvert*

## ACROSS

**1** "What did Delaware?" "I don't know, but ___" (old joke)
**7** "I ___ bored!"
**11** Score components: Abbr.
**14** Decorate flamboyantly, in slang
**15** Simon ___
**16** Noisy fight
**17** King who was the son of Pepin the Short
**19** "___ Rocker" (Springsteen song)
**20** Electron's path
**21** River that ends at Cairo
**22** Cinematographer Nykvist
**23** Post-copyright status
**26** Sister of Snow White
**29** Smack hard
**30** Intuition, maybe: Abbr.
**31** Darkens
**34** Big name in vacuums
**37** La Choy product
**41** Russian country house
**42** F.B.I. guys
**43** Ming of the N.B.A.
**44** Puts away plates
**46** French carmaker
**49** Easternmost U.S. capital
**53** Graph paper pattern
**54** Food thickener
**55** For face value
**59** Cabinet dept. overseeing farm interests
**60** Fancy equine coif
**62** No. on a calling card
**63** Zealous
**64** Not polished
**65** Pothook shape
**66** Till compartment
**67** Like Dracula

## DOWN

**1** Classic record label for the Bee Gees and Cream
**2** Bert who played a cowardly lion
**3** Emirate dweller
**4** Indicator of rank
**5** Civilization, to Freud
**6** Distant cousin of humans
**7** Sapporo competitor
**8** ___ Johnson
**9** Church councils
**10** Sugar suffix
**11** Philip Marlowe or Sam Spade
**12** Actress Marisa
**13** Ex-Steeler Lynn
**18** Crown ___
**22** Unctuous flattery
**24** "Venerable" monk
**25** "Geez! That stings!"
**26** Shipping dept. stamp
**27** Dept. of Labor arm
**28** Scary, Baby, Ginger, Posh and Sporty
**32** Year McKinley was elected to a second term
**33** First American in space
**35** "Gotta go!"
**36** Muscle malady
**38** Hot: Fr.
**39** Kit ___ (candy bars)
**40** "Dedicated to the ___ Love"
**45** Excessively fast
**47** Japanese eel and rice dish
**48** Lose patience and then some
**49** Ornamental quartz
**50** Earnestly recommends
**51** "To repeat . . ."
**52** Dust busters
**56** Peel
**57** Jug handle, in archaeology
**58** Stalk in a marsh
**60** Face the pitcher
**61** Old French coin

| | | | | | | | | | | | | | | |
|---|---|---|---|---|---|---|---|---|---|---|---|---|---|---|
| 1 | 2 | 3 | 4 | 5 | 6 | ■ | 7 | 8 | 9 | 10 | ■ | 11 | 12 | 13 |
| 14 | | | | | | ■ | 15 | | | | ■ | 16 | | |
| 17 | | | | | | 18 | | | | | ■ | 19 | | |
| 20 | | | | | ■ | 21 | | | | ■ | 22 | | | |
| ■ | ■ | ■ | 23 | | 24 | | | | | 25 | | | | |
| 26 | 27 | 28 | | | | | ■ | ■ | 29 | | | | ■ | ■ |
| 30 | | | ■ | ■ | 31 | | 32 | 33 | ■ | 34 | | | 35 | 36 |
| 37 | | | 38 | 39 | | | | | 40 | | | | | |
| 41 | | | | | ■ | 42 | | | | ■ | ■ | 43 | | |
| ■ | ■ | 44 | | | 45 | ■ | ■ | 46 | | 47 | 48 | | | |
| 49 | 50 | | | | | 51 | 52 | | | | | ■ | ■ | ■ |
| 53 | | | | ■ | 54 | | | | ■ | 55 | | 56 | 57 | 58 |
| 59 | | | ■ | 60 | | | | | 61 | | | | | |
| 62 | | | ■ | 63 | | | | ■ | 64 | | | | | |
| 65 | | | ■ | 66 | | | | ■ | 67 | | | | | |

*by Paula Gamache*

30 

## ACROSS

**1** Tiny
**7** End of a Shakespeare play
**11** MP3 holders
**14** Artist Diego
**15** One who talks only about himself, say
**16** Egg layer
**17** Genesis duo
**19** Historical time
**20** Fish-fowl connector
**21** It's found on a nightstand
**23** ___-Wan with the Force
**26** Chum
**28** "Enough!"
**29** Certain mustache shape
**33** Not great, but not awful either
**34** TV part
**35** Computer capacity, informally
**38** Means of staying toasty at night
**43** Yankee nickname starting in 2004
**44** Control, as expenses
**46** Treated, as a sprained ankle
**50** American symbol
**52** "Let's play!"
**55** Major coll. fraternity
**56** Sunburned
**57** Made possible
**59** "___ moment!" ("Don't rush me!")
**61** French pronoun
**62** Street weapon . . . or a hint to the circled letters in this puzzle
**68** Under the weather
**69** Bond girl Kurylenko
**70** Spotted feline
**71** Profs.' helpers
**72** Wall Street inits.
**73** Darcy's Pemberley, e.g., in "Pride and Prejudice"

## DOWN

**1** Parabola, e.g.
**2** ___ Maria
**3** Prefix with duct
**4** Target audience of Details magazine
**5** Country with a Guardian Council
**6** One use of a Swiss Army knife
**7** Lawyers' org.
**8** Ty with batting titles
**9** Sequoias, e.g.
**10** Open grassland
**11** Penny-pincher, slangily
**12** Skin layer
**13** Wake with a start
**18** Blah
**22** ___ Lonely Boys (rock band)
**23** Cries of surprise
**24** "The Well-Tempered Clavier" composer
**25** Memo starter
**27** Greek L's
**30** Org. monitoring narcotics smuggling
**31** "___ thousand flowers bloom"
**32** Bible study: Abbr.
**36** Tool you can lean on
**37** Snick's partner
**39** When you entered this world: Abbr.
**40** Seoul-based automaker
**41** Hwy. planner
**42** 10-point Q, e.g.
**45** Actor Beatty
**46** "That's clear"
**47** Kind of oil
**48** Contacts via the Net
**49** Girl with a coming-out party
**51** Secular
**53** Johnny who used to cry "Come on down!"
**54** As of late
**58** Shovels
**60** Rudimentary education
**63** ___ Bo
**64** Redo, in tennis
**65** ___ mode
**66** Half of a colon
**67** Summer on the Seine

*by Oliver Hill*

## ACROSS

**1** Dudley Do-Right's org.
**5** Banjo sound
**10** Video recorders, briefly
**14** Anticipatory cry
**15** Tend to, as plants
**16** "So true!"
**17** Disk-shaped sea creature
**19** Bit of dialogue
**20** Oral hesitations
**21** Bruins' sch.
**22** High-I.Q. crew
**23** Actress Carrere
**24** Shift blame to another
**27** More posh
**29** Approx. takeoff hour
**30** Bashful
**31** Routing abbr.
**32** Immeasurably vast
**35** Chowder ingredient
**40** Tater Tots brand
**41** Santa ___ (hot California winds)
**43** Exclamation in Berlin
**46** Leatherworker's tool
**47** Current unit
**49** Hit that just clears the infield
**53** Short smoke?
**54** Turkish money
**55** Jean who wrote "The Clan of the Cave Bear"
**56** Hydroelectric project
**57** "He loves," in Latin
**58** Auto-racing designation
**61** "Scrubs" actor Braff
**62** Not abridged
**63** Baseball great Musial
**64** Ones who've been through divorce court
**65** Horseshoers' tools
**66** Pain in the neck

## DOWN

**1** Stone discovery site
**2** "Ben-Hur" racers
**3** Global agricultural company
**4** Advanced deg.
**5** Kind of garage
**6** Masons' creations
**7** Muscular Charles
**8** Union with 3+ million members, in brief
**9** Junkyard dog's greeting
**10** Novelist Carr
**11** Pretty good grade
**12** Stand-up guy
**13** Deceitful
**18** Hornswoggle
**22** Battlefield doc
**25** Rival of Edison
**26** WWW code
**28** "For more ___ . . ."
**32** Hot dog topper
**33** U.K. lexicon
**34** Sound of thunder
**36** Golf hazards
**37** Wields a needle
**38** Short reminiscence
**39** ___ Trench (deepest point on Earth's surface)
**42** Orange part, e.g.
**43** In flames
**44** Part of a book where you're unlikely to stop
**45** Poet who originated the phrase "harmony in discord"
**47** Indigenous Alaskans
**48** Pell-___
**50** Courtroom rituals
**51** Feds who make busts
**52** Ruin, informally
**58** Stole material
**59** "Not ___ bet!"
**60** African slitherer

*by Doug Peterson*

32

## ACROSS

**1** Defeat, barely
**5** Word on a bar worker's jar
**9** Gem
**14** Pasta or potato, for short
**15** Savoie sweetheart
**16** Still in the game
**17** Brag
**18** Beekeeper played by Peter Fonda
**19** Recurring melody
**20** Tiger and Elin Woods's 37-Across order?
**23** Super, slangily
**24** Sign on a locked lavatory
**25** Vast amounts
**27** It might start "E FP TOZ LPED"
**30** Party that's a wow
**31** Posh
**32** One pitied by Mr. T
**33** Doo-___ music
**36** Actor's rep: Abbr.
**37** Cocktail called "the elixir of quietude" by 4-Down
**40** 1950s campaign nickname
**41** ___'easter
**42** Apple originally marketed to schools
**43** New car sticker fig.
**44** Figure of Greek myth with a statue at Rockefeller Center
**46** 1889 statehood achievers, with "the"
**49** Ringtoss game
**51** A marathon has about 26 of these
**52** Runnin' Rebels' sch.
**53** Paula Abdul's 37-Across order?
**58** "Later, amigo!"
**60** French cleric
**61** Foot: Prefix
**62** It's not good to run one
**63** Potter's oven
**64** Mineral in hemoglobin
**65** The hapless Corleone
**66** Things that modest people lack
**67** "Peter Pan" fairy, for short

## DOWN

**1** Shoe company founded in Denmark
**2** "Phooey!"
**3** Small cavern, in poetry
**4** "The Elements of Style" updater
**5** Sign after Aries
**6** "Please help me with directions!"
**7** Jigsaw puzzle element
**8** Be "it," in a game
**9** Wing it, musically
**10** Skips the dos before the I do's?
**11** O. Henry's 37-Across order?
**12** Aquafina rival
**13** Some turns and boxing punches
**21** Opposite WSW
**22** Wise old Athenian
**26** City known as Colombia's sports capital
**27** Pizazz
**28** "Car Talk" dubbed it "the worst car of the millennium"
**29** Popeye's 37-Across order?
**30** Avril Lavigne's "Sk8er ___"
**32** Consumer protection agcy.
**34** Vegetable in Cajun cuisine
**35** Livens, with "up"
**37** Cheesy sandwich
**38** Collect
**39** Dorm figures, for short
**43** Frenzied place at a rock club
**45** Recorded for later viewing
**46** Cisco Kid's horse
**47** "The X-Files" figures
**48** Big beer buy
**49** Hearty drink
**50** Hypnotized or anesthetized
**51** Head honcho
**54** Help oneself to
**55** Garr of "Tootsie"
**56** Noodles with tempura
**57** Medium-rare steak color
**59** B'way success sign

*by Keith Talon*

## ACROSS

**1** Kansas City university formerly known as College of Saint Teresa
**6** Prefix with conference
**10** Stds. important to the health-conscious
**14** Gore who wrote "Lincoln" and "1876"
**15** Eddie's character in "Beverly Hills Cop"
**16** Commercial prefix with México
**17** Retired general?
**20** Surgeon's order
**21** Speaker's place
**22** Antlered animal
**23** Part of the mailing address to Oral Roberts University
**25** Field for Dem Bums
**28** Was loud
**31** Poetic work by Tennyson
**32** Old cracker brand
**35** University wall covering
**36** Stringy
**37** Late nobleman?
**41** Grades 1-6: Abbr.
**42** That: Sp.
**43** "The Thin Man" terrier
**44** Glass-encased item in "Beauty and the Beast"
**45** Seattle team, for short
**48** Residue locale
**50** Set one's sights
**55** Unit a little longer than an arm's length
**56** Chest muscles, for short
**58** "The Time Machine" race
**59** Carillon call?
**63** Groening who created "The Simpsons"
**64** Together, in music
**65** Egyptian peninsula
**66** Sit (for)
**67** Greek letters that look like pitchforks
**68** Seven-year stretch

## DOWN

**1** "Stop!" at sea
**2** Objets d'art
**3** Unimprovable
**4** Cobblers' forms
**5** Optional hwy. route
**6** 1970s Japanese P.M. Kakuei ___
**7** W.W. II vet, e.g.
**8** A majority of August births
**9** Tolkien creature
**10** Horse-racing devotees, slangily
**11** Dressed to the nines
**12** "___ you happy now?"
**13** Sisters' org.
**18** Hero to many
**19** Library Lovers' Mo.
**24** "___ Ben Adhem" (Leigh Hunt poem)
**25** Big name in ice cream
**26** Impatient sort
**27** Done with a wink
**29** Wisconsin town where the Republican Party was born
**30** "Little" Stowe character
**32** Signs of goodness
**33** Giant glaciers
**34** Catcher's location
**38** Comfy spot
**39** General on Chinese menus
**40** Hoeing the garden, e.g.
**41** Chronology segment
**46** Urges
**47** Word in many Perry Mason titles
**49** "___ say!"
**51** Fear-inspiring
**52** How hermits like to be
**53** Des Moinesian or Davenporter
**54** Modest dresses
**56** Opium poppies have them
**57** Decorative sewing kit
**59** Hi-fi component
**60** Kung ___ chicken
**61** Access, as a resource
**62** 23-Across winter setting: Abbr.

*by Ken Bessette*

# 34

## ACROSS

**1** Option for a H.S. dropout
**4** Yaks
**8** Ford misstep
**13** Dispense, as milk
**14** Surrounding glow
**15** Throw water on
**16** Big name in athletic shoes
**18** Still asleep
**19** Site of a tkt. booth
**20** J. Edgar Hoover's org.
**21** "Enough, you're killing me!"
**22** Prince
**28** Singer Guthrie
**29** Electronics giant
**30** Reader of omens
**31** Supermodel Carol
**34** Defendant's plea, for short
**36** Neither's partner
**37** End of a Napoleonic palindrome
**40** Mensa figs.
**42** "Wiseguy" actor Ken
**43** Mediterranean, for one
**44** Boring routines
**46** Laments
**48** Rock's Better Than ___
**52** Black-and-tan purebred
**56** Bush's "___ of evil"
**57** Priestly vestment
**58** Sgt. or cpl.
**59** Three-card con
**61** Carrier with a shamrock logo
**64** Slang
**65** Bird with an olive branch
**66** Zaire's Mobutu ___ Seko
**67** "Fargo" brothers
**68** Singles
**69** "What ___ the chances?"

## DOWN

**1** Possible result of iodine deficiency
**2** Provider of a pass abroad
**3** Basketball's Erving, familiarly
**4** Greta of "Anna Christie," 1930
**5** I.R.S. scares
**6** Article under a blouse
**7** ___ Diego
**8** Mrs. Woodrow Wilson
**9** Patrons of the arts, perhaps
**10** Court summons
**11** Chicago-to-Pittsburgh dir.
**12** Commanded
**13** Turkish pooh-bah
**17** Frequently, to a poet
**21** Modes
**23** Engine sound
**24** Puff the Magic Dragon's frolicking place
**25** Sufficient, for Shakespeare
**26** Prefix with con
**27** "To ___ is human . . ."
**32** Dr. Kildare player Ayres
**33** Pageant toppers
**35** Corrida cry
**37** Alienate
**38** Synagogue
**39** 1930s heavyweight champ Max
**40** Tax planner's plan, for short
**41** On the ___ vive
**45** Church groundskeeper
**47** Go hungry
**49** Clever comeback
**50** Disqualify, as a potential juror
**51** Got up from sleeping
**53** Removes excess poundage
**54** Monthly fashion issues
**55** Category in which the single-season record is 191
**59** Bub
**60** Gold, in Guadalupe
**61** Hubbub
**62** Long, long time
**63** Code-crackers' org.

*by Andrea Carla Michaels*

## ACROSS

**1** Music played by Ravi Shankar at Woodstock
**5** "There it is!"
**10** Disconcert
**14** Historic periods
**15** Pianist Claudio
**16** "I'll get right ___!"
**17** Use of a company car, e.g.
**18** Wherewithal
**19** Emulates Lil' Kim or Lil Wayne
**20** Fairy tale's start
**23** Greeted, with "to"
**24** Destination for a W-2
**25** Thor Heyerdahl craft
**28** That, to Tomás
**29** "Exodus" author
**32** "Brrrr!"
**34** Grandpa's start
**36** Plus
**39** Adlai's opponent in '52 and '56
**40** Rod's partner
**41** Mom's start
**46** "The Count of Monte ___"
**47** Blueprint detail
**48** Broadway's Hagen
**51** Cooke who sang "You Send Me"
**52** Indianapolis-to-New Orleans dir.
**54** Like some patches
**56** Legend's start
**60** Balletic leap
**62** Location of a starry belt
**63** Cole Porter's "Well, Did You ___?"
**64** Lab medium
**65** Quitter's cry
**66** It produces more than 20 billion bricks annually
**67** Popular Microsoft product
**68** Expressed disapproval
**69** White blanket

## DOWN

**1** Period of rest
**2** Gladiators' locales
**3** Ice cream flavor Cherry ___
**4** Made an inquiry
**5** Anne Rice's Lestat, for one
**6** Cookie with a floral design on it
**7** Ahmadinejad's land
**8** Island veranda
**9** Where Schwarzenegger was born
**10** W-2, e.g.
**11** Bacterium that doesn't need oxygen
**12** Address ending, informally
**13** Some "Stargate SG-1" characters, in brief
**21** Guttural refusal
**22** Ideological beliefs
**26** ___ vera
**27** Pastoral composition
**30** The G, W or B in G.W.B.
**31** Followers of Guru Nanak
**33** Grant in four Hitchcock films
**34** Chinese cookers
**35** Sob
**36** Rudiments
**37** Yuri's love in "Dr. Zhivago"
**38** Curved saber
**42** Start of a spider's description, in song
**43** Barely beat
**44** Condescended
**45** Prefix with phobic
**48** Not level
**49** Trinidad's partner
**50** Be that as it may
**53** Gives a yellow flag
**55** Law school newbies
**57** Geek
**58** Cafe proprietor in "Casablanca"
**59** It's commonly filleted
**60** Talk on and on, slangily
**61** Sense of self

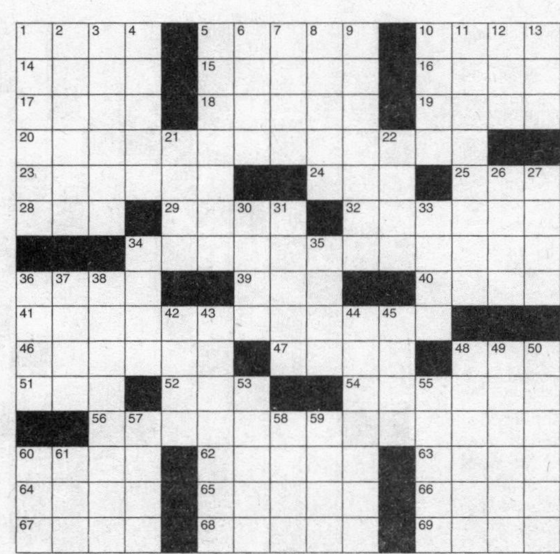

*by Leonard Williams*

# 36 

**ACROSS**

**1** Requests for a saucer of milk, maybe
**6** Film vixen Bara
**11** Woebegone
**14** Central courtyards
**15** Sahara sights
**16** Blubber
**17** "2, 4, 6, 8 ___ who do we appreciate?," e.g.
**18** Competitive noshers' event?
**20** Room under the roof
**22** Iraq's second-largest city
**23** One cured of a sleep disorder?
**26** Cyberjunk
**29** British Conservative
**30** Demonic
**31** Letter between eta and iota
**32** Like some winks
**33** Pupil surrounder
**34** Transferred, as property
**35** Sarcastic comment?
**37** Glad rival in the kitchen
**40** Shipshape
**41** LP speed
**44** Newspaper columnist Goodman
**45** Cargo
**46** Nautical leader?
**47** Kazan of Hollywood
**48** Brushoff from the Ottomans?
**50** ___ Empire, conquered by Cortés
**52** Doled (out)
**53** Terrible-twos tantrums?
**57** Hole-making tool
**59** Round-faced flier
**60** Daisylike bloom
**61** Low-tech office recorder
**62** Pint-size
**63** Bassoonists' buys
**64** On edge

**DOWN**

**1** Apple on a desk
**2** Biofuel option
**3** Speaker's art
**4** Cold and raw
**5** French composer Erik
**6** Super Bowl stat
**7** Attila the ___
**8** Tooth protector
**9** Remodeler's planning
**10** Seeks assistance
**11** Like some tickets and Western pioneers
**12** Rocket's path
**13** Artificial color
**19** Fraternity recruit
**21** Church official
**23** Parts of P.O. labels
**24** Roman poet banished by Augustus
**25** Acapulco agreement
**27** Wolfed down
**28** Loony
**31** Sherpa shelter
**33** Informed about
**34** Headgear fit for a queen
**35** Disreputable
**36** Tap mishap
**37** Last of 26
**38** Indisposed
**39** Easily bent
**41** Goes back (on)
**42** Sensible
**43** Gangster group
**45** Clear plastic
**46** Discerning
**48** On edge
**49** Moonshine ingredient
**51** Romanov ruler
**53** What a violinist may take on stage, in two different senses
**54** Amaze
**55** Brother of Jack and Bobby
**56** Most univ. applicants
**58** Pop artist Lichtenstein

*by Lynn Lempel*

## ACROSS

**1** "Casablanca" star, informally
**6** Rio automaker
**9** Legendary cowboy ___ Bill
**14** Brings in
**15** Dijon denial
**16** Bejeweled topper
**17** Mediocre F. Scott Fitzgerald novel?
**20** Whopping
**21** Gibbons of TV talk
**22** Gas company that sells toy trucks
**23** "Evil Woman" band, for short
**25** Daisy ___, who went to Marryin' Sam
**27** Mediocre place to scuba?
**36** It merged with the WB to form the CW
**37** Yarn buy
**38** Atoll makeup
**39** Bow-wielding god
**41** Quick-witted
**43** "Lovely" Beatles girl
**44** Sony competitor
**46** Cold war–era blast, in headlines
**48** Mean mutt
**49** Mediocre Steve McQueen film?
**52** Unlock, to a bard
**53** Kiev's land: Abbr.
**54** Like a trim lawn
**57** Unyielding
**61** Asia's ___ Sea
**65** Mediocre Jerry Lee Lewis hit?
**68** In the ___ of life
**69** Barbie's beau
**70** Novelist Calvino
**71** Zesty dip
**72** Match part
**73** Hose material

## DOWN

**1** "Little Women" woman
**2** Honolulu's home
**3** Kinnear of "Little Miss Sunshine"
**4** "For sure!"
**5** Suffix with journal
**6** See 29-Down
**7** Actress Skye
**8** 1998 animated film with a queen
**9** Group that usu. meets at a school
**10** "Take your pick"
**11** Scope out, pre-heist
**12** Planets or stars
**13** Comes out with
**18** Items of apparel for Dracula
**19** Willing to go along
**24** Barbell abbr.
**26** ___ welder
**27** Spare-room user
**28** First name in book clubs
**29** With 6-Down, ready to propose
**30** Place to get clean
**31** Cowpoke's rope
**32** How mistakes are often marked
**33** "All My Children" vixen
**34** Thoroughly enjoy
**35** S O S signal
**40** Roget's listings
**42** False start?
**45** Alley ___
**47** Terse reproof
**50** Trillion: Prefix
**51** Cunningly evil
**54** Unruly dos
**55** Gumbo vegetable
**56** Banshee's sound
**58** Types
**59** High spirits
**60** George Harrison's "___ It a Pity"
**62** Omani money
**63** Folkie Guthrie
**64** Trotsky of Russia
**66** Arthur of "Maude"
**67** One of a snorkeler's pair

*by David Kwong and Emily Halpern*

# 38

## ACROSS

**1** Woodworking tool
**5** Real-life scientist played by David Bowie in "The Prestige," 2006
**10** Dwarf or giant, maybe
**14** Perjured oneself
**15** Work that begins "Sing, goddess, the wrath of Peleus' son . . ."
**16** Older brother of Michael Jackson
**17** Writer who created the character Vivian Darkbloom
**20** Edgar ___ Poe
**21** Suffer
**22** Keep ___ on
**26** Spleen
**27** Singer who nicknamed himself Mr. Mojo Risin'
**32** Sine ___ non
**35** Words said with a nod
**36** Unwakeful state
**37** Newspaperman Harold
**39** The 40 of the Top 40
**40** "Saturday Night Live" bits
**42** End of an illness?
**43** Mr. T series, with "The"
**45** Inter ___
**46** "Toodles!"
**47** Talk smack about
**48** Author/illustrator who used the pseudonym Ogdred Weary
**51** Caustic cleansing agent
**52** Stagger
**53** Unidentified man
**57** Upper crust
**62** What the clues for 17-, 27- and 48-Across all contain
**66** Teeming (with)
**67** Besmirch
**68** Shake alternative
**69** British gun
**70** Adlai's 1956 running mate
**71** Revolutionary car part?

## DOWN

**1** Thomas ___ Edison
**2** Salmon garnish
**3** Fervor
**4** Snorri Sturluson work
**5** Late newsman Russert
**6** With 10-Down, ABC series starring Jonny Lee Miller
**7** Walter Scott title
**8** Superboy's crush
**9** Samuel Barber's "___ for Strings"
**10** See 6-Down
**11** "Kon-___"
**12** All-inclusive
**13** Travel the country
**18** Preoccupied with
**19** Carried
**23** They may be drawn with compasses
**24** Tom who wrote "The Greatest Generation"
**25** Akin
**27** Fanatics wage it
**28** Last Supper query
**29** Doles (out)
**30** Badlands sight
**31** "Saturday Night Live" genre
**32** Doha's land
**33** Hook up
**34** Analyze, as ore
**38** Don Corleone
**41** Marquis de ___
**44** "The Great Gatsby" gambler Wolfsheim
**49** Lower the allowed electrical capacity of
**50** Narrow valley
**51** Three-star officer: Abbr.
**53** Location of Olympus Mons
**54** Still alive
**55** Out's opposite
**56** Brief holiday?
**58** One-L person, in an Ogden Nash poem
**59** Big movie fan's option?
**60** Distinguish
**61** Dirección from which the sun rises
**63** Cambridge sch.
**64** Suffix with ethyl
**65** The shakes, for short

*by Joon and Caroline Pahk*

**ACROSS**

**1** Just for guys
**5** Rice dish
**10** Colleague of Clark at the "Daily Planet"
**14** Oscar winner Kedrova
**15** Amorphous critter
**16** Ultimatum's end
**17** State firmly
**18** Musical genre for Destiny's Child
**19** Concert halls of old
**20** TV game show that places spouses at risk?
**23** "Crocodile Rock" singer John
**24** Fresh talk
**25** Chemical in Drano
**27** Belittle, slangily
**28** Toe the line
**32** Chocolate trees
**34** Red Bordeaux
**36** Outback avians
**37** TV game show that quizzes oenophiles?
**40** Morales of "N.Y.P.D. Blue"
**42** Lease signer
**43** Winter topper
**46** Hawaii's state bird
**47** Hood's pistol
**50** Do-over at Wimbledon
**51** Pint-size
**53** Reads closely, with "over"
**55** TV game show that eliminates coy contestants?
**60** Super server
**61** ___ to (in on)
**62** Nair competitor
**63** "Comin' ___ the Rye"
**64** First name in TV talk
**65** Gabor and Longoria Parker
**66** Colon, in an emoticon
**67** Not the sharpest pencil in the box
**68** Place for a blotter

**DOWN**

**1** Left rolling in the aisles, as an audience
**2** Copenhagen's ___ Gardens
**3** Native Alaskans
**4** Reclusive Greta
**5** A comb makes one
**6** "If ___ suggest . . ."
**7** Last name in TV talk
**8** Co-panelist of Cowell
**9** It's sold by the yard
**10** Sainted fifth-century pope
**11** Former inamorato or inamorata
**12** "Peekaboo" follower
**13** Neptune's realm
**21** ___ Gay" (W.W. II bomber)
**22** New Deal org.
**26** Pothook shape
**29** Lawman Masterson
**30** Once, once
**31** Aden's land
**33** Coin whose front was last redesigned in 1909
**34** In vogue
**35** Newcastle's river
**37** "Don't move ___ I'll go for help"
**38** Hardly ruddy
**39** All thumbs
**40** Night school subj.
**41** Lacking details
**44** "How cute"
**45** Espied Godiva, e.g.
**47** Show sorrow
**48** Trojan War hero
**49** "You should have known better"
**52** Country rocker Steve
**54** Had title to
**56** Cupid's Greek counterpart
**57** Ceramist's oven
**58** Times to revel
**59** January 1 song word
**60** Broke bread

*by Ray Fontenot*

# 40

## ACROSS

**1** Admirer of Beauty, with "the"
**6** Sing like Ella Fitzgerald
**10** Genesis victim
**14** Longtime G.E. chief with the best seller "Jack: Straight from the Gut"
**15** Mrs. Dithers in "Blondie"
**16** 1950s–'70s Yugoslav leader
**17** Loud, as a crowd
**18** Place for a roast
**19** Not duped by
**20** "Huh?"
**23** And others of the same sort: Abbr.
**24** Circle section
**25** Comment after 20-Across
**34** Not just once
**35** Word from the crib
**36** Etiquette maven Vanderbilt
**37** Restrain, with "up"
**38** Andrea Bocelli deliveries
**40** Sicilian spewer
**41** Male gobbler
**42** Say "one club," say
**43** Like something communicated with a wink and a nod
**44** Comment after 25-Across
**48** MSN rival
**49** Lode load
**50** Comment after 44-Across
**59** ___ Inn
**60** Wild cat
**61** Rodeo contestant
**62** Neutral shade
**63** The "U" in 21-Down
**64** Puccini opera
**65** In the public eye
**66** Head of France?
**67** Like a cigar bar

## DOWN

**1** N.Y.C. theater district, for short
**2** One of the Saarinens of Finland
**3** Baseball's Moises
**4** "The Lion King" villain
**5** Bases loaded
**6** Burn with an iron
**7** Place to moor a boat
**8** See 58-Down
**9** Big mugs
**10** "A.S.A.P.!"
**11** Cherry variety
**12** Caesarean rebuke
**13** Chicago district, with "the"
**21** Abbr. on an appliance sticker
**22** "___ la Douce"
**25** Desert flora
**26** "Ha! That's ___ one!"
**27** One of the Judds
**28** Litter cry
**29** Minneapolis suburb
**30** Fine bond rating
**31** "But of course!"
**32** ___ vincit amor
**33** Jane of "Father Knows Best"
**38** Well said
**39** Tape deck button
**40** Have a bite
**42** ___ about (roughly)
**43** Opera, ballet and so on
**45** Bygone Japanese car name
**46** Until now
**47** Dernier ___
**50** When 12-Down was uttered
**51** Valentine decoration
**52** Stringed instrument of old
**53** Letter in a mysterious inscription
**54** Throw off
**55** Appear ominously
**56** ___ facto
**57** Chicken part that's good for soup
**58** With 8-Down, source of an ethical dilemma

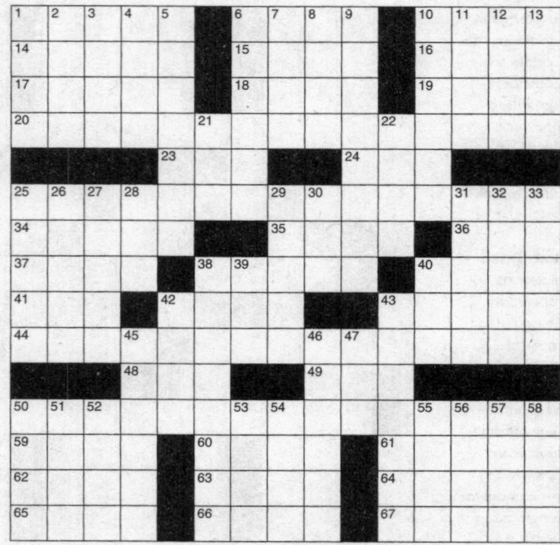

*by Harriet Clifton*

# 41

## ACROSS

1 Fix firmly
6 Bust ___ (laugh hard)
10 Colombia's second-largest city
14 Walled city of Spain
15 "Forbidden" perfume brand
16 Service closer
17 Focus of some contemplation
18 Control tower word
19 Cozy corner
20 Hoopsters turn down singer Stevie?
23 Singing the blues
24 Filled fare
25 Taxonomic suffix
26 Misplace comic Costello's privies?
31 "The Square Egg" author
34 Keen on
35 Maximilian I's realm: Abbr.
36 20-, 26-, 46- and 56-Across, homophonically speaking
40 Yup'ik and others
42 Like a petty officer: Abbr.
43 Martinique et Corsica
45 Org. with a closing bell
46 Apportion hamburgers to track runners?
51 Get-up-and-go
52 Candidates for witness protection programs
53 Secretary Geithner
56 Compose the appropriate ceremony?
60 Austria's capital, to Austrians
61 Kind of tide
62 Rushed
63 Grp. including Nigeria and Venezuela
64 "Mon Oncle" star
65 Speedy Washington-to-Boston link
66 Chinese toy, for short
67 German admiral who went down with the Scharnhorst
68 Custodian's supply

## DOWN

1 Admiral and others
2 The first Mrs. Trump
3 Like some imaginations
4 T.V.A. output
5 Have a word with
6 On the double
7 Filled fare
8 Alpine goat
9 Rat race casualties
10 Alternative to "Continue" in an online order
11 In a frenzy
12 13 popes, so far
13 Tattooist's supply
21 Airline in the Star Alliance
22 "No harm, no foul"
26 Sass
27 Pee Wee Reese, for the Dodgers
28 "Heavens!"
29 Top prizes at the Juegos Olímpicos
30 Zaire's Mobutu ___ Seko
31 Part of many musical notes
32 Former Minnesota governor Carlson
33 Piper's wear
37 The sky, it's said
38 Things on a table
39 "Get it?"
41 Cause of a turnover: Abbr.
44 Make furrows in
47 Show clearly
48 Heckle or Jeckle of cartoons
49 Haile Selassie's land: Abbr.
50 Like some planetarium projections
53 Sticking points
54 Author Calvino
55 Like most golf woods, nowadays
56 Towelette, e.g.
57 Need a bath badly
58 Take in
59 Blue
60 Doo-___

| | | | | | | | | | | | | | | |
|---|---|---|---|---|---|---|---|---|---|---|---|---|---|---|
| 1 | 2 | 3 | 4 | 5 | ■ | 6 | 7 | 8 | 9 | ■ | 10 | 11 | 12 | 13 |
| 14 | | | | | ■ | 15 | | | | ■ | 16 | | | |
| 17 | | | | | ■ | 18 | | | | ■ | 19 | | | |
| 20 | | | | | 21 | | | | | 22 | | | | ■ |
| 23 | | | ■ | 24 | | | | ■ | 25 | | | ■ | ■ | ■ |
| ■ | ■ | ■ | 26 | | | | | 27 | | | | 28 | 29 | 30 |
| 31 | 32 | 33 | | ■ | ■ | ■ | 34 | | | | ■ | 35 | | |
| 36 | | | | 37 | 38 | 39 | ■ | 40 | | | 41 | | | |
| 42 | | | ■ | 43 | | | 44 | ■ | ■ | ■ | 45 | | | |
| 46 | | | 47 | | | | | 48 | 49 | 50 | | ■ | ■ | ■ |
| ■ | ■ | ■ | 51 | | | ■ | 52 | | | | ■ | 53 | 54 | 55 |
| ■ | 56 | 57 | | | | 58 | | | | | 59 | | | |
| 60 | | | | ■ | 61 | | | | ■ | 62 | | | | |
| 63 | | | | ■ | 64 | | | | ■ | 65 | | | | |
| 66 | | | | ■ | 67 | | | | ■ | 68 | | | | |

by Kenneth J. Berniker

# 42

## ACROSS

**1** "___ you serious?"
**4** Equilateral quadrilateral
**10** Went like the dickens
**14** Former Yankee pitcher and coach Stottlemyre
**15** Had dinner
**16** Hammy "Now I see!"
**17** Tatyana of "The Fresh Prince of Bel-Air"
**18** Like the Canadian flag . . . and a hint to the first names of 24- and 48-Across
**20** Number on a tag
**22** Where Orvieto can be found
**23** The N.F.L.'s Papa Bear
**24** 1939 role for 57-Across, for which she won a 38-Across
**28** Go like the dickens
**29** Kim of "NYPD Blue"
**32** Fancy neckwear
**35** Nothing more than
**36** Paternity confirmer
**37** Eight the hard way, e.g.
**38** See 24- and 48-Across
**40** Fox News star
**41** CBS show set in Las Vegas
**42** Breyers alternative
**43** Challenges
**44** Town that failed to pay the piper
**46** Ralph who was the 1974 N.L. batting champ
**48** 1951 role for 57-Across, for which she won a 38-Across
**53** "Not me"
**55** "___ Fool to Want You"
**56** Miss from Mex.
**57** See 24- and 48-Across
**61** Big tractor, informally
**62** Follower of "for ever and ever"
**63** Kim who sang "Bette Davis Eyes"
**64** ___ king
**65** Emperor who married his stepsister
**66** Woodwind player
**67** Dict. offering

## DOWN

**1** Pile up
**2** Excavated item
**3** Henry's tutee
**4** Lith. or Est., once
**5** Its flag sports four fleurs-de-lis
**6** Modernize
**7** Disconnected
**8** Cartoon pooch
**9** Former "Tonight Show" announcer Hall
**10** Most of Mali
**11** Fool around
**12** This, to Picasso
**13** They might bring in a few bucks
**19** Starbuck's quarry
**21** "Captain Blood" star Flynn
**25** Atlas fig.
**26** Old music halls
**27** Frau's mate
**30** Suffix with confer
**31** Shaggy Tibetans
**32** Eyebrow shape
**33** Slugger Sammy
**34** Traverse, as a mountain ridge
**35** Hosts, for short
**38** Husband of Frigg
**39** Lip- ___
**40** Digs
**42** Make ecstatic
**43** Actress Joanne
**45** Meteorological phenomenon
**46** Early Cape Canaveral program
**47** "Make hay while the sun shines" and others
**49** Sacred: Prefix
**50** Menaces from the deep
**51** Where Orvieto can be found
**52** Pitchfork wielder
**53** Director Reitman
**54** Five-and-___
**58** Sgt. or cpl.
**59** Part of many a psych course
**60** D.D.E.'s predecessor

*by Peter A. Collins*

★★

**ACROSS**

**1** President before Jack
**4** City on a bay
**9** One of the Bushes
**12** Early Atari offering
**14** Calculus calculations
**15** Bone connected to the supinator muscle
**16** 90 degrees from sur
**17** Key building support
**19** Across the entire United States
**21** Dispatch boat
**22** Put into words
**26** Unable to run
**30** Seconds, at dinner
**31** "That's ___!"
**32** Letterman list, e.g.
**34** Boomerang, in a way
**39** Order to relax
**40** Perfectly
**41** Marquee name
**42** Publisher of The New Yorker
**47** Cry of praise
**50** Guardian spirits
**51** Be disadvantageous to
**55** Reasonably priced . . . or a hint to 17-, 19-, 26-, 34-, 42- and 51-Across
**58** Ex-Runaways guitarist Ford
**59** ___ d'amore (instrument)
**60** 100, in Italy
**61** In the public eye
**62** "Horrors!," online
**63** Name registered at many an escort service
**64** Some homecoming float makers: Abbr.

**DOWN**

**1** Drug for a poisoning victim
**2** Disputed Balkan territory
**3** Necessarily involve
**4** Skill not displayed by asking "Have you put on weight?"
**5** Suffix with buck
**6** Chicago exchange, for short
**7** Prove successful
**8** "Save me ___" (latecomer's request)
**9** Selena portrayer, familiarly
**10** Minnesota twins?
**11** Cricketer's need
**13** Painter's undercoat
**15** Musically bouncy
**18** String after Q
**20** Ark scrolls
**23** Prefix with tiller
**24** "___ Tu" (1974 hit)
**25** Make an impression on?
**27** Penguin's hangout
**28** Objective
**29** Get done
**32** Repulsive sort
**33** Salsa brand
**34** Word before cow or crop
**35** "Beetle Bailey" bulldog
**36** Tsp. or tbsp.
**37** Malady treated with drops
**38** Whole lot
**42** A.T.M. button
**43** Simon and Diamond
**44** John Denver's "___ Song"
**45** Woman with vows
**46** Tennessee gridders
**48** "___ will not!"
**49** Never, in Nogales
**52** Literature Nobelist Morrison
**53** Terrier in whodunits
**54** Classic Pontiac muscle cars
**55** Try to win
**56** Big Blue
**57** Dress (up)

*by Gary Steinmehl*

44

**ACROSS**

1 U.S. political scandal involving a fictional sheik
7 Sport whose name has two accents
11 Some tablets
14 Puget Sound city
15 Classic theater name
16 Alley ___
17 Twine cutter?
19 Time for the history books
20 Words after cross, down or over
21 Setting of an April marathon
23 Thurman of "Pulp Fiction"
24 OPEC production cutback?
27 Reservoir producers
29 Louvre Pyramid architect
30 Suffix with myth
31 Bygone monarchs
34 Legal precedent setter
37 March figure . . . or, when split into three parts, a title for this puzzle
39 Buzzer in the kitchen, maybe
42 Onetime South African P.M. Jan
45 Years in old Rome
46 Reuters competitor
48 Strait-laced
50 Pen for a pet pig?
55 Suffix with project
56 Imam, e.g.
57 Be postponed
59 Folded-over skirt part
60 Ice hockey in prison?
63 "The Raven" writer's inits.
64 Rental for an outdoor reception
65 Will's focus
66 Banned bug spray
67 Some valuable 1920s–'40s baseball cards
68 Fur wraps

**DOWN**

1 Offered for breeding
2 Shower room sight
3 Fun house sounds
4 Stamp purchase
5 Prenatal exam, briefly
6 Great: Prefix
7 Directional ending
8 Polynesian paste
9 Like some private dets.
10 "I've got my ___ you!"
11 Horace's "Ars ___"
12 Mexican beer choices
13 Glittery glue-on
18 Seaweed variety
22 Bank teller's fear
25 Make up galleys for printing
26 Layer
28 Less respectful
32 Map no.
33 Hawaiian Tropic no.
35 What your mom might call your aunt
36 RKO film airer, maybe
38 Grad
39 Came out of one's shell
40 Being walked, as Fido
41 Disheveled
43 Of no matter
44 End of life as we know it?
47 Archipelago's makeup: Abbr.
49 Becomes one
51 Tissue: Prefix
52 Quarterfinals qualifiers, e.g.
53 Little ones: Var.
54 Brewing need
58 One of four Holy Roman emperors
61 Bankbook fig.
62 Football linemen: Abbr.

by Patrick Merrell

## ACROSS

**1** Go over the wall, maybe
**7** Asia's Trans ___ Range
**11** "Great" creature
**14** Peter Pan lost his
**15** Serenades the moon
**16** Either of two A's rivals
**17** Word after yes or no
**18** Ancient concert halls
**19** Don Ho adornment
**20** Wagner's earth goddess
**21** Conveyances at 40-Across
**24** Revue bits
**26** Nintendo's Super ___
**27** Collagist Max
**28** Some tides
**30** 1936 foe of Franklin D.
**31** Beaufort ___, area above Alaska
**33** Prickly plants
**36** "Voice of Israel" author
**40** City with a landmark spelled out by the circled letters, reading left to right
**43** Former Wall St. letters
**44** Thoroughly frustrate
**45** Early seventh-century year
**46** ___-pah band
**48** Holiday visitor, maybe
**50** Org. headquartered on N.Y.C.'s First Avenue
**53** Part of B.Y.O.B.
**55** Letter before beth
**58** 1904 event at 40-Across
**61** Coin with the words REPVBBLICA ITALIANA
**62** One may stand in it
**63** Needle holder
**64** Problem drinker, e.g.
**66** Actor Cage, familiarly
**67** Project, as a 14-Across
**68** Arm-twisting
**69** Come down with
**70** See 65-Down
**71** Soviet agcy. in Bond novels

## DOWN

**1** Slalom maneuvers
**2** Dodge, as a duty
**3** Pro team in 40-Across
**4** Madison Ave. cost
**5** Creator of Roderick Usher
**6** Basin go-with
**7** Superior to
**8** Does dock work
**9** Yesterday, in the Yucatán
**10** Juan Perón's third wife
**11** Narnia lion
**12** 5-Down and others
**13** Be
**22** Refuse to bend
**23** Monteverdi opera partly set in the underworld
**25** "Elephant Boy" boy
**29** Spectrum-forming solid
**30** Words after ugly or guilty
**31** Govt.-issued ID
**32** Info from the cockpit, for short
**34** "Rehab" singer Winehouse
**35** Adriatic Riviera city
**37** Brand associated with 40-Across
**38** ___ cosine
**39** Shoot down
**41** Two-time N.L. batting champ Lefty
**42** Emmy winner Ward
**47** Next in the order
**49** Cafe aroma, say
**50** Vocal nasality
**51** TV host Mandel
**52** Way to stand
**53** Worth having
**54** Ralph of "The Waltons"
**56** Defensive strategy in basketball
**57** Like Russian winters
**59** Ollie's partner
**60** X-ray dosage units
**65** With 70-Across, cause of a limp

*by Peter A. Collins*

# 46

## ACROSS

**1** Billionaire Bill
**6** Sleeping in, say
**10** Bolshevik's foe
**14** Lake of the Ozarks feeder
**15** Eins und zwei
**16** Streamlined, in brief
**17** How a former product may be brought back
**20** Louisville sports icon
**21** Like steak tartare
**22** Provokes
**23** Tale of a hellish trip
**28** Biochem strand
**29** Faulty, as a plan
**32** "City Without Walls" poet
**35** Shell alternative
**37** Trifling amount
**38** Redistributionist's catchphrase . . . or a hint to the words formed by the circled letters
**42** "Piggy"
**43** Actor Jonathan ___ Meyers
**44** ___ dust (so-o-o boring)
**45** Suffering torment
**48** Ruling party in Johannesburg: Abbr.
**49** Upscale shoe brand
**55** Eccentric
**57** Soybean relative
**58** Valéry's vacation time
**59** Escapes via luxury liner
**64** Puzzling jumble: Abbr.
**65** Izmir native
**66** "Good question"
**67** Half-baked
**68** "Buy It Now" site
**69** Impudent lady

## DOWN

**1** Sprout mold, say
**2** Places of respite
**3** Anticlimactic putt
**4** Elitist's problem
**5** Patriot Day mo.
**6** Dwight's two-time opponent
**7** Brain's counterpart
**8** Unceasingly, to Burns
**9** Accomplished
**10** Spanish road
**11** With fervor
**12** Obama education secretary ___ Duncan
**13** Concrete reinforcers
**18** Bear overhead?
**19** Muffs
**24** Dendrologist's subject
**25** Central Sicilian city
**26** Amalgamates
**27** Adequate, in verse
**30** Part of N.B.
**31** Cries from the momentarily stupid
**32** Moscato d'___ (Italian wine)
**33** Knowledgeable of
**34** Superstar assembly
**35** Alcohol type used as biofuel
**36** Short
**39** Fleming supervillain
**40** Cross-dressing "Dame" of humor
**41** Roman aqueduct support
**46** Mustang's place
**47** Vending machine input
**48** Former orchard spray
**50** Teatro La Fenice offering
**51** Tom Sawyer's crush
**52** Snuggles
**53** Lovey-dovey pairs
**54** Merry Prankster Ken
**55** Queensland gem
**56** It parallels the radius
**60** RAV4 or TrailBlazer, briefly
**61** Chafe
**62** Cry made while holding the nose
**63** Note from a busted person

*by Chuck Deodene*

## ACROSS

**1** Prefix with lateral
**5** Frame side
**9** Was in the arms of Morpheus
**14** Ward who played Robin
**15** Baseball family name
**16** Conductors' platforms
**17** Wait
**18** Symbol of uncommunicativeness
**19** Hockey no-no
**20** One who plunders boatloads of jack-o'-lanterns?
**23** Published
**24** Zilch
**25** Pet store offering
**29** Pick-me-up
**31** ___-devil
**34** One way to read
**35** Shook out of dreamland
**36** In among
**37** First-rate chastisement?
**40** Tree of Life locale
**41** Destination for a ferry from Livorno
**42** Get stuffed
**43** Words from the Rev.
**44** One may be in waiting
**45** Ship of fuels
**46** "The tongue of the mind": Cervantes
**47** Stage design
**48** Nickname for an unpredictable Communist?
**55** Family
**56** Skyrocket
**57** Love of Spain
**59** Preceding on the page
**60** "I'm off!"
**61** Egypt's third-largest city
**62** Arab League member
**63** Yoked pair
**64** What ". . . . . . . ." means to a typesetter

## DOWN

**1** A drop in the ocean?
**2** Will Rogers specialty
**3** Official language of Pakistan
**4** News clipping
**5** Follower who does the dirty work
**6** Bushed
**7** Sound stressed, maybe
**8** Traffic slower
**9** Ghost
**10** Neighborhood pub
**11** Ready for release
**12** Tar source
**13** It's game
**21** Fall preceder
**22** Draw a conclusion
**25** Krypton and others
**26** Not get caught by
**27** Rodeo specialist
**28** Use as fuel
**29** Hotel area
**30** Furniture chain
**31** Show of smugness
**32** Pivotal point
**33** Trimming tool
**35** Ironworker's union?
**36** Loads
**38** Had in view
**39** Banded gemstone
**44** Heavy
**45** Home of the Azadi Tower
**46** Establish as fact
**47** Union member
**48** Hamburg's river
**49** Leeway
**50** Part of an analogy
**51** Sweet-talk
**52** Car wash gear
**53** Shoot out
**54** Snooze
**55** Dark horse
**58** Chinese calendar animal . . . or the key to this puzzle's theme

*by Richard Silvestri*

# 48

## ACROSS

**1** Painter's primer
**6** Mex. miss
**10** Big Apple neighborhood west of the East Village
**14** English novelist Canetti who wrote "Crowds and Power"
**15** Thing to look under
**16** Privy to
**17** Dear
**20** Actress Thompson
**21** When la Tour Eiffel lights up
**22** Rock band with a lightning bolt in its logo
**23** What children should be, so the saying goes
**27** Electees
**28** Mount in the Bible
**29** "___ the last rose of summer" (start of a Thomas Moore poem)
**30** ___ the day
**31** Head out on the ranch?
**33** Korean money
**34** What Justin Timberlake's "bringin' back," in a song
**35** Home of the Ivy League
**39** Director Preminger
**42** Palindromic exclamation
**43** Many sand castle molds
**47** Not con
**48** Take to court
**49** Carmaker whose name means "arise out of Asia"
**51** ___ Mustard
**52** It's a relief in Athens
**56** Princess with a blaster
**57** "That's big news, dude!"
**58** Sentence segment: Abbr.
**59** Likely to change everything
**62** Baseball's Moises
**63** Like lemonade sans sugar
**64** Oscar-winning "Tootsie" actress
**65** Cold War news source
**66** Canine command
**67** Comedian Wanda

## DOWN

**1** Book that spans 2,369 years
**2** Gold or silver, but not bronze
**3** Like the cats in "Lady and the Tramp"
**4** Clear kitchen wrap
**5** Sunrise direction in Berlin
**6** Hoot and holler
**7** 1998 De Niro film
**8** In direct competition
**9** Google moneymakers
**10** Lisa Simpson, to Patty or Selma
**11** How one might go bungee jumping
**12** Receptacle for Voldemort's soul in Harry Potter
**13** Que. neighbor
**18** Burden
**19** Derisive laughs
**24** Prefix with -meter
**25** Fey of "30 Rock"
**26** Susan of "L.A. Law"
**32** Musician Brian
**33** ". . . that's ___!"
**34** Where to catch a bullet?: Abbr.
**36** Player/preyer
**37** "And after that?"
**38** Exchange jabs or gibes
**39** Right to left, e.g.: Abbr.
**40** Light refrain
**41** Stars in a ring
**44** Place to see a flying camel
**45** Drop down one's throat?
**46** Big busting tools
**48** Persian monarch
**49** Full of difficulties
**50** "___ first you . . ."
**53** "___ Andronicus"
**54** John who wrote "Appointment in Samarra"
**55** Start of an appeal
**59** Drop down one's throat
**60** Urban grid: Abbr.
**61** Chi-town trains

*by Jonah Kagan*

## ACROSS

**1** Resell quickly, as a house
**5** No longer insure
**9** Native to
**13** Passed-down stories
**14** Voodoo accessories
**16** Flintstones' pet
**17** Scary figure
**18** Conclude
**19** Med school subj.
**20** Garden intruders
**22** Denver's ___ University
**24** Command to Rex
**25** Ones flying in formation
**27** Driveway applications
**29** Rigel or Spica
**32** Thérèse, for one: Abbr.
**33** Pioneer in instant messaging
**34** Protection: Var.
**36** Himalayan legends
**40** Easy way of pulling in . . . and a hint to the six circled words
**44** 2005 documentary subtitled "The Smartest Guys in the Room"
**45** Orderly
**46** Word for word?
**47** U.S. Dept. of Justice raiders
**49** Items for urban dog-walkers
**52** Toga go-withs
**56** Pound and others
**57** "What ___ the chances?"
**58** Day spa facial procedures
**60** "___ the Sheriff" (Eric Clapton hit)
**63** Watch from a hidden position
**65** Half of a giant 1999 merger
**67** ___-shanter
**68** International shoe company
**69** Skit collection
**70** Composer Khachaturian
**71** Lucy's love
**72** Counterparts of dahs
**73** Belgrade native

## DOWN

**1** Rap component, to a rapper
**2** Special seating area
**3** Asymmetric
**4** River with its source in the Appalachians
**5** Onetime White House monogram
**6** Liberal pundit with a conservative father
**7** Shoppe modifier
**8** Cord ends
**9** Rx overseer
**10** Dishwasher cycle
**11** Broadcasting
**12** Big name in applesauce
**15** Black and white Mad magazine figures
**21** Paris possessive
**23** Woodland reveler of myth
**26** British submachine gun
**28** Welsh national emblem
**29** Wished
**30** Pork cut
**31** Stirs up
**35** Visits la-la land
**37** Vacation plan
**38** "___ out?" (question to a pet)
**39** Some cops: Abbr.
**41** Prod
**42** Ready for use
**43** One-volume encyclopedia range
**48** Topps competitor
**50** ". . . ___ quit!"
**51** Olive Garden dishes
**52** Garden dish
**53** As ___ (usually)
**54** Willy Wonka Candy Company brand
**55** Determined the gender of
**59** M years before the Battle of Hastings
**61** Epps or Sharif
**62** Mausoleum
**64** Decorative pond fish
**66** Super ___ (1980s-'90s game console)

*by Peter A. Collins*

# 50

## ACROSS

1 Appetite arouser
6 Show appreciation, in a way
10 Busyness
13 Reporting to
14 "Gladiator" setting
15 Groucho's cigar, e.g.
16 Attila, for one?
18 First-rate stand-up comic
19 Bird sounds
20 Neck and neck
21 Is tiresome
22 How some things are set
24 When said three times, a dance
25 Cowardly boxer?
31 Voice opposition
35 Food with lots of fiber
36 North Carolina's ___ University
37 Jefferson's religious belief
39 "L'___ c'est moi"
40 Like a photon
42 Herders' tools
43 Where to find a genie?
46 Colony worker
47 Polite reply that may be accompanied by eye-rolling
52 The Destroyer, in Hinduism
55 Relative of Bowser
57 Concerning
58 Trek
59 Holders of some pipe joints?
61 Start the bidding
62 Middling
63 Nimbi
64 Carry-on checkers: Abbr.
65 Bit of laughter
66 Teapot part . . . or a two-word hint to 16-, 25-, 43- and 59-Across

## DOWN

1 Early counters
2 Military drone's job, for short
3 Spreads in bars
4 Like towelettes, typically
5 Barley bristle
6 Lily-livered
7 Prospector's strike
8 Word of agreement
9 A pop
10 "Habanera" from "Carmen" is one
11 "Let's Make a Deal" choice
12 Stops waffling
15 Flock leader
17 Caesar's "I came"
21 Taylor or Tyler
23 Norris Trophy winner for eight consecutive years
24 One to hang with
26 Miller's need
27 N.Y.S.E. listings
28 Green Hornet's sidekick
29 "Yikes!"
30 Pulls in
31 Prefix with god
32 Zip
33 Kind of votes a candidate wants
34 Stubbly
37 Cardholder's woe
38 That, in Toledo
41 ___ the Hyena of "Li'l Abner"
42 Foot, to a zoologist
44 Popular bathroom cleaner
45 First pope with the title "the Great"
48 Fixed fashionably
49 Summer month in South America
50 Pianist Claudio
51 Change, as an alarm
52 It may precede a chaser
53 They may swivel
54 Self-assembly retail chain
55 Ice sheet
56 She said "Play it, Sam"
59 "I know what you're thinking" skill
60 "If I Ruled the World" rapper

*by Andrea Carla Michaels and Peter L. Stein*

## ACROSS

**1** With 69-Across, 1930s-'50s bandleader
**5** Brand name in the kitchen
**10** Suit to ___
**14** Bellicose deity
**15** One who's "toast"
**16** Comparison word
**17** Japan, to the U.S., once
**19** Sleek, in car talk
**20** 1966 Mary Martin musical
**21** Fleet elite
**23** Ex-lib, maybe
**24** "I'm ___!" ("Can do!")
**25** Views that reality is a unitary whole
**29** ___ Martin (cognac brand)
**32** Ancient Greek sculptor of athletes
**36** "Golly!"
**37** Hogwash
**39** Eagle's claw
**41** Place for une île
**42** Brickyard 400 entrant
**43** Use weasel words
**44** All there
**46** Makes a cat's-paw of
**47** Sizzling sound
**48** "Baby Baby" singer, 1991
**51** Sushi-rolling accessories
**53** Good-humored
**58** Carbon 14 and uranium 235
**62** Subtitle of 1978's "Damien"
**63** Shark on some menus
**64** 1976 Eric Carmen hit
**66** Pulitzer-winning author Robert ___ Butler
**67** Homeric sorceress
**68** Word with family or fruit
**69** See 1-Across
**70** Made bearable
**71** Criteria: Abbr.

## DOWN

**1** Oral vaccine developer
**2** Take for ___ (hoodwink)
**3** Copycat's cry
**4** Old Connecticut whaling town
**5** Science for farmers
**6** See 50-Down
**7** Wintour of fashion
**8** More than desire
**9** One with yellow ribbons, maybe
**10** Game maker since 1972
**11** Courtroom antics, e.g.
**12** Sandwich man?
**13** Fourth book of the Book of Mormon
**18** Esau's descendants' land
**22** Brass or woodwind: Abbr.
**26** Chinese menu notation
**27** Start of a rumor report
**28** Ancient city that lent its name to a fig
**30** Tool for a duel
**31** Actor Mike
**32** That you should feed a cold and starve a fever, and others
**33** Explorer John and actress Charlotte
**34** Snowy peak of song
**35** Creamy beverage
**38** Former German president Johannes
**40** "Cool!"
**45** Ate up, so to speak
**49** Popular social networking site, and this puzzle's theme
**50** With 6-Down, 1994 Olympic gold medalist in downhill skiing
**52** Thing to do on Yom Kippur
**54** Endows (with)
**55** Hard to combine, chemically
**56** Was indisposed
**57** Thomas Hardy's "___ Little Ironies"
**58** "Don't worry about me"
**59** Part of una casa
**60** London Magazine essayist
**61** Some cameras, for short
**65** Pre-A.D.

*by Dan Schoenholz*

# 52

## ACROSS

**1** Specialty
**6** 1970s sitcom that included Carlton the Doorman
**11** "___ you one"
**15** "___ Majesty's Secret Service"
**16** Hatch in the Senate
**17** Country music pioneer Ernest
**18** Boarding place?
**19** Test group?
**20** Attempt
**21** Short trip
**22** Civil War inits.
**24** Some footnotes, for short
**26** Person on your bad side?
**29** Cannoli ingredient
**32** Contradict
**33** Flower of the buttercup family
**35** Gmail alternative
**36** Passport info
**38** "Mazel ___!"
**39** Green gem source
**41** Some surprises . . . and what you'll find in the circled areas of this puzzle
**45** Israel's Dayan
**46** ___ Miss
**47** Superscript number in math: Abbr.
**48** More than -er
**49** Woman in Sartre's "No Exit"
**52** Number two: Abbr.
**56** Doughnuts are fried in it
**58** Short piano piece
**60** Shoe brand named for an antelope
**62** Former N.B.A. star Unseld
**63** Hip-hop's ___-A-Fella Records
**64** It's better than ace-high
**66** Tchaikovsky's black swan
**68** Madison Sq. Garden player
**70** Woodworking tool
**71** Branch gripper
**72** Regular's request, with "the"
**73** Goes on and on
**74** Religious assembly
**75** Word-processing command

## DOWN

**1** Took the cake, perhaps
**2** Smitten
**3** "Fantaisie" composer
**4** In the know, old-style
**5** Standing
**6** 1915 Literature Nobelist ___ Rolland
**7** Realm ended by Napoleon: Abbr.
**8** "Yes ___?"
**9** Confute
**10** Tylenol competitor
**11** "___ die for"
**12** Defeat in a don't-blink contest
**13** Tate and Bowe were once champions of it: Abbr.
**14** Decline
**23** Person often pictured with crossed legs
**25** Where trays may be stacked
**27** "Dune" director David
**28** Irritate
**30** Santa's sleighful
**31** "Is that ___?"
**34** Bris parties
**37** Michael of "Caddyshack"
**40** American in Paris, perhaps
**41** Singer Feliciano
**42** What a record may have
**43** "Another time, perhaps"
**44** Designer Geoffrey
**45** Kind of school
**50** Cousins of clogs
**51** Subwoofer's zone
**53** Bright spot in Canis Major
**54** Back-country winter transport
**55** Take on
**57** They did it
**59** Invite to one's penthouse, say
**61** Oven
**64** Meddle
**65** Org. with a sign at many motels
**67** Head of Buckingham Palace?
**69** Secretive org.

by Pete Muller

# 53

## ACROSS

1 "The aristocrat of pears"
5 Daytime TV staple
10 "In addition . . ."
14 Parrot
15 More than miffed
16 Boot
17 *1986 Newman/Cruise film
20 Jazz session highlights
21 Kind of master
22 Squabble
23 Vintner's valley
25 Deletes, as expletives
26 *Ritzy delicacy
31 Woodworking tool
32 Meddlesome
33 Marvelous, in slang
36 Symbols of industry
37 Heavyweight champion of the world, e.g.
39 Dance with a wiggle
40 China's Lao-___
41 Languish
42 Key of Beethoven's Fifth
44 *Showboating type
46 Half of an old comedy duo
49 #2: Abbr.
50 Navel type
51 Alternative to Gmail
53 90 degrees from norte
57 Dr. Seuss book . . . or a description of the answers to the three starred clues
60 Dinghy pair
61 Weight-watcher's order, maybe
62 "Never follow" sloganeer, once
63 Gin flavorer
64 Iron
65 Try out

## DOWN

1 Takes a risk
2 Cuatro y cuatro
3 "Where the Sidewalk Ends" author Silverstein
4 Milk sources
5 Standard ___
6 Disposition pick-me-up
7 Label in a bibliophile's catalog
8 Immensely
9 Mag mogul beginning in the '50s
10 More in need
11 Kendo motion
12 Exhaust
13 Eye sores
18 Missouri River tributary
19 Language of Kuala Lumpur
24 Like early election night returns
25 Halves
26 Grill option, for short
27 Seemingly forever
28 Renaissance instrument
29 Put in a stake
30 L x w x h
33 It may be mutual
34 Balm ingredient
35 Attorney general after Thornburgh
38 Tolkien's The Prancing Pony, e.g.
39 Subtly suggested
41 Groom
43 Secret order member
44 Dolphins Hall-of-Fame QB Bob
45 Dances to some of Gloria Estefan's music
46 Symbols of industry
47 Heard, but not seen
48 In ___ (not yet born)
51 Gelatin substitute
52 Watch like a wolf
54 Actress Elisabeth
55 Small amounts
56 Discharge
58 Seer's gift
59 Pitches

*by Daniel Kantor*

# 54

## ACROSS

**1** More fitting
**6** Sound in a hatchery
**10** Mexican muralist Orozco
**14** "The ___!" (perturbed cry)
**15** Major-league team member through 2004
**16** Month before Nisan
**17** "I'm ___ and didn't know it"
**18** Stationer's unit
**19** Year Cortés conquered Cuba
**20** "Rhoda" and "Frasier"
**22** Keen insight
**24** Part of a heartbeat
**25** Suffix with moon
**26** Util. bill
**27** Mathematician's "ta-da!"
**28** 15-Across now, informally
**31** Where the cows come home
**34** Words to a traitor
**36** Glue
**38** They're often twisted apart
**40** Supermodel Carangi
**41** More trustworthy
**42** Long (for)
**43** Growing room?
**45** "___ boy!"
**46** "My Gal ___"
**47** Former Notebook maker
**49** Final, e.g.
**51** Sugar ___
**53** Stimulus response
**57** Centers
**59** Like some missiles
**60** First word of "The Raven"
**61** Tickle Me Elmo maker
**63** "The Secret Life of Walter ___"
**64** Suffix with origin
**65** "The first word of the answer to each of the six starred clues describes the number of that clue," e.g.
**66** "That's ___!"
**67** Pitcher Wilhelm
**68** Chemical endings
**69** Horne and Olin

## DOWN

**1** Jawbone of ___ (biblical weapon)
**2** Spirited
**3** Number of Dumas's Mousquetaires
**4** *Balance in personality
**5** Overhaul
**6** *Pitcher's dream
**7** Split personalities?
**8** Waste watchers: Abbr.
**9** Crushed pulp
**10** Clog
**11** *They don't belong
**12** Old German duchy name
**13** Land o' blarney
**21** Take off
**23** Citadel student
**25** *Basic Scout ties
**29** Dungeons & Dragons weapons
**30** Banks on the runway
**31** Word before and after "will be"
**32** Side by side?
**33** *It's no fake
**35** Quirk
**37** *It follows the evening news
**39** Marsh bird
**44** ___ row
**48** Cheerful
**50** 20 Questions category
**52** Open-eyed
**54** Squelched
**55** Prefix with venous
**56** Some terriers
**57** Ancient mariner
**58** Gay Talese's "___ the Sons"
**59** Bad marks?
**62** Feminine side

*by Tim Wescott*

Note: The eight two-letter answers in this puzzle are all state postal abbreviations, representing (in some order) the Beaver State, Beehive State, Big Sky Country, Heart of Dixie, Pine Tree State, Show Me State, Sunflower State and Volunteer State.

**ACROSS**

**1** 1889 Jerome K. Jerome comedy novel
**16** Undesirable alternatives
**17** Bear, in old Rome
**18** Some feds
**19** Bill
**20** See note
**21** Office rewards
**23** Carlo who married Sophia Loren
**24** Anne who married Henry VIII
**26** Not guzzle
**27** See note
**28** New Orleans-to-Indianapolis dir.
**29** Put into office: Var.
**33** Gas pump abbr.
**34** Cry interrupting a prank
**35** Bank book entry
**36** Schubert's "The ___ King"
**37** Comparative suffix
**38** Like a certain route
**39** "You mean me?"
**40** Telecom setup
**41** More, it's sometimes said
**43** Langley, e.g.: Abbr.
**44** Yearbook div.
**45** Indulge
**46** Something with this is not neat
**47** See note
**48** Game piece in Hasbro's The Game of Life
**49** One who knows what's suitable?
**51** Alternative to "take out"
**53** Young haddocks
**56** See note
**57** Jefferson bills
**58** Classic TV role for Ronny Howard
**59** Beautiful woman of paradise
**61** Dessert not for the calorie-conscious
**64** Some awards for accomplishment

**DOWN**

**1** Outline
**2** Whence the line "A person's a person, no matter how small"
**3** Purview of the I.C.C.
**4** Accustom (to)
**5** Made an effort
**6** See note
**7** Certain newts
**8** Finger
**9** Time of danger
**10** "Delta of Venus" author
**11** See note
**12** Swing alternative
**13** Warning sign
**14** Something customary
**15** Pushing beyond proper limits
**22** Superior canal locale
**23** Painter Mondrian
**25** Overhears, perhaps
**26** Heel style
**30** Short burst
**31** Joe who was twice A.L. Manager of the Year
**32** Light ___
**33** Forward
**41** Footwear giant Thom ___
**42** One who won't move over
**48** 1973 War hit "The ___ Kid"
**50** "God ___ refuge" (start of Psalm 46)
**52** Pixar drawing
**53** Not really fight
**54** Part of a mileage rating
**55** Shoot in a swamp
**58** Pay extender?
**60** Service
**62** See note
**63** See note

*by Joe Krozel*

# 56

**ACROSS**

**1** Coors product
**5** N.Y.C. theater area
**9** Frank in the Rock and Roll Hall of Fame
**14** ___-Tass news agency
**15** Surrealist Magritte
**16** Apple instant-messaging program
**17** Lovers of fine fare
**19** River flowing into and out of Lake Geneva
**20** Recital player
**21** Madden, and how
**23** Keebler cracker brand
**25** Aurora's Greek counterpart
**26** Sci-fi sidekick, maybe
**29** Restaurateur Toots
**30** Assumed name
**34** "That feels great"
**35** Honeybee genus
**37** Bit of dental work
**38** Free pass, of sorts
**39** Theme of this puzzle
**41** One of eight Eng. kings
**42** "___ regret it!"
**44** Famous Amos
**45** Nutritionist's std.
**46** Birthplace of composer Richard Strauss
**48** Guitarist Lofgren
**50** "For example . . ."
**51** Highlands refusal
**52** Madison Ave. trade
**54** Redlines
**58** Begins slowly
**62** "Be ___ and . . ."
**63** Queen ___ Maria, mother of England's Charles II and James II
**65** Stiller's comic partner
**66** Sacramento's ___ Arena
**67** "___ as I can tell . . ."
**68** Ball's comic partner
**69** Secluded area
**70** Animated film hit of 1998

**DOWN**

**1** Goes this way before that
**2** Langston Hughes poem
**3** Rough up
**4** Ingrediente en paella
**5** Military bigwig
**6** Deteriorated
**7** What's more
**8** Sammy Davis Jr.'s "___ Can"
**9** Cubic ___ (gem)
**10** Truman's last secretary of state
**11** Unit of loudness
**12** Producers' fears
**13** Faultlessly, after "to"
**18** Architect Ludwig ___ van der Rohe
**22** Three R's org.
**24** Flagstaff's place
**26** Child in a 1980s custody case
**27** "What a kidder!"
**28** N.Y.C. country club?
**31** Cubs, but not Bears, for short
**32** When said three times, "et cetera"
**33** Ol' Blue Eyes classic
**36** Harsh quality
**39** The Rock
**40** Getty or Rockefeller
**43** Ancient Cretan writing system
**47** Part of a bray
**49** "Of course, señor!"
**53** Ethan Frome's wife
**54** Lady of Spain
**55** German river to the Fulda
**56** Show preference
**57** Layered haircut
**59** 9-mm. gun of W.W. II
**60** "Let's leave ___ that"
**61** Onetime "Concentration" host Jack
**64** Schubert's "The ___-King"

*by Henry Quillen*

Note: When this puzzle is finished, the 11 circled letters in reading order will spell the subject of the quote starting at 20-Across.

**ACROSS**

**1** Symbol of gentleness
**5** Goober ___
**9** Direction for playing a dirge
**14** Like some hygiene
**15** Homecoming returnee
**16** "It floats" sloganeer
**17** Home to Columbus
**18** Thompson of TV's "Family"
**19** Birth-related
**20** Part 1 of a quote attributed to Sam Goldwyn
**23** Partook of
**24** Comb maker
**25** Gangster's target, maybe
**29** Word part: Abbr.
**30** Nervous
**31** Irish red, for one
**32** Places for crow's-nests
**35** Blackthorn
**36** Stooges, e.g.
**37** Part 2 of the quote
**40** ___ undisclosed location
**41** Pest
**42** Horses of a certain color
**43** .001 inch
**44** Rheinland residence
**45** Hardly a gulp
**46** Kind of lettuce
**48** Foxtail feature
**49** ___ candidate
**52** End of the quote
**55** Succotash ingredients
**58** Trampled (on)
**59** Mixture
**60** "Wheel of Fortune" category
**61** Where St. Patrick's Day is a national holiday
**62** "___ and Monsters" (1998 film)
**63** "La Toilette" artist
**64** Actress Charlotte and others
**65** W.W. II foe

**DOWN**

**1** Spa sponge
**2** Enlightened Buddhist
**3** "Murder, She Wrote" locale
**4** Inky mess
**5** Large quantity
**6** Gladden
**7** Auto make owned by Volkswagen
**8** Wrestling show
**9** Leading lady Laura
**10** Avoid
**11** "___ an option"
**12** ___-la
**13** Popeye's Olive
**21** Chasm
**22** Reaction to a snub, maybe
**26** Magna ___
**27** Unfamiliar
**28** Lowly types
**29** Laurel from England
**30** ___ Island, museum site since 1990
**32** City on Biscayne Bay
**33** Dusty place, traditionally
**34** Low marshland
**35** Cream
**36** Sporty car feature
**38** A sad way to grow
**39** Skater Slutskaya
**44** The job in "The Italian Job," and others
**45** Early colonists along the Delaware
**47** Swahili form of address
**48** Previous to, once
**49** Jacob's-ladder, for one
**50** Shirley Temple title role
**51** Cast-off material
**53** Verdi's "E il sol dell'anima," for one
**54** "Julius Caesar" costume
**55** Played the first card
**56** "Now ___ seen everything!"
**57** Computer unit, informally

*by Elizabeth A. Long*

58

## ACROSS

**1** Capital on the Arabian Peninsula
**5** Drone, e.g.
**9** Recommended reading for www newbies
**13** Religious leader in a turban
**14** "___ blame you"
**16** Lummox
**17** "Santa Baby" singer, 1953
**18** Lose one's amateur standing
**19** Give ___ of approval
**20** 1972 Charles Grodin film, with "The"
**22** Drugs, informally
**23** Toil (away)
**24** Spice Girl Halliwell
**26** 1984 Ralph Macchio film, with "The"
**29** Below
**33** Three sheets to the wind
**36** General whose name is associated with chicken
**37** San ___, Tex.
**38** Dijon seasons
**40** Canadian lout
**42** Dos cubed
**43** "Il Postino" poet
**45** Public health agcy.
**46** Word that's missing from 20-, 26-, 48- and 59-Across and 9- and 39-Down
**47** Protein acid
**48** Willie Mays's sobriquet
**51** "Agreed!"
**53** They all lead to Rome, in a saying
**56** TV viewer's vantage point
**59** 1965 Steve McQueen title role
**63** Have too much of, briefly
**64** Sainted ninth-century pope
**65** Rio and Sedona
**66** Setting of many a Monet painting
**67** 15 mg. of zinc, e.g.
**68** "Night" novelist Wiesel
**69** Henry who once headed the House Judiciary Committee
**70** Chinese weight
**71** Jane who loved Rochester

## DOWN

**1** Many a Punjabi
**2** French girlfriends
**3** ___ chart
**4** Train company with a portmanteau name
**5** Long-range German gun of W.W. I
**6** Stench
**7** Weapon in Clue
**8** Make sputtering mad
**9** 1984 Matt Dillon title role
**10** Top status
**11** Part of Q.E.D.
**12** Norms: Abbr.
**15** Puff
**21** F.D.R. creation
**25** Homer's outcome
**27** Japan's largest active volcano
**28** Opera about an opera singer
**30** Kayo
**31** K-12
**32** Crucifix
**33** River of Irkutsk
**34** Agenda addition
**35** Hatcher of "Desperate Housewives"
**37** Malfoy, to Harry Potter
**39** Nickname for Harry Longabaugh
**41** Big name in ice cream
**44** A deer, a female deer
**48** Most cunning
**49** Long, long time
**50** Munson, Maris or Mantle
**52** Rights org.
**54** Like bread in the Lord's Prayer
**55** Way up, maybe
**56** Not yet a jr.
**57** Anita who was nicknamed the Jezebel of Jazz
**58** Crossing, of a sort
**60** Charles of mysteries
**61** Murderous suffix
**62** "Got it"

by *Caleb Madison*

★★

**ACROSS**

**1** Forces
**6** Show off at the gym, say
**10** Fingered, briefly
**14** Come ___ of the rain
**15** Disappeared
**16** Rise by the shore
**17** Kitty
**20** Hardly anything
**21** Melville title
**22** Atlantic City casino, with "the"
**23** Résumé datum
**25** Things from faraway lands
**27** Kitty
**29** Poetic preposition
**30** "We ___ not amused"
**31** Place to kick back
**32** Grant portrayer
**35** Annual coll. basketball contest
**37** Where to get off
**41** Gasoline choice: Abbr.
**43** ___ Smiley of "Sesame Street"
**45** Cellular carrier?
**46** Kitty
**52** Flatter, in a way
**53** Binds in a bundle
**54** Therapists' org.
**55** Humble reply to praise
**57** ___ Book Club
**59** Kitty
**62** The Stooges, e.g.
**63** Main idea
**64** "S.N.L." alum Cheri
**65** Members in a 100-member club: Abbr.
**66** Maker of moving walkways
**67** Pesach feast

**DOWN**

**1** Lock feature
**2** Canines' neighbors
**3** Available
**4** Terrarium denizen
**5** Like an inscribed pillar
**6** Some N.F.L. scores: Abbr.
**7** Plumb crazy
**8** Paint type
**9** Reproduced, in a way
**10** "Rise and Fall of ___ Amin" (1981 film)
**11** Hoffman who has won two Oscars
**12** Tie up
**13** Wedding hiree
**18** Spring Air rival
**19** Was imminent
**24** Adventurers' tale
**26** Music quality
**27** Soup spherule
**28** Neutral hue
**33** Lead-in to while
**34** Stick
**36** Spots for soaks
**38** Served as an intro to
**39** Corporate gadfly's purchase, maybe
**40** Make use of
**42** "Bye now!"
**44** Gleeful shout
**46** Super Bowl XLII winners
**47** Diamond authority
**48** Vitamin in liver
**49** Miss Piggy's pal
**50** Dupes
**51** Dojo discipline
**56** "___ Can" (Sammy Davis Jr. autobiography)
**58** Move a bit
**60** Ring victories, for short
**61** Sumter and McHenry: Abbr.

*by Victor Fleming*

# 60

**ACROSS**

**1** Formed for a specific purpose
**6** Good (at)
**11** "Next" network
**14** Pipe type
**15** Inlay material
**16** Back
**17** See 55-Down
**19** Like Abner
**20** Prefix with -cardial
**21** Badlands feature
**22** Deprived
**24** Rapper Kanye
**25** Stood up to
**26** Astaire wear
**29** Capote wearers
**32** Munch Museum's home
**33** Starts of some brawls
**35** Marshal under Napoleon
**36** Hitcher's digit
**38** "I'd like to buy ___"
**39** Straphanger's buy, once
**41** Hosp. procedure
**42** Ones in matching tuxes
**45** "Whip It" band
**46** Bulwark
**48** Minded
**50** Some sculptures
**51** ___ Gailey of "Miracle on 34th Street"
**52** Talented Zero
**54** Great Trek emigrant
**55** Diner cupful
**58** Guitar, in slang
**59** See 55-Down
**62** Water around Polynésie
**63** Gobi greenery
**64** Comedy club host
**65** Pantry raider
**66** "It is equally an error to ___ all men or no man": Seneca
**67** Canon competitor

**DOWN**

**1** Up to it
**2** IV flow
**3** Rec room item of old
**4** Granola morsel
**5** Yalta's peninsula
**6** Recurring Woody Allen theme
**7** Flash drive filler
**8** Writer Umberto
**9** Validation of a will
**10** Put on the tube
**11** See 55-Down
**12** End-of-workweek cry
**13** Pioneering General Motors electric car
**18** Homes of twigs
**23** McCarthy quarry
**24** Part of T.W.I.M.C.
**25** Goodie bag goodie
**26** Clan symbol
**27** Milo of Hollywood
**28** See 55-Down
**29** See 55-Down
**30** A Chaucer pilgrim
**31** Church council
**34** Comedy club outbursts
**37** Commuters' terminus
**40** Had need of an E.R., maybe
**43** Top-notch
**44** Philosopher Kierkegaard
**47** Granola morsel
**49** Candice of "Murphy Brown"
**51** Palm off
**52** Word from the crib
**53** Teamed beasts
**54** Tournament passes
**55** Word that can define 17- and 59-Across and 11-, 28- and 29-Down
**56** Modern ice cream flavor
**57** Scene of a fall
**60** Tempe sch.
**61** Early 10th-century year

*by Allan E. Parrish*

★★

**ACROSS**
**1** Gathering clouds, e.g.
**5** Smooth-talking
**9** Some N.C.O.'s
**14** Centers of attention
**15** Rock's partner
**16** Sierra ___
**17** Unencumbered
**19** Shop group
**20** Some fruit still lifes?
**22** Parka wearer, maybe
**25** Orbital extreme
**26** Showy dance intro?
**30** Security concerns
**31** Diva's asset
**32** Where one might get steamed
**35** Suffix with buoy
**36** Chocolate-caramel candies
**37** In short order
**38** Terse reproof
**39** Actor Rutger ___
**40** Political philosopher John
**41** Gobbler in a powwow musical group?
**43** Comical Boosler
**46** Call for more
**47** Chocolate's journey?
**51** Prickly plant
**52** Stateside
**56** Where élèves study
**57** Hosiery shade
**58** "Hairspray" mom
**59** Writer who went to hell?
**60** Get blubbery
**61** Novelist Jaffe

**DOWN**
**1** Not quite oneself
**2** Jersey sound
**3** System starter?
**4** Sweating the small stuff
**5** Gradually appeal to
**6** In the ___
**7** Rick's film love
**8** Totally bungled
**9** 7-Eleven cooler
**10** Like half of U.S. senators
**11** In action
**12** It takes up to 10 yrs. to reach maturity
**13** Pick up on
**18** Priests of the East
**21** Hunger signals
**22** Super success
**23** Composer Camille Saint-___
**24** Natural ability
**27** "Are you in ___?"
**28** Archaeologist's prefix
**29** Huge, in verse
**32** Super, in Variety
**33** Cincinnati and lowball are versions of this
**34** In the blink of ___
**36** Japanese bowlful
**37** Dungeons & Dragons character
**39** Roasted one
**40** Fencing move
**41** Capulet murdered by Romeo
**42** Get together for a task
**43** Fell back
**44** Poet Federico García ___
**45** Negative particle
**48** Penthouse asset
**49** It's enough, for some
**50** Easy to maneuver, at sea
**53** Oath affirmation
**54** "The Situation Room" airer
**55** Rte. suggester

*by Donna Hoke Kahwaty*

# 62

## ACROSS

1 Legree's creator
6 Pants part
10 Grain containers
14 They may crunch when you bite into them
15 Mound
16 One
17 Providers of excellent service?
18 Hungarian city known for its thermal baths
19 Frozen dessert chain since 1981
20 Printer's type: Abbr.
21 Colossus
23 Part that's cut off and thrown away
24 Conn. summer hours
25 Singer Easton
28 Carnival food on sticks
31 Law partner?
32 Coral reef dweller
33 ___ flakes (cereal)
35 It may be found in a box in the basement
36 Subject of this puzzle
40 Subway fare?
41 Club ___
42 Cathedral city near Cambridge
43 More men do this than women, studies show
45 Raises, as a surface design
49 Treeless area
51 Part of E.U.: Abbr.
52 Walked
54 As expressly said
56 Macbeth or Lady Macbeth
57 Beautiful race in an H. G. Wells novel
59 Israeli flag carrier
60 "Same here"
61 Author L. Frank ___
62 Jamaica or Barbados
63 ___ shooting
64 Word often prefixed with kilo-
65 Snipers' place
66 Bit of sleepwear

## DOWN

1 It may lead to a landing
2 Ploy
3 El Atlántico, por ejemplo
4 What each of seven 36-Across events at the 2008 Olympics ended in
5 Tee preceder
6 Brand name associated with 36-Across
7 Singular achievement by 36-Across at the 2008 Olympics
8 Protected from the wind
9 Provisions
10 One technique used by 36-Across
11 Increased slowly
12 Pen point
13 Pen
21 Madhouse
22 Comment of surprise
26 Tight end?
27 Go for, in price
29 O.T. book
30 Chump
34 Something to be tested
36 List of alternatives
37 Smooths over
38 Wide shoe spec
39 Chicago carriers
40 Pres. elected in '48
44 Procter & Gamble detergent
46 The Baltimore ___ (nickname of 36-Across)
47 Like some banks
48 Performed without help
50 Didn't do takeout
53 Saturn or Venus
55 "Anything ___?"
57 Decline
58 Set (down)
60 Bygone aircraft, briefly

by David J. Kahn

★★

## ACROSS

**1** Easy catch for an infielder
**6** Jazz (up)
**11** Slumber party attire, for short
**14** Greeted the day
**15** Voice above a baritone
**16** Debtor's note
**17** 1966 Beatles #1 hit
**20** Pub brews
**21** Object of Indiana Jones's first quest
**22** Military engagement
**23** Non-Rx
**24** Blow off steam
**25** Louisville landmark
**32** Not the main bank
**33** Stanford rival, familiarly
**34** Thou, today
**35** "Oui" and "sí"
**36** Danson of "Cheers"
**37** Floored
**39** Select, with "for"
**40** Moo ___ pork
**41** Icon in an Internet forum
**42** Command Kirk never really gave
**46** Billions of years
**47** Lew Wallace's "Ben-___"
**48** Develop gradually
**51** It might say "Welcome"
**52** Floored it
**56** Standard degrees for scientists?
**59** Hawaiian Punch alternative
**60** Too trusting
**61** Employee's desire
**62** ___ Miss
**63** Sheen
**64** Private . . . or a hint to the words spelled by the circled letters

## DOWN

**1** "Come to ___"
**2** Face-to-face exam
**3** Successor of St. Peter
**4** Functions
**5** For each
**6** Pasta has it
**7** Atticus Finch portrayer . . . or something finches do
**8** Tattoo, slangily
**9** It may be heard in a herd
**10** Item on a to-do list
**11** Pennsylvania university, for short
**12** "Piano Man" singer
**13** "Absolutely!"
**18** Sheet of cookies
**19** "Gotta hand ___ ya . . ."
**23** Menaces to hobbits
**24** ___ the Impaler
**25** Brunch serving
**26** "___ la vista, baby!"
**27** Article in Arles
**28** Freeze over
**29** Lawman Earp
**30** "Inconceivable!"
**31** Plaintiff
**32** Letters on some invitations
**36** Ergo
**37** Actor and songwriter Novello
**38** Turner who led a revolt
**40** Nation where Wolof and French are spoken
**41** Obtuse's opposite
**43** Become squishy, like chocolate
**44** Emotional
**45** Secret Service eyewear
**48** It may be heard in a tunnel
**49** Bit of bridal wear
**50** First word of "The Raven"
**51** Dallas team, to fans
**52** Survey
**53** Cause of a wince
**54** "Or ___!"
**55** A fawn is a young one
**57** Brazilian vacation destination
**58** ___ Lanka

*by Lucas Gaviotis Whitestone*

**ACROSS**

**1** Some electrical plugs
**6** Kid-___ (film genre)
**9** Neither-here-nor-there state
**14** Volunteer's words
**15** Enzyme suffix
**16** Bygone
**17** Typical date activity
**18** ___ few rounds
**19** Joie de ___
**20** See 10-Down
**21** Sean Connery: "The Man Who ___" (1975)
**24** Turn over
**26** It flows with the wind
**27** President Sadat
**29** Ticket datum
**30** Hardly ruddy
**33** Rubber hamburger, e.g.
**35** Like a moonscape
**37** Hokkaido seaport
**38** Golfer's concern
**39** Climber of Mount Sinai
**40** Hid from view
**42** Attends homecoming, say
**43** Velvet finish?
**44** Put on
**45** "Zip your lip!"
**46** Log holder
**48** How-to unit
**51** David Bowie: "The Man Who ___" (1976)
**55** Shakespearean prince
**56** Get out of
**57** "___ funny!"
**58** The end
**60** Maui veranda
**61** Words on a card
**62** Signal to pull over
**63** Biscotti flavoring
**64** Ernie on the links
**65** Bring to bear

**DOWN**

**1** Chimp, at times
**2** Came to
**3** Boris Karloff: "The Man Who ___" (1936)
**4** Gridder Manning
**5** Knocked off
**6** Not so clear
**7** Sicilia e Sardegna
**8** Like paper vis-à-vis electronic
**9** Burt Reynolds: "The Man Who ___" (1983)
**10** With 20-Across, '50s slogan
**11** Year of Columbus's death
**12** It's on the Aare
**13** NASA force unit, briefly
**22** Oil of ___
**23** Book jacket blurbs
**25** ___ nous
**28** Lloyd Nolan: "The Man Who ___" (1942)
**30** Billy Bob Thornton: "The Man Who ___" (2001)
**31** Suit to ___
**32** Top Untouchable
**33** Two caplets, e.g.
**34** "Top ___ mornin'!"
**35** Executed
**36** Vuitton of fashion
**38** Defendant's hope, at sentencing
**41** Thickhead
**42** Go ballistic
**45** Conqueror of Mexico
**46** Wanted poster info
**47** Holocaust hero Wallenberg
**49** Raring to go
**50** Carnival shill, e.g.
**51** F.D.R. dog
**52** Sen. Bayh
**53** Anderson of "Stroker Ace"
**54** Cheat, slangily
**59** Be sociable

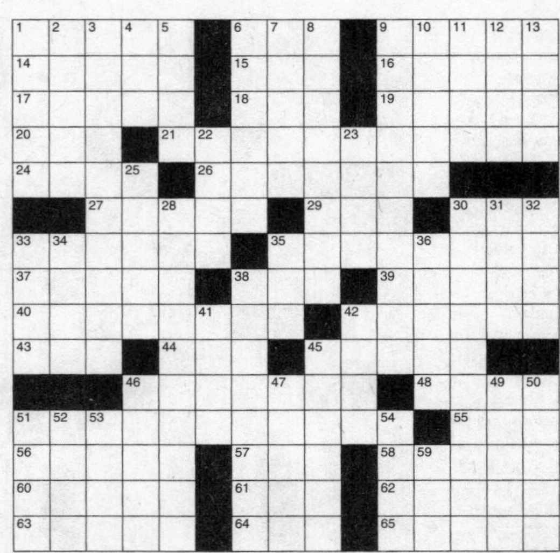

*by Edward Safran*

## ACROSS

1 Empty-headed sort
6 Battle to remember, with "the"
11 "And ___!"
14 Frequent Jacques Brel song subject
15 Like the Battle of Trafalgar
16 Work by Gray or Spenser
17 One of the "dumbest dumb animals," according to 60-Across
19 Eye protector
20 Polynesian land
21 Walton who founded Wal-Mart
22 Some Jim Beam quaffs
23 Classic Main Street liners
25 Unpaid factory worker
27 Start of the reason the 17-Across is one of the "dumbest dumb animals"
33 Pics for docs
34 Corn locale
35 Shown in full
36 Course number
37 Chairs
40 Car wash item
41 Award for Best Novel won three times by Dick Francis
44 Person to bum around with
45 Driver's warning?
46 End of the reason
50 Tropical vine
51 Unpleasant look
52 "The Grapes of Wrath" surname
54 Easter egg brightener
56 Goddess of home and family
59 "Golly!"
60 See 17-Across
63 F.D.R. employment initiative
64 Craze
65 Steaming
66 Trip provider?
67 Wilderness walks
68 Conical home

## DOWN

1 "Humph!"
2 "___ in the Morning"
3 Guggenheim alternative in N.Y.C.
4 Lousy breaks
5 Orange-and-black flier
6 Taiwanese-born director Lee
7 Where many cultures thrive
8 Home for a 5-Down, maybe
9 Rockies rodent
10 Out of vogue
11 Imp plus
12 Jon's comics canine
13 Ends an engagement
18 M.V.P. of Super Bowl III
22 Home of the Galleria Borghese
24 Gin flavoring
26 Something to drool over?
27 Force
28 Vocation
29 "Le Morte d'Arthur" figure
30 Took a giant step
31 Found out
32 Outer reaches
38 "Fantastic Mr. Fox" author
39 Elbow locale
42 Perennially parched
43 Protein-producing substance
45 Definitely
47 Make lovable
48 The beginning
49 Tad
52 Bloodhound feature
53 Bungler's cry
55 "CHiPs" actor Estrada
57 Decoy
58 Start to date?
60 Clock setting at 0 degrees longitude: Abbr.
61 Fuel on the range
62 Witness

by Lynn Lempel

# 66

## ACROSS

**1** Antiaircraft missile
**6** Au ___
**10** Apple offering
**14** NPR's "Only ___"
**15** Ubangi tributary
**16** Choice at checkout
**17** Inspiration for "Troilus and Cressida"
**18** "Look at me, ___ helpless . . ." (opening to "Misty")
**19** See 23-Across
**20** When said three times, a yuletide song
**22** Picnics, e.g.
**23** With 19-Across, borderer of four states
**24** Frees, in a way
**25** Follow relentlessly
**28** Simple sort
**31** Not so attractive
**33** Mixed
**38** Clod
**39** Title role in a 1950s TV western
**41** Bear in the sky
**42** Stick-to-it-iveness
**44** Artisan whose work is featured in this puzzle?
**46** County seat on the Des Moines River
**48** ___ pal
**49** Well-defined
**53** Bean pot
**55** Is too cool
**56** 1957 Disney tearjerker
**61** One in civvies who maybe shouldn't be
**62** Lost traction
**63** Santa ___, Calif.
**64** Scratch
**65** What a getaway car may be waiting in
**66** Literary invalid
**67** Remnants
**68** It's not good for conducting
**69** Oddballs

## DOWN

**1** Fly (through)
**2** "Sleeping" sensation
**3** Amble, e.g.
**4** P.D.A. communiqué
**5** Delay cause
**6** Neighbor of Liberia
**7** San ___, Italy
**8** "There oughta be ___!"
**9** Parts opposite some handles
**10** Freeze over
**11** Happy hour order
**12** Petula Clark's "___ of the Times"
**13** Knight's activity?
**21** Emmy-winning Tom of "Picket Fences"
**22** Not conned by
**24** In a very generous manner
**25** Main, e.g.
**26** Figure in Magic: The Gathering
**27** Valley ___, redundantly named California community
**29** RCA competitor
**30** Actor John
**32** 1986 showbiz autobiography
**34** Some punch for punch
**35** H.S. math
**36** "Cómo ___?"
**37** Gary who invented the Pet Rock
**40** "___ be a pleasure"
**43** Regulated pollutants, for short
**45** "Eeny-meeny-miney-mo" activity
**47** Walk unsteadily
**49** Captain of the Golden Hind
**50** Any resident of 46-Across
**51** Termagant
**52** Bell sounds
**54** "Abandon hope ___ . . ."
**56** ___ English 800 (Miller brand)
**57** Oscar winner Kedrova
**58** Missing the boat, say
**59** Senta's suitor in "The Flying Dutchman"
**60** Some butters
**62** 1960s event

| 1 | 2 | 3 | 4 | 5 | ■ | 6 | 7 | 8 | 9 | ■ | 10 | 11 | 12 | 13 |
|---|---|---|---|---|---|---|---|---|---|---|---|---|---|---|
| 14 | | | | | ■ | 15 | | | | ■ | 16 | | | |
| 17 | | | | | ■ | 18 | | | | ■ | 19 | | | |
| 20 | | | | | 21 | | | | ■ | 22 | | | | |
| ■ | ■ | ■ | 23 | | | | ■ | ■ | 24 | | | | | |
| 25 | 26 | 27 | ■ | 28 | | | 29 | 30 | | | ■ | ■ | ■ | ■ |
| 31 | | | 32 | | | ■ | 33 | | | | 34 | 35 | 36 | 37 |
| 38 | | | | ■ | 39 | 40 | | | | ■ | 41 | | | |
| 42 | | | | 43 | | | | ■ | 44 | 45 | | | | |
| ■ | ■ | ■ | ■ | 46 | | | | 47 | | | ■ | 48 | | |
| 49 | 50 | 51 | 52 | | | ■ | ■ | 53 | | | 54 | ■ | ■ | ■ |
| 55 | | | | | ■ | 56 | 57 | | | | | 58 | 59 | 60 |
| 61 | | | | ■ | 62 | | | | ■ | 63 | | | | |
| 64 | | | | ■ | 65 | | | | ■ | 66 | | | | |
| 67 | | | | ■ | 68 | | | | ■ | 69 | | | | |

*by Holden Baker*

★★

## ACROSS

**1** Proceed without notes, say
**6** How kids grow up, it's often said
**13** Soviet space dog
**14** *One who dislikes unruly hair?
**15** Spy satellite's acquisition
**16** Bygone emporium
**17** ___ position
**18** Housewares brand
**19** Felipe Calderón's land: Abbr.
**20** Night class subj.
**21** *Alternative way to get directions?
**26** Heroic verse
**28** Artist's portfolio
**32** "Molly ___," popular Irish song
**34** *Better, in hip-hop slang?
**35** Spanish waves
**36** Church perch
**37** "___ in London" (jazz album)
**38** *Kitchen or living room?
**41** Like XX vis-à-vis X, sizewise
**43** "American Beauty" setting
**44** Canadian station sign
**45** *Via Veneto?
**47** Villainous member of the Serpent Society, in Marvel Comics
**50** 39-Down vote
**53** FedEx rival
**54** Half of a 1980s sitcom duo
**56** Football's Adam Vinatieri, e.g.
**60** Sewers have them
**61** *Be funnier than comedian Bill?
**62** Pick
**63** 2003 hip-hop hit by Fabolous
**64** Pharmacy units

## DOWN

**1** Subtitle of many biographies
**2** The majority of Jutlanders
**3** Mary's charge
**4** Retail giant founded by a 17-year-old
**5** Swell
**6** Song sung by an orphan
**7** Expose, poetically
**8** Sounds of surprise
**9** Stout
**10** ___ smasher
**11** Very dry
**12** "The Lost World" menace
**14** Answer to each of the six starred clues, literally
**16** Play-___
**22** Literary monogram
**23** Chip, maybe
**24** Amaze
**25** Piccolo players, e.g.
**27** Affected one
**29** Masked men with blades
**30** Big blow?
**31** Alpha, beta or gamma
**32** Eponymous scale developer
**33** Diamond family name
**36** Devotional bench
**39** Voting 50-Across
**40** 1972 treaty subj.
**41** Judge's cry
**42** Red-faced
**46** Pilot's abbr.
**48** "___ when?"
**49** Gadflies, e.g.
**50** Hairy Himalayan
**51** Nebraska senator succeeded by Hagel
**52** Datebook entry: Abbr.
**55** "Fiesque" composer
**57** I love, to Livy
**58** Scotland's Firth of ___
**59** Greek character

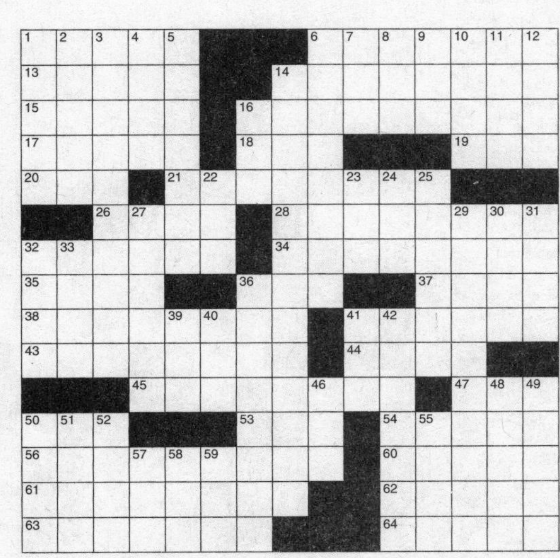

*by David J. Kahn*

NOTE: When this puzzle is finished, the six circled letters can be arranged to spell an answer to the catchphrase reading diagonally from upper left to lower right.

## ACROSS

**1** One crossing through the strike zone?
**5** "Speak" response
**9** Gin runs
**14** "We Need a Little Christmas" musical
**15** ___ all-time high
**16** Infiniti rival
**17** Grammy winner from County Donegal
**18** Incantation #1
**20** It may pay off if it has your number
**22** Some brothers and sisters
**23** ___ Titanic
**24** Lab monitor?
**25** Confederate flag flier
**26** ___-majesté
**27** Nine-digit ID
**28** Former Dodgers third baseman whom Chris Berman nicknamed "Born in the U.S."
**31** "It's time to fly" advertiser
**33** ___ Green, 1987 L.P.G.A. Rookie of the Year
**36** Somewhat
**37** Incantation #2
**39** Grab bag
**40** Ancient Britain
**41** Rolling features of some golf courses
**43** Rathskeller cooler
**44** Polo Grounds legend
**47** Carmaker since 1899
**48** "Alphabet web," to Variety
**51** Former capital of Crete
**53** Texas N.B.A.'er
**54** "Welcome to the islands"
**56** Olympian Jesse
**57** Incantation #3
**60** Vacation time in France
**61** ___ Bok, former Harvard president
**62** "The Reader" actress Lena
**63** About
**64** Dissertation defenses
**65** Classic Jags
**66** ___ off (began)

## DOWN

**1** Needs airing out, maybe
**2** Paddlers' craft
**3** "The Joy Luck Club" author
**4** Jack Kerouac, Allen Ginsberg and others
**5** Rejection interjection
**6** From ___ (the works)
**7** Speed demon
**8** Coach Rockne
**9** Google feature
**10** Modern prefix with balance
**11** Mrs. James A. Garfield
**12** Equipment that comes with sticks
**13** Mouthed off to
**19** "Elephant Boy" actor
**21** Top 10 hit for Neil Sedaka
**26** First sign of fall
**29** ___ Savahl (couture label)
**30** "It's fun to stay at the ___": Village People
**32** Acronym associated with Oreos
**33** Security that matures in a year or less, briefly
**34** Janis who sang "At Seventeen"
**35** Margin
**37** Herbalist's supply
**38** "When We Were Kings" subject
**39** In theory
**41** ___ dragon (largest living lizard)
**42** Kind of price
**44** New Year's Day, datewise
**45** Professor's privilege
**46** Took a sample of
**49** Bronx Bombers' foes
**50** Lesson writer?
**52** Stand by for
**54** Expresses wonder?
**55** Billet-doux writer
**58** "Volare (___ Blu Dipinto di Blu)"
**59** Junior officer: Abbr.

*by John Farmer*

## ACROSS

**1** Tijuana dishes
**8** Relegated to a state of oblivion
**15** Middle name of Sen. Joe Lieberman
**16** Resting place for the deceased
**17** False start's result, in football
**19** Red ___ (sushi order)
**20** "Do me ___ and . . ."
**21** Reference abbr.
**22** Ming's 7'6" and Bryant's 6'6", e.g.: Abbr.
**24** "Resolved: that . . . ," for debaters
**26** D.O.E. part: Abbr.
**28** "'Tis a pity"
**30** Tiberius' "to be"
**32** Last test before starting some advanced deg. programs
**33** Request of a frog in a fairy tale
**36** Missions, for short
**37** Laptop key
**38** [Refer to blurb]
**40** Last name in ice cream
**42** Laborer's suffix
**43** Lance
**44** Reversible preposition
**45** Double-bladed ___ II razor
**47** Fated for ruin
**51** Doily material
**53** Rent down the center
**56** Milk: Prefix
**57** Time-share unit
**59** Latin motto "Ars ___ artis"
**61** Tilly of Tinseltown
**62** Doughbags
**65** Renaissance cradle city
**66** Resident of the Winter Palace before 1917
**67** Last-column element on the periodic table
**68** Relatively piquant

## DOWN

**1** Rémy Martin units
**2** Lasagna cheese, sometimes
**3** Late New York senator Jacob
**4** Lanthan- suffix
**5** Michael's sister La ___
**6** Mideast peace conference attendee, 1993
**7** Regulator mechanism, for short
**8** Doesn't let go?
**9** Refusal for Rob Roy
**10** Millet's moon
**11** Reverse of "bring together"
**12** Mishmashes
**13** Mister Belvedere and others
**14** Record of 1947 "Peg ___ Heart"
**18** Lamebrain
**23** "Reginald" writer
**25** Large bill, slangily
**27** Remote button
**29** "Far out, man!"
**31** Michigan, e.g., to a Spaniard
**34** Fashionista ___ Moon Zombie
**35** Does in with a rope
**38** Factual info on a dating service questionnaire
**39** Fatal virus
**40** Sole alternative?
**41** Fanged villain
**46** Laptop key
**48** "Rebecca of Sunnybrook Farm" was published in this year
**49** Timeless, old-style
**50** Reader's place marker
**52** Restaurant order
**54** Repeat New York City Marathon winner Grete ___
**55** Lazy
**58** Solving, as a puzzle
**60** Miscellanies
**62** Dow Chemical, e.g.: Abbr.
**63** Mineral in sheets
**64** Michelangelo's field

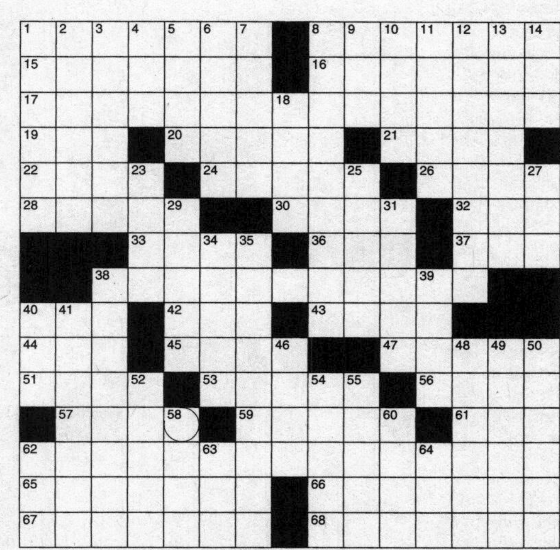

by Daniel A. Finan

## ACROSS

**1** Kobe Bryant's team, on scoreboards
**4** Boxing champ Hector
**11** Earlier
**14** Near East honorific
**15** Like boot camp vis-à-vis day camp
**16** Annihilate, with "down"
**17** Odd sign at a Michelin dealership?
**20** Roast, e.g.
**21** In agreement with the group
**22** Photography pioneer
**26** Goes after
**28** Part of an academic title
**30** ___ cheese
**31** The Black Stallion and others
**35** Choreographer Lubovitch
**36** Odd sign at Victoria's Secret?
**40** Carrier to Tokyo
**41** Shortcut, perhaps
**42** Computer innards, for short
**44** Issues
**48** Like slow students, sometimes
**52** Summerlike
**53** Kind of disorder
**55** Alphabet string
**56** Odd sign at Men's Wearhouse?
**60** Sch. in Brooklyn, N.Y.
**61** ABC daytime staple since 1997
**62** U.R.L. ending
**63** Program holders
**64** Extra
**65** ___ Accord (1998 Mideast peace agreement)

## DOWN

**1** Physical expense
**2** Radiant
**3** Who wrote "He who does not trust enough will not be trusted"
**4** Comedian Margaret
**5** Jr. Olympics sponsor
**6** "The A-Team" muscleman
**7** Concerning
**8** Popular wedding gift
**9** Tea flavorings
**10** Sandwiches for dessert
**11** Panhandle city
**12** Bookbinding decoration
**13** Get behind
**18** Symbol of limpness
**19** Car whose name is an acronym
**23** Stuck
**24** ___ 2600
**25** Nile Valley region
**27** Roar producer
**29** More than a raid
**32** "Oh, give me ___ . . ."
**33** Frequent spoilers
**34** Grade
**36** Milk: Prefix
**37** For everyone to see
**38** Spiral-shelled creature
**39** Talents
**43** Soaks (up)
**45** 61-Across, e.g.
**46** Bistro
**47** Gunk
**49** One-sided contests
**50** Electrical pioneer Thomson
**51** Antique dealer, at times
**54** Answer
**56** Frequent Winter Olympics site
**57** The "S" in 54-Down
**58** Romanian currency
**59** Jimmy Stewart syllables

by Dan Naddor

## ACROSS

**1** Talks little
**6** Short chest, for muscles
**10** Funny co-star in "Barbra's Girl"
**14** Washington's Sound ___
**15** Main contents of the Spanish
**16** Clothing court
**17** Like the clues in all the words in this puzzle
**19** The Terrible ___
**20** As a grasshopper prepares
**21** Food process
**23** Faith without a person
**26** Years of plenty
**27** Fine with choked sand
**28** Date for many a place
**29** Visitor space
**30** Drive off the top?
**31** "___ Dies"
**34** Music backdrop of "The Sound"
**35** Alley ___
**38** General program for a future, maybe: Abbr.
**39** Of kind society
**41** Supply nursery
**42** Faces sulky
**44** Places small American flags for
**46** Mouse ___
**47** Old like some painted cars
**49** Cleared home at the plate?
**50** Tool fencing
**51** Union in the European capital
**52** Channel game
**53** Like the clues in all the words in this puzzle
**58** Some served veterans there: Abbr.
**59** Cry ___
**60** Brief blowup, in "Big"
**61** Opening China?
**62** Example, for boxers
**63** For one square

## DOWN

**1** Revival of a cause, briefly
**2** Cry of partner
**3** Respect of Eastern title
**4** Of a colony member
**5** Having a sound grating
**6** Show part of a game
**7** With spurs on
**8** Go on to signal
**9** Low on the side
**10** Craft paper
**11** Like the clues in all the words in this puzzle
**12** In lower rank
**13** Letters for checks
**18** In a split way
**22** Cooler drink
**23** Stern violinist
**24** Wafer ___
**25** Like the clues in all the words in this puzzle
**26** Attitude with singers
**28** Secret thieves of slang
**30** Worker routine
**32** Half of a musical second
**33** City steel in Europe
**36** Drivers of love
**37** Judges of written works
**40** Part of drain
**43** Heaven, not in here
**45** A dreary poet upon midnight, once
**46** Off tee
**47** Fountain ___
**48** "When Flower ___ Knighthood" (1922 film)
**49** Opportunities to speak so
**51** Does partner for
**54** Light sky, maybe
**55** Traffic group that may stop: Abbr.
**56** To know one way
**57** Offering G.P.S.

*by Lee Glickstein*

72 

## ACROSS

**1** *4:00 in the afternoon
**8** *To make holes
**14** Form of writing of ancient Crete
**15** Sought food
**16** It comes in fifths
**17** Poetry performance
**18** Add zest to
**19** *To go round and round
**20** Catcher's spot?
**21** Wrap up
**23** Wrapped up
**24** *Fearsome, swift-moving creature with snapping jaws
**30** It's 71% cookie, 29% creme
**31** Chucklehead
**35** Emulate the dodo
**38** Indian tourist city
**39** Means of unloading?
**43** Unnamed others, briefly
**44** Writer who was the source of all the words with asterisked clues in this puzzle
**47** Wonderland food for Alice
**50** A bit nasty
**51** "Say what?"
**52** *Grass plot around a sundial
**54** Put away
**59** Some buffalo hunters of old
**61** Variety of grape
**62** Confronts
**63** Positions (oneself)
**64** *Lithe and slimy
**65** *Smiling radiantly

## DOWN

**1** Lesage hero Gil ___
**2** Make stew?
**3** Certain ancient mummy
**4** Affectionate, fiery types, supposedly
**5** Pakistan's so-called "Garden of Mughals"
**6** Person whose work is decreasing?
**7** Miss
**8** Church annex?
**9** ___ caelestes (divine wrath: Lat.)
**10** ___ Hatter
**11** Old-time floozie
**12** "From Russia With Love" actress Lotte
**13** Beaten (out)
**15** Browner
**19** Sharks, e.g.
**22** Long-running CBS hit
**23** Beer, sometimes
**24** Vintner's concern
**25** "O patria mia," e.g.
**26** Opposite of alway
**27** Drawing in a margin, maybe
**28** Waits in music
**29** "Curiouser and curiouser!," e.g.
**32** Mysterious Mr.
**33** Kazakh river
**34** Bears do it
**36** Take advantage of
**37** Playing marble
**40** Departure point for explorer Vasco da Gama
**41** Feudal laborer
**42** It goes after poli and before fi
**45** Urge formally
**46** Objects employed to show everyday life
**47** Online discussions
**48** Not visual
**49** Uniform coloring
**52** Wadi
**53** Stern cry?
**55** Detail
**56** Lawyer/civil-rights activist Guinier
**57** Tolkien creatures
**58** Tach's location
**60** Dear
**61** [I'm heartbroken!]

*by Matt Ginsberg*

# 73

## ACROSS

**1** Ladies' man
**5** Mentally out of it
**10** H.S. class member
**14** The Ponte Santa Trinita spans it
**15** Prefix with car
**16** "Lullaby," for one
**17** Areas in northern forests?
**19** Grinding location
**20** Digging further, say
**21** Amos of "Amos 'n' Andy"
**22** ISP with a butterfly logo
**23** Chatty bird alliance?
**27** Big bushes
**29** Doctor's recommendation, often
**30** "Mission: Impossible" figure
**31** Capital on the Dnieper
**32** Stuff
**35** Time when laboratories came into vogue?
**40** "Celeste Aida" singer
**41** Commander, in Arabic
**42** Some G.P.S. lines
**45** Late stand-up comic Richard
**46** Foreign pen pal, perhaps
**47** Witch's hamper?
**51** Lightning org.
**52** Co-producer of the film "Precious"
**53** Wading bird with an upcurved bill
**55** R&B singer Shuggie ___
**56** Heavenly food for the Duke?
**60** Beverage with a lizard logo
**61** Even up
**62** Jackie O, e.g.
**63** Follow
**64** Rushed
**65** Lizardlike creature

## DOWN

**1** Collected dust
**2** Fascinate
**3** One who labors for labor's sake?
**4** Feet, slangily
**5** Three-term governor of New York
**6** Nut with a cupule
**7** Place for exhibits
**8** Defensive ___
**9** 27-Across, e.g.
**10** Margaret Mead's "Coming of Age in ___"
**11** Some gaskets
**12** Accumulate
**13** Title admiral in a Paul and Linda McCartney hit
**18** Targets
**21** Beetle's cousin?
**22** Fashion
**24** Temple of ___, one of the Seven Wonders of the Ancient World
**25** Poet whose works were set to music by Schumann, Strauss and Brahms
**26** Some college srs. take them
**28** [Turn the page]
**32** Song that people flip for?
**33** Big name on the range?
**34** ___ sch.
**36** Howdah occupant, maybe
**37** Prestige
**38** "No, I meant tomorrow . . . duh!"
**39** Kazakh/Uzbek ___ Sea
**42** Sneaker symbol
**43** Sneak, in a way
**44** Writer
**46** Unit proposed by Leucippus
**48** Scoped out
**49** "Winnie-the-Pooh" character
**50** Calendar entry
**54** Crop farmer of Genesis
**56** Classic one-word headline
**57** Like
**58** The dark side
**59** Soldier ___

| | | | | | | | | | | | | | | |
|---|---|---|---|---|---|---|---|---|---|---|---|---|---|---|
| 1 | 2 | 3 | 4 | ■ | 5 | 6 | 7 | 8 | 9 | ■ | 10 | 11 | 12 | 13 |
| 14 | | | | ■ | 15 | | | | | ■ | 16 | | | |
| 17 | | | | 18 | | | | | | ■ | 19 | | | |
| ■ | 20 | | | | | | ■ | ■ | ■ | 21 | | | | |
| 22 | | | ■ | 23 | | | 24 | 25 | 26 | | | | | |
| 27 | | | 28 | | ■ | ■ | 29 | | | | ■ | 30 | | |
| 31 | | | | ■ | 32 | 33 | | | | | 34 | ■ | ■ | ■ |
| 35 | | | | 36 | | | | | | | | 37 | 38 | 39 |
| ■ | ■ | ■ | 40 | | | | | | | ■ | 41 | | | |
| 42 | 43 | 44 | ■ | 45 | | | | ■ | ■ | 46 | | | | |
| 47 | | | 48 | | | | | 49 | 50 | | ■ | 51 | | |
| 52 | | | | | ■ | ■ | ■ | 53 | | | 54 | | | ■ |
| 55 | | | | ■ | 56 | 57 | 58 | | | | | | | 59 |
| 60 | | | | ■ | 61 | | | | | ■ | 62 | | | |
| 63 | | | | ■ | 64 | | | | | ■ | 65 | | | |

*by Brendan Emmett Quigley & Joon Pahk*

# 74

## ACROSS

**1** Like saddle shoes and bell-bottom pants
**6** Beehive contents
**10** Cooking amts.
**14** Send
**15** It's found in arms
**16** Syngman ___, first president of South Korea
**17** Israeli political party
**18** One who's available when needed
**20** Need for a link
**21** Pilot, for one
**23** Baseball Hall-of-Famer Roush
**24** With 40-Across, key to the "map" of this puzzle
**26** Like a small egg
**28** "___ quam videri" (North Carolina's motto)
**29** Rushing goal
**33** Eastern royal
**34** Gordon of "Oklahoma!"
**36** "One Life to Live" airer
**37** ___ Wayne with the platinum album "Tha Block Is Hot"
**40** See 24-Across
**42** Dir. from Springfield, Mass., to Providence
**43** 2009 Peace Nobelist
**45** Pays (for)
**47** Hefty refs.
**48** Be Ciceronian
**49** Novel subtitled "A Narrative of Adventures in the South Seas"
**53** Enters, as data
**55** Asked a hard question in public, say
**57** Director Lee
**58** Flows
**62** End of a series
**63** "Mmm! So satisfying!"
**65** Prep
**67** Star followers
**68** Dish (out)
**69** Elegiac music
**70** Dutch export
**71** Those: Sp.
**72** Nickel and dime in gaming?

## DOWN

**1** Choice
**2** Warnings
**3** Raga accompaniers
**4** W.W. II inits.
**5** Zoolander of "Zoolander"
**6** Certain trekker
**7** Book after Joel
**8** Chat room opener
**9** Parts of sonatas
**10** "Give it a shot!"
**11** It may be on the tip of the tongue
**12** Jewelry often used in hypnosis
**13** Libido
**19** Battle Born State: Abbr.
**22** Demoralize, with "out"
**25** Band with the 2008 album "Accelerate"
**27** City area, informally
**30** Backward
**31** Bob Marley, e.g.
**32** Point along a line
**35** ___ loss
**36** Nibbled away
**37** Cry for attention
**38** Dupe's shout
**39** Singer born Stefani Germanotta
**41** Early aft. hour
**44** In-box stock: Abbr.
**46** Alky
**48** Punctual
**50** "La Clemenza di Tito" composer
**51** Antsy
**52** Sunflower-like daisies
**54** Suffix with hawk
**56** Std. on food labels
**59** Delivery drivers' assignments: Abbr.
**60** "Cómo ___?"
**61** Graph lines
**64** Enchanter in "Monty Python and the Holy Grail"
**66** German "a"

*by Caleb Madison*

## ACROSS

**1** Rattlebrains
**6** Winter hours in Colo.
**9** Fix, in a way
**14** Stiff-backed
**15** "Every day ___ new day"
**16** Clear
**17** With 37- and 54-Across, curious property of this crossword
**20** "Whether ___ . . ."
**21** Common item in a purse
**22** Mellow, say
**23** King with a statue in Trafalgar Square
**25** Imitates a penguin
**27** It may actually be a hunch
**28** "Interest paid on trouble before it falls due," per W. R. Inge
**29** What hawks do
**32** Asian spiritual guide
**36** "Jerusalem Delivered" poet
**37** See 17-Across
**38** Nail's partner
**39** Enter surreptitiously
**41** Dictionary listing
**42** Lizard that chirps
**43** Something that may be let out
**44** Actress Harper
**47** Quiet
**51** "___ fancy you consult, consult your purse": Benjamin Franklin
**52** Foundation
**53** Hold over the fire, say
**54** See 17-Across
**59** W.W. II blockade enforcer
**60** Hagen with three Tonys
**61** Salon supply
**62** Smooths
**63** Some sports scores, briefly
**64** U.S. term for a British "saloon"

## DOWN

**1** Subpar grade
**2** 60 minuti
**3** Rot
**4** Autumn shade
**5** Maurice of Nixon's cabinet
**6** Peruvian volcano El ___
**7** Dir. from Paris to Bordeaux
**8** Olympic sport since 2000
**9** Parch
**10** Procter & Gamble's first liquid laundry detergent
**11** ___ metabolism
**12** Dictionary topic
**13** Code carriers
**18** "___ did not!"
**19** Abrogate a peace treaty, maybe
**23** Isn't serious
**24** City on the Nile
**26** Big name in vacuum cleaners
**28** Conjoined with
**30** County name in Kansas, Missouri and Oklahoma
**31** Pot contents
**32** Totally beat
**33** For the reason stated
**34** French beings
**35** Gun, for one
**40** Less welcoming
**44** Mythological subject for Titian and Botticelli
**45** One of the ABC islands
**46** It may be found often in a shop
**47** Mini-section of an almanac
**48** Who wrote "I was never kinder to the old man than during the whole week before I killed him"
**49** Walks
**50** First name in perfume
**55** Misbehaving
**56** Busy co. on Mother's Day
**57** Material in protein synthesis
**58** Colorado's ___ Luis Peak

*by David J. W. Simpson*

76 

## ACROSS

1 ___ City (computer game)
4 Columbia org.
8 N'awlins sandwiches
14 Cable channel
15 Actor Omar of "House"
16 Surfing site
17 Suffix with robot
18 Barbecue comfortably?
20 "Are your Southern breakfast vittles satisfactory?"
22 Victorious
23 When doubled, a #3 hit of 1968 or a #1 hit of 1987
24 Nonmigratory goose
25 Some TV drama settings
26 Anticipates
28 Jeans brand
31 Actress Merrill
32 Marvelous golf club?
35 Purple outfit?
37 Rules regarding tile setting?
40 Wild ___
43 Won handily
44 "Little" title figure in a Beach Boys hit
46 Enzyme suffix
47 Stag
50 "___ Jury"
51 Silents star Nita
54 Big black bird?
56 Passenger gorging on fried chicken and potato chips?
58 Grossglockner, for one
59 "Take your pick"
60 Pulitzer winner James
61 ___ chi
62 Family of George's fiancée on "Seinfeld"
63 Narcissist's love
64 Preposition before now

## DOWN

1 Hester Prynne's "A," e.g.
2 Clique
3 Name of many hospitals and cemeteries
4 Darkroom production, for short
5 They come with strings attached
6 Lace
7 Lion of Narnia
8 Org. that usually has a fall start-up meeting
9 "___ be in England": Browning
10 Lived
11 Carousing
12 "Don't evade the question!"
13 Hamlet, to Claudius
19 A corrosive
21 Snarling
27 Pâtisserie offering
28 Animal with a silent head?
29 Numbskull
30 It went down in history
32 3.0, e.g.
33 Opposite of FF
34 Numbskull
36 Municipal pol.
37 19th-century farmer
38 Karen's maid on "Will & Grace"
39 Egg foo yung dishes, basically
41 Measure the strength of, in a way
42 Book burrower
44 Sushi offering
45 Kind of doll
47 Restaurant V.I.P.: Abbr.
48 Met expectations?
49 Shelf
52 Morse bits
53 "Gotcha"
55 Not kosher
57 Sentence units: Abbr.

by Dan Naddor

## ACROSS

1 Archaeologists usually find things in this
5 Cutlass part
9 1992 Jack Nicholson title role
14 Asta in the book "The Thin Man," e.g.
16 Pang
17 Instruction to an overexcited Frenchman?
19 Bartolommeo and Angelico
20 Call from the field
21 Common Hebrew name
22 Oriole or Tiger, informally
23 Really wet grass expected tomorrow morning?
27 Tattoos, e.g.
29 Hack
30 Wirers, say: Abbr.
31 Box office
33 Interruption causes
34 What quilting farmers do?
36 Restrictive wear
38 Auvers-sur-___, last home of Vincent van Gogh
39 Top of a suit?
42 Commodity for John Jacob Astor
43 Camera innovator George
45 Whitecaps next to an underpriced beachfront property?
49 Some jellied dishes
50 Oscars prop: Abbr.
51 Put in one's ___
52 Date maker
53 Simplify things at a ricotta factory?
59 Old Dodge hatchbacks
60 Box office request
61 Henpeck
62 Hockey's Steve and baseball's Mel
63 Retired fleet

## DOWN

1 Missoula-to-Boise dir.
2 Seal's resting place, perhaps
3 Great American Ball Park team
4 Heedless
5 Color
6 Suffix with color
7 Eager beaver's word
8 Some scouts
9 Dearborn ___, MI
10 "___ don't know about that"
11 Bronze statue on top of the U.S. Capitol
12 Bobbles
13 Lofty stronghold
15 Sounds of comprehension
18 Signal of comprehension
22 "The Simpsons" grampa
23 Tournament starting points
24 Jazzy James
25 They repeat whatever you say
26 "That's finally done!"
28 Realtors, e.g.
32 Musician Brian
33 Evaluate
34 Lemon ___
35 Object of a French prayer
36 Beach locale of song
37 Gunning
39 Some Amys, Emmas and Mias
40 Least rocky
41 Not the longest dashes
44 Tempts
45 Victors' cry
46 Salaam
47 Unsophisticated boob
48 London borough containing Wembley Stadium
52 Chum
54 Fashion model Carangi
55 Only 20th-century prez without a coll. degree
56 ___ again
57 Mini-albums, briefly
58 Hi-___

*by Patrick Merrell*

78 

## ACROSS

1 "___ Si Bon" (1950s Eartha Kitt hit)
5 Post-diet, ideally
9 Surfaces
14 Dinosaur National Monument locale
15 ___ bar
16 "Scenes of Clerical Life" author, 1858
17 1958 World Cup hero
18 50/50
19 See 24-Across
20 What this answer could use?
23 Record producer Brian
24 With 19-Across, language from which "steak" and "eggs" come
25 On intimate social terms with
28 Alaska vacation destination
30 Spray on a pan
32 Federally funded program since '65
33 Coiner
35 Coin toss call
37 Like this answer's error
40 Upset
41 Prize
42 Un cuarto of 62-Across
43 Compete in a biathlon, in part
44 "Sweet ___"
48 Sound choice?
51 "Years ___. . ."
52 ___ Jemison, first black woman in space
53 This answer contains one
57 Top celebs
59 Jordanian queen
60 Queen of the heavens
61 Hanukkah staple
62 Cuatro times 42-Across
63 Help with a prank
64 "___ Eyes" (1969 hit)
65 Irwin who wrote "Rich Man, Poor Man"
66 Took in

## DOWN

1 Like beggars' hands
2 Timeless, to Shakespeare
3 Watering hole
4 One of the "Cosby Show" kids
5 First-rate
6 Long-___
7 Company founded by Ingvar Kamprad
8 Take exception to
9 Pasta choice
10 Isolated
11 Atlantic Coast Conference team
12 Mother of the stars and the winds
13 ___-Julie, Que.
21 Page numbers
22 Tour's end?
26 Dudley Do-Right's girlfriend
27 Ozone, for one
29 Concert hall equipment
30 It "hits the spot" per an old jingle
31 "Was it ___ I saw?" (classic palindrome)
34 Migration, maybe
35 Steering system part
36 Pinnacle
37 Instruction at a horse show
38 Home of the 1,612-foot Ribbon Falls
39 Property divider
40 Music sources
43 Saturate
45 Tiny blob
46 Defective
47 Calm
49 Takes a chance on
50 First name in beauty products
51 "Hawaii ___" (island song)
54 "The Dukes of Hazzard" spinoff
55 Scotland's ___ Awe
56 Pow!
57 PC key
58 ___-di-dah

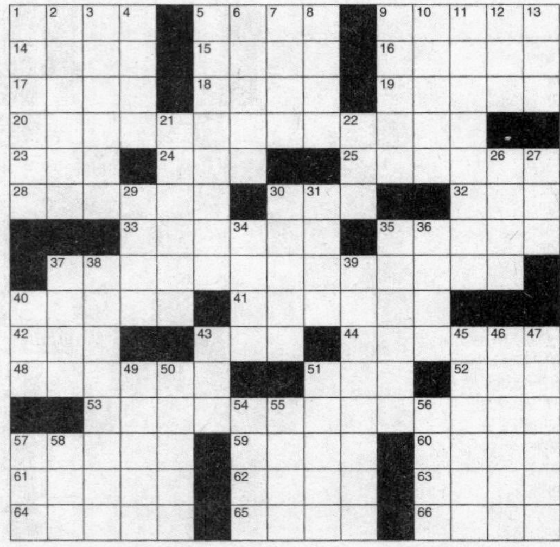

*by Keith Talon*

## ACROSS

**1** Gave an order to
**5** Fork
**10** Woods call
**14** Platinum Card offerer, for short
**15** Shopping center
**16** Shuffle or 67-Across, e.g.
**17** Eliminate, with "out"
**18** Symbol of thinness
**19** Alternatives to creams
**20** Arctic explorer post-fight?
**23** Hatch or Byrd: Abbr.
**24** Formerly, in high society
**25** Possible cover for a siesta
**27** Mood
**29** Some offensive linemen: Abbr.
**32** Off
**33** "___ Love," 1975 Jackson 5 hit
**35** "THAT guy!"
**37** Past
**38** Bows and arrows for Midas?
**43** Was on the ticket
**44** Major Indonesian export
**45** Big inits. in Hollywood
**46** 1985 John Malkovich drama
**49** Beseech
**51** Convinced
**54** Choice poultry
**56** Use (up), as savings
**58** Common suffix on chemical elements
**60** Storage area for ribbed fabric?
**64** Ladies' man
**65** Inspector of crime fiction
**66** Yearn (for)
**67** See 16-Across
**68** Model
**69** Horse-drawn carriage
**70** Switch possibilities
**71** Level . . . or a three-word hint to 20-, 38- and 60-Across
**72** Proctor's call

## DOWN

**1** Unpleasant remarks
**2** Item worn around the neck, maybe
**3** Presidential middle name
**4** Prez, e.g.
**5** Binge at the mall
**6** Ladies' man
**7** What many do on a day off
**8** Polo alternative
**9** Temporary covers
**10** Singer of Rossini's "Largo al factotum"
**11** Zero personality?
**12** Pudgy
**13** Money managers?: Abbr.
**21** Massage
**22** Night of poetry
**26** Tight ___
**28** Not even a little
**30** Shakespearean title
**31** English title
**34** Big Apple cultural attraction, with "the"
**36** Hosts
**38** Enormous
**39** Candy box size
**40** Pen point
**41** "___ mañana"
**42** The "I" of Claudius I
**43** Boombox button
**47** Like some skiing
**48** Not the party type?: Abbr.
**50** Yellowstone Park attraction
**52** Chinese fruit tree
**53** Duke's home
**55** Water pits
**57** Copycatting
**59** "The hell you say!"
**61** Source
**62** Roughly
**63** Thomas with a pointed pen
**64** Little, to Robert Burns

*by Ari Halpern*

80

**ACROSS**

**1** Salt or smoke
**5** Starr of the Old West
**10** Boom
**14** Type type: Abbr.
**15** Bay window
**16** ___ colada
**17** Like a bell
**18** Pale purple
**19** Pancake Day is the day before this begins
**20** Make rustle, as foil
**22** Writes odes to, e.g.
**24** U.N. secretary general from Ghana
**25** Not straight up
**26** Bits
**29** Winter melon
**33** Colorful lawn or garden fixture
**37** Soundtrack annoyance
**38** Slithering danger
**39** Hebrews, for example
**43** A pitcher should keep it low
**44** Something you might want to get to the heart of?
**46** Annoy
**50** Sale day feeling
**51** They cross here
**53** ___ salts
**57** One of TV's Gilmore Girls
**60** Unfolds
**62** Pen pal in Paris, perhaps
**63** Agreement
**65** Exercised a legal option
**66** Police protection
**67** Doha's domain
**68** "___ This Last" (series of John Ruskin essays)
**69** ___ place
**70** Stood out, in a good way
**71** Say no

**DOWN**

**1** Around
**2** Often-illegal maneuver
**3** Entered quickly
**4** Percussion instrument in an orchestra
**5** Cotton pod
**6** Pennsylvania's northwesternmost county
**7** One of TV's Rugrats
**8** Bounded
**9** Coterie
**10** Forks
**11** "The Worst ___ in London" ("Sweeney Todd" song)
**12** Monarch immediately after William and Mary
**13** Headliner
**21** Small hill
**23** Mobile home?: Abbr.
**25** "___ see it . . ."
**27** Railroad crossbeam
**28** Tourist city between Jaipur and Lucknow
**30** Middle range
**31** Hesitate
**32** Author James
**33** Bird with speckled eggs
**34** Fabled racer
**35** "Take ___ face value"
**36** "___ life!"
**40** Fraternity jewelry
**41** More likely to cause slipping
**42** Quits misbehaving . . . or a literal hint to 4-, 9-, 13-, 49- and 57-Down
**45** Abbr. in real estate ads
**47** Chirps
**48** Ha-ha, nowadays
**49** Unhip person
**52** Alice's pet cat in "Alice in Wonderland"
**54** Hot spot
**55** "The Country Girl" playwright, 1950
**56** Many PCs once ran on it
**57** Racetrack
**58** Impending clouds, e.g.
**59** Small hill
**60** Avant-garde filmmaker Brakhage
**61** Funeral sight
**64** "What am ___ do?"

*by Elizabeth A. Long*

81

## ACROSS

1 Warm-blooded shark
5 Blood's partner
10 Klingon on "Star Trek: T.N.G."
14 With 46-Down, writer of "The Autobiography of Malcolm X"
15 Originator of the equation e to the power (pi * i) + 1 = 0
16 Airline that doesn't fly on Saturday
17 Hollow-point projectiles
19 Title cocker spaniel in a Disney film
20 Bazaar
21 Pixie-esque
22 Mutually beneficial interaction
25 Roughly triangular racket
28 Chemistry Nobelist Hahn, who co-discovered nuclear fission
29 "___ Majesty" (last track on "Abbey Road")
30 Reconciled
35 Jacqueline Susann novel, and the problem with some of the answers in this puzzle
39 Follows temporally
40 Order at a French restaurant
41 Berlin article
42 Delight
45 Puerto Rican–born P.G.A. star
50 Lacks, briefly
51 Impoverished
55 "___ Want for Christmas"
56 Child's fair-weather wish
58 Usher's offer
59 Agreeing (with)
60 "Your Majesty"
61 "Really!"
62 Annual awards presented in Los Angeles
63 Legis. meeting

## DOWN

1 Synthetic
2 Fund-raising target, briefly
3 Dole's 1996 running mate
4 River bends
5 Like a leopard
6 Beauts
7 Incense resin
8 Volleyball action before a spike
9 9 a.m. and 5 p.m.
10 Rich
11 Norwegian king who converted the Vikings to Christianity
12 Portion of an advertising budget
13 One of the Mudville players on base when the mighty Casey struck out
18 "Trinity" author
21 Taken in
23 Tugboat warnings
24 ___ Reader
25 Dice, say
26 Slots spot
27 "The Lord of the Rings" army
30 Lay to rest
31 Preschoolers?
32 "I'm Gonna Wash That Man Right ___ My Hair"
33 Oral grimaces
34 What you used to be
36 Forever
37 "You ___!" (cry while hitting oneself on the head)
38 Levee material
42 Mass dismissals
43 Duke Atreides in "Dune"
44 New York bridge toll option
45 Wide divide
46 See 14-Across
47 Its symbol is a crescent moon
48 Go for broke, e.g.
49 ___ Weasley of Harry Potter books
52 Toddler's cry of pain
53 They're found in banks
54 Bar stock
56 Charlotte of "The Facts of Life"
57 Cash cache

*by Matt Ginsberg*

# 82

**ACROSS**

**1** Temple activity
**8** Tex-Mex treats
**15** Wedding gown material
**16** Distinguished
**17** Dean Martin, for one
**18** Bach work
**19** 1979 Bee Gees chart-topper
**21** Civvies
**23** ___ change
**24** QB's stat.
**25** Great Plains tribe
**26** County of St. Andrews, Scotland
**28** Part of a seal
**30** Professor Lupin in Harry Potter books, e.g.
**33** Creator of the Bennet family
**34** Band with the 1970 hit "Get Ready"
**36** One of the four evangelists, briefly
**39** Many Latin compositions
**43** Come up
**44** Shot (off)
**45** Yes, in Yokohama
**46** Let go
**47** Author of a once-popular book of quotations
**48** Devil
**50** 1979 AC/DC seven-time platinum album
**55** Blow up
**56** Emit
**59** Smaller than small
**60** Where the buoys are?
**61** Puts under
**62** Takes over

**DOWN**

**1** Fighters' org.
**2** 1967 N.H.L. rookie of the year
**3** Support, at a game
**4** Tear out
**5** Radio ___ (onetime propaganda source)
**6** Footnote word
**7** Locale for Che Guevara in "The Motorcycle Diaries"
**8** Computer whiz
**9** Menotti title character
**10** Harbor danger
**11** Architectural pier
**12** Michael ___, Bush secretary of health and human services
**13** Accord
**14** Suffragist Elizabeth Cady ___
**20** One that's "perky" in the morning
**21** Shorten, in a way
**22** Multipurpose truck
**26** Chess tactic that involves attacking two pieces at once
**27** Spot in la mer
**28** Half-and-half, maybe
**29** Department of Labor agcy.
**31** Post–Civil War Reconstruction and others
**32** Pottery
**33** Unimaginative
**35** Koko who communicates through American Sign Language, e.g.
**36** Lingerie drawer items
**37** Drill instructor's charge
**38** Got around at a get-together
**40** Military wing
**41** Eggs Benedict ingredient
**42** Hardly a chug
**44** Football Hall-of-Famer Gale
**47** Patrick ___, 1996 Tony recipient for "Marat/Sade"
**48** Q45 or Grand Marquis
**49** "Walkin' After Midnight" hitmaker, 1957
**51** Mandlikova of tennis fame
**52** Judicial directive
**53** Killer whale
**54** Violin virtuoso Hilary
**57** Gadget for 58-Down
**58** Golfer dubbed "the Big Easy"

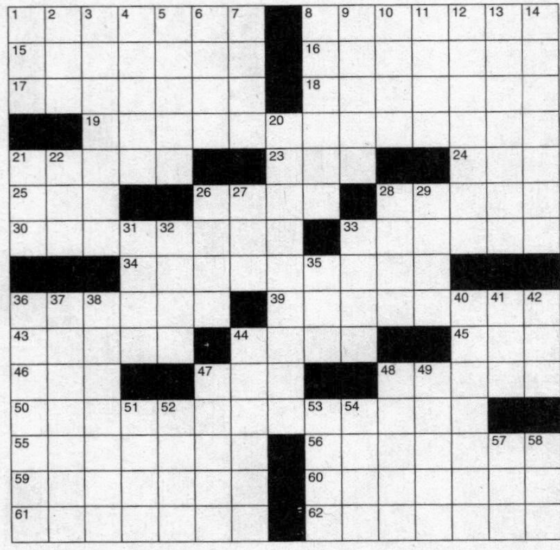

*by Allan E. Parrish*

☆☆

## ACROSS

**1** Quatrain form
**5** Latin lover's word?
**9** BlackBerry output: Abbr.
**13** Co-star of the film whose title is hidden sequentially in 20-, 34-, 41- and 52- Across
**15** Inflict upon
**16** Squabbling
**17** "Not so loud!"
**19** Costa ___, Calif.
**20** About to collapse, say
**22** DHL delivery: Abbr.
**23** Subject for Freud
**24** Amu ___, Asian river
**27** Singles players
**30** When brunch may be scheduled
**33** Poetic preposition
**34** Plea from the plate
**37** Some yeses
**39** Like some columns
**40** Take off
**41** Canine coat
**44** Apt name for a fiftyish Roman woman?
**45** Show host
**46** It makes pets pests
**47** Usher's domain
**49** Eliot Ness, notably, for short
**51** Bull Halsey in W.W. II, e.g.: Abbr.
**52** Some W.W. I code talkers
**59** Leaf feature
**60** Aesthetically pleasing ratio of antiquity
**62** German-built auto
**63** Verdi's "Di Provenza il mar," e.g.
**64** Another co-star of the film hidden in this puzzle
**65** Beatles song that begins "Is there anybody going to listen to my story"
**66** Hard wood
**67** Point out

## DOWN

**1** Not the main rte.
**2** "To ___ not to . . ."
**3** Japanese aborigine
**4** Spook's employer, with "the"
**5** Wing: Abbr.
**6** Eponymous instrument maker Robert
**7** Retired Audi supermini
**8** British weight
**9** Giant tusk holders
**10** Items unlikely to be stored on the top shelf
**11** Essence
**12** Command to Fido
**14** Suggest
**18** Anniversary gift for the year after pottery
**21** Was at the Colosseum?
**24** Al ___
**25** Get ___ for the night
**26** Object of a hunt in a 1984 best seller
**27** Queen's subject?
**28** ___ Brothers (pop trio)
**29** Dips
**31** What a server may serve
**32** Brass
**35** Get shaking
**36** Hotel freebie
**38** Subject of modern research
**42** Coppers
**43** Bill of ___ (shipping document)
**48** 1965 Yardbirds hit
**50** Pester
**51** It's made in a squeeze
**52** Backup cause
**53** Literally, "peaceful" person
**54** Eroded
**55** Hip bones
**56** Locale of Sitting Bull Coll.
**57** Mountain where Moses died, in the Bible
**58** Curer
**61** Alumna identifier

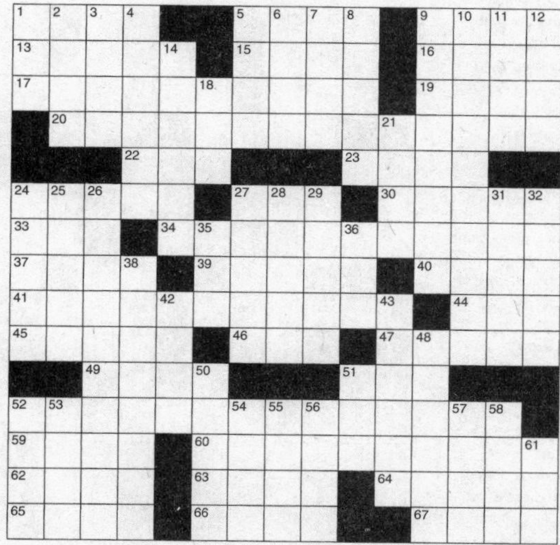

*by Peter A. Collins and Joe Krozel*

## ACROSS

**1** Mythical hammer wielder
**5** Nickname for a namesake of Mary's husband
**9** Burn, in a way
**14** ___ wave
**15** First name in folk
**16** "Institutiones Calculi Integralis" writer
**17** Castle stronghold
**18** Like some interest
**20** Unauthorized preview, say
**22** Ocasek of the Cars
**23** Apology starter
**24** Resettle
**28** Serious
**30** Strip joint, euphemistically
**31** My ___
**32** Joan Miró's "L'___"
**33** Prefix for many cold-weather product names
**34** Glacial ridges
**38** Like 1-Across
**41** Lee of Hollywood
**43** Position
**44** Part of a veterinarian's job
**46** Aegean island near Naxos
**48** The Tigers of the Ohio Valley Conf.
**49** General for whom a style of chicken is named
**50** Crab
**53** Roly-poly
**56** Defiling
**57** German pronoun
**58** Lawyers' org.
**60** Faithful, to a Scot
**61** Went on
**65** Goddess in the hand of the statue of Athena in the Parthenon
**68** Poe-ish
**69** Call to Rover
**70** Taking care of things
**71** Some histrionics
**72** Career division, in sports
**73** Capt.'s inferiors

## DOWN

**1** Finger wagger's sound
**2** Speed
**3** Comic's stock
**4** Adjusts, as a currency rate
**5** Crooks' lackeys
**6** Sch. in Tulsa, Okla.
**7** State tree of Massachusetts
**8** Not their
**9** Port locale
**10** Director's cry
**11** Out on ___
**12** It holds water
**13** Gloomy, literarily
**19** Thread type
**21** Fly ball's path
**24** Fix
**25** Little brother's cry, perhaps
**26** Deli sandwich choice
**27** Vernacular that came into prominence in 1996
**29** One of a candy box duo
**35** Making necessary
**36** Balsam, e.g.
**37** Burned
**39** In ___ (positioned naturally)
**40** Tangles
**42** Sticky stuff
**45** "___ with you" (parting words)
**47** Smoke a little
**51** "American ___"
**52** Grasslands
**53** More red, maybe
**54** Papery sheath on a plant stem
**55** Protective protrusion
**59** Wan
**62** "Shoo!"
**63** Match
**64** Reconstruction, e.g.
**66** Do-it-yourselfer's aid
**67** Uranians, e.g., in brief

*by Damon J. Gulczynski*

## ACROSS

**1** Capital on Lake Victoria
**8** Morrow and Murrow, e.g.
**15** Part of a floor décor
**16** War movie sound effect
**17** Innards
**18** Hostility
**19** Musical group that stays together?
**21** Bulldogger's event
**22** Herd: buffalo :: knot : ___
**26** Part of Eastern Europe, once: Abbr.
**29** Cryptanalysis org.
**32** Ancient theaters
**33** Mountain West Conference player
**34** Faith healing service?
**38** Iowa county named for an Indian tribe
**39** Death on the Nile cause?
**40** Thurman of the "Kill Bill" films
**41** Frolicsome
**42** Stadium's dome?
**45** Home of Samuel Beckett: Abbr.
**46** Designer Saab
**47** Beach shade
**48** Red Cross supply
**49** City near Dayton
**51** Infatuation
**55** Donation to the Salvation Army?
**61** 1960s sitcom title role
**64** Three-dimensional scene
**65** Played the role of
**66** Ready to blow
**67** Most brazen
**68** Eternal . . . and a hint to 19-, 34-, 42- and 55-Across

## DOWN

**1** Intoxicating Polynesian drink
**2** Parched
**3** Jersey material
**4** Conseco Fieldhouse team
**5** "Am not!" rejoinder
**6** Shocking
**7** Tequila source
**8** Chi-town daily, with "the"
**9** Cow: Sp.
**10** Tour of duty
**11** It's hot in an Indian restaurant
**12** Put away
**13** Univ. dorm supervisors
**14** G.P.S. data: Abbr.
**20** Stretches of history
**23** How "Moon River" is played
**24** Take off
**25** Give permission
**26** Northernmost county in New Jersey
**27** Chase scenes, in action films
**28** Bring back, as silver dollars
**30** String before W
**31** "Whatever shall I do?!"
**34** Ring surface
**35** Entry-level position: Abbr.
**36** Pet lovers' org.
**37** Plug place
**43** Held sway
**44** One way to store data
**48** Beethoven's ___ Symphony
**50** Former "Biography" channel
**52** "___ cock-horse to Banbury Cross"
**53** Not abstaining
**54** Germ
**56** Narrow inlets
**57** Oscar superlative
**58** Brush material?
**59** ___ Building, first skyscraper in Boston
**60** Schoolboys
**61** Boxer's setup
**62** Prefix with -cide
**63** U.S./U.K. divider

*by Gary J. Whitehead*

# 86

## ACROSS

1 Poor dating prospects
5 Central Africa's Lake ___
9 Place for a motto
14 M.P.'s quarry
15 Bloody, so to speak
16 Early British automaker Henry
17 Hot strip?
18 Washington has some big ones
19 Mountaineering equipment
20 Historical 1976 miniseries
23 $C_7H_5N_3O_6$
24 Toy at the beach
25 Close, old-style
27 Record holder
30 Refrigerator part
32 Big name in Gotham City
33 "Mens sana in corpore ___"
34 California's ___ Music Festival, since 1947
36 Goon
37 Juliet, e.g., in Gounod's "Romeo and Juliet"
40 Chapel Hill sch.
41 Only player to be part of three World Cup-winning teams
43 Poland's second-largest city
44 Tear
46 Obeys
48 Didn't raise
49 ___ light: Var.
50 Lay person?
51 Reverence
53 Punny hint to answering 20-Across, 11-Down and 29-Down
58 Sends
60 Object of ridicule
61 After-lunch bite
62 Black tea
63 Stick on a dish
64 Scraggy
65 It may be rounded up in a roundup
66 European capital
67 "Do the Right Thing" pizzeria

## DOWN

1 Part of a pound
2 Out
3 Siesta
4 Abate
5 Hatch
6 Global legal venue, with "The"
7 Yankee nickname starting in 2004
8 1940s–'50s film/TV star with two stars on the Hollywood Walk of Fame
9 Cause for using a hot line
10 Sinbad's avian attacker
11 Classic 1947 detective novel
12 Process, in a way, as documents
13 Transcript
21 Biographies
22 ___ Station
26 Delivery notation: Abbr.
27 Give and take
28 It's sometimes grabbed
29 Bygone political slogan
30 '06 Series winner
31 Eastern royal
33 Title TV character in Bikini Bottom
35 Put away
38 Liquid fat
39 Prefix with sclerosis
42 Night school class, for short
45 Soldiers' jobs
47 Come-on
48 Not punishing sufficiently
50 One of the "Brady Bunch" kids
51 Cold-blooded killers
52 Stimulate
54 Holiday season
55 Quarter
56 "Hud" Oscar winner
57 Ones with charges
59 Writer who wrote "I became insane, with long intervals of horrible sanity"

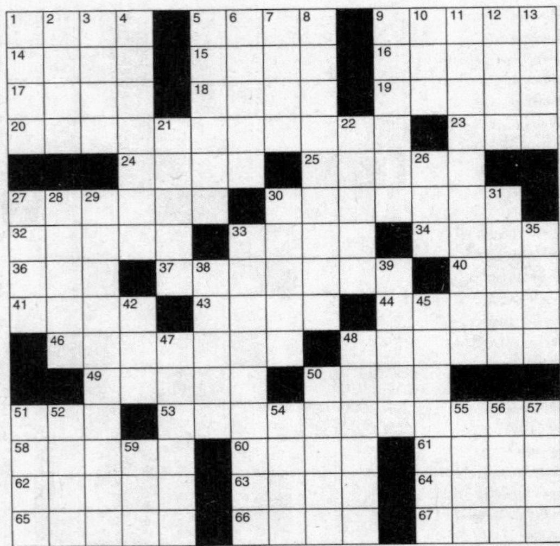

by Sheldon Benardo

# 87

## ACROSS

**1** Feature of an acacia tree
**6** 1986 showbiz autobiography
**11** W.W. II hero, for short
**14** Historical biography that won a 1935 Pulitzer
**15** With 16-Across, boxing result, often
**16** See 15-Across
**17** Certain feed
**18** Slow
**20** Delphic quality
**22** Hawaii's annual ___ Bowl
**23** With 24-Across, curious case in psychology
**24** See 23-Across
**26** Free
**28** Watch brand
**32** Where Nixon went to law school
**35** Much of central Eur., once
**36** Life, liberty and the pursuit of happiness
**37** Married
**38** With 39-Across, instant
**39** See 38-Across
**40** Nod, say
**41** Sped (by)
**43** G.R.E. takers, generally: Abbr.
**44** Locale for four World Series
**45** The last 10% of 110%
**46** Three-wheeled Indian taxi
**48** With 50-Across, grammatical infelicities
**50** See 48-Across
**54** Quiet cough
**57** From southern Spain
**59** Patent holder's income
**61** Total
**62** With 63-Across, go Dutch
**63** See 62-Across
**64** Comparatively considerate
**65** Seed alternative
**66** They're usually washed separately
**67** Medical flow enhancer

## DOWN

**1** "The Sound of Music" name
**2** Soixante minutes
**3** "Wait till you're ___" (parent's reply)
**4** Bing Crosby's "White Christmas," again and again
**5** Hawk, maybe
**6** Lay off
**7** Pubescent, say
**8** Makeshift dagger
**9** American-born Japanese
**10** The Sun Devils, for short
**11** Diable battler
**12** Sweetie
**13** Irish singer with eight platinum U.S. albums
**19** Trample, for example
**21** Proceeded slowly
**25** Former E.P.A. chief Christine ___ Whitman
**27** It's produced by a Tesla coil
**29** Singly
**30** Affix
**31** Where Melville's Billy Budd went
**32** Not be alert
**33** Operating system developed at Bell Labs
**34** Stayed fresh
**36** Impart gradually: Var.
**38** Grammy-winning reggae artist ___ Paul
**39** TV planet
**42** ___ facie
**43** Tanner's locale
**44** Attire that often includes a hood
**46** More minute
**47** Flip-flops
**49** Jazz's Earl Hines, familiarly
**51** Wrestling promoter McMahon
**52** Gone, in a way
**53** Bar belt
**54** Wiles
**55** Twinkie alternative
**56** Assessed visually
**58** Poses posers
**60** Plasma alternative, briefly

| 1 | 2 | 3 | 4 | 5 | ■ | 6 | 7 | 8 | 9 | 10 | ■ | 11 | 12 | 13 |
|---|---|---|---|---|---|---|---|---|---|---|---|---|---|---|
| 14 | | | | | ■ | 15 | | | | | ■ | 16 | | |
| 17 | | | | | ■ | 18 | | | | | 19 | | | |
| 20 | | | | | 21 | | | | | ■ | 22 | | | |
| 23 | | | | | | ■ | 24 | | | 25 | | ■ | ■ | ■ |
| ■ | ■ | ■ | 26 | | | 27 | | | ■ | 28 | | 29 | 30 | 31 |
| 32 | 33 | 34 | | ■ | 35 | | | ■ | 36 | | | | | |
| 37 | | | ■ | 38 | | | ■ | 39 | | | ■ | 40 | | |
| 41 | | | 42 | | | ■ | 43 | | | ■ | 44 | | | |
| 45 | | | | | ■ | 46 | | | | 47 | | ■ | ■ | ■ |
| ■ | ■ | ■ | 48 | | 49 | | | ■ | 50 | | | 51 | 52 | 53 |
| 54 | 55 | 56 | | ■ | 57 | | | 58 | | | | | | |
| 59 | | | | 60 | | | | | ■ | 61 | | | | |
| 62 | | | ■ | 63 | | | | | ■ | 64 | | | | |
| 65 | | | ■ | 66 | | | | | ■ | 67 | | | | |

*by Matt Ginsberg*

Note: When this puzzle is done, connect the circled letters in alphabetical order, and then back to the start, to reveal something seen on the 32-Down 4-Down.

## ACROSS

1 Waxed
5 First name in erotica
10 They might be chocolate
14 ___ Flynn Boyle of "Twin Peaks"
15 Request at a laundry
16 Like some keys
17 Dye plant
18 Popular women's fragrance
19 Together, in music
20 Makes people offers they can't refuse?
22 Apportionment
23 Set of values
24 View from Marseille
25 Relatives, slangily
27 You might end up with a bum one
30 Actress Tyler
31 Child, for one
34 Adler who outwitted Sherlock Holmes
36 ___ impulse
38 ___+ grenadine + maraschino cherry = Roy Rogers cocktail
39 Illumination of manuscripts, and others
40 Headline-making illness of 2002–03
41 Dis
42 Mushroom maker, for short
43 Tony nominee for "Glengarry Glen Ross"
44 Interrogator's discovery
45 Cultural org.
46 Retain
48 Rand who created Dagny Taggart
49 Striped quartz
53 ___ pop, music genre since the 1980s
55 Nocturnal bloodsucker
60 Tony Musante TV series
61 Extracted chemical
62 Punishment unit
63 Frost
64 Options during computer woes
65 James of jazz
66 Competitor of Ben & Jerry's
67 "Thus . . ."
68 Spotted

## DOWN

1 Ruiner of many a photo
2 Charged
3 Filmmaker Von Stroheim
4 Theme of this puzzle
5 Without ___ (riskily)
6 It may be wrinkled
7 Ancient Semitic fertility goddess
8 Bakery employee
9 Elvis Presley's "___ Not You"
10 Detective's need
11 Like some six-packs
12 See 32-Down
13 Vile smile
21 That, to Tomás
26 Home of "The Last Supper"
27 Place for picnicking and dog-walking
28 Hill dwellers
29 ___ alla genovese (sauce)
30 City where 32- and 12-Down is found
31 Also sends to, as an e-mail
32 With 12-Down, locale of the 4-Down
33 "Ishtar" director
35 You might give a speech by this
37 Ultrasecret org.
47 "That mad game the world so loves to play," to Jonathan Swift
48 ___ ready
50 Peter out
51 It's often unaccounted for
52 Allen in American history
54 All ___
55 Lynn who sang "We'll Meet Again"
56 Port near the Red Sea
57 Yellow squirt?
58 Pie chart figs.
59 "Wishing won't make ___"

by Caleb Madison

## ACROSS

**1** Eric's "Will & Grace" co-star
**6** Language from which "divan" is derived
**11** Dunderhead
**14** Thin as ___
**15** Strand, somehow
**16** Nickname for #6 on the Sixers
**17** [See circles]
**19** D.D.E.'s W.W. II command
**20** Well-dressed, photogenic male
**21** [See circles]
**23** Delays set them back: Abbr.
**25** "No horsing around!"
**26** Negligent
**29** A.B.A. member's title
**30** Burger order
**31** "How Do ___" (1997 LeAnn Rimes hit)
**33** One pointing and clicking
**35** Oenophile's interest
**39** 80, for Hg
**40** Northern Europeans
**41** Start time for many a military mission
**42** Colonel's div.
**43** Check box option on a Spanish survey?
**44** "Dream Lover" singer, 1959
**45** CNBC news topics, for short
**47** Business with a register
**49** Paris's Basilique ___-Clotilde
**50** Language that treats "dz" as a single consonant
**53** Use a cell phone outside one's calling area
**55** [See circles]
**58** Recess
**62** Dick
**63** [See circles]
**65** Egypt's ___ Simbel historical site
**66** Defensive retort
**67** Scottish child
**68** Seedy sort?
**69** Majority of a crowd at a Jonas Brothers concert
**70** "I'm outta here!"

## DOWN

**1** Family pet in "Hi and Lois"
**2** Former "ER" co-star La Salle
**3** Having one's heart set (on)
**4** Change colors?
**5** Oliver Twist, for one
**6** Hi-___
**7** Result of overstrain
**8** Concrete
**9** Court huddles
**10** Taken-aback response
**11** Start of many dedications
**12** ___-Detoo
**13** Finger of the ocean
**18** Forms a union
**22** Program
**24** Occupies an abandoned building
**26** Either of two guests on "To Tell the Truth"
**27** Der ___ (Konrad Adenauer)
**28** Deer ___
**30** Garage job
**32** Like some candles
**34** When flowers bloom: Abbr.
**36** Crew members
**37** "M*A*S*H" co-star
**38** Feminizing suffix
**40** Attention-getting cry
**44** Test sites
**46** Handles roughly
**48** Linguist Chomsky
**50** Relatively cool red giant
**51** Remain inactive
**52** How actors should appear
**54** Jazz's Carmen
**56** Drop paper in a box, maybe
**57** Coll. major
**59** Tex's neighbor
**60** Especially
**61** It's about 2½ times as high as Vesuvius
**64** W.B.A. finales

*by Mike Nothnagel*

90

## ACROSS

**1** Fifth stroke, often
**5** Tatter
**8** Shoeboy's offering
**14** Tony player on "NYPD Blue"
**15** Home of the Clearwater Mtns.
**16** Not necessarily rejecting
**17** Draws
**19** Edberg who won two Wimbledons
**20** 1972 musical with the song "Summer Nights"
**22** Actress Graff
**23** Ancient Romans' attire
**26** Draws
**28** Graduate
**30** "Isn't ___ bit like you and me?" (Beatles lyric)
**31** Retired barrier breaker, for short
**32** Law or medicine, e.g.
**33** Sole support
**34** Weight
**35** Awakens
**37** Sermonizer in France
**41** Tiant in the Red Sox Hall of Fame
**42** Angiogram sight
**44** Pollen holder
**47** Porter, e.g.
**48** Pest eradicator
**49** Draws
**52** Having steam come out the ears, say
**53** W.W. II blockade enforcer
**54** Old Athenian ally against Persia
**56** What fools do, per an adage
**58** Draws
**62** ___ Green, Scottish town famous for runaway weddings
**63** Head lines, in brief?
**64** What may ensure the show goes on?
**65** Annapolis graduate
**66** Gridiron stat.
**67** Hightailed it

## DOWN

**1** By means of
**2** "What's the ___?"
**3** Middle X, say
**4** Draws
**5** Rather smelly
**6** Attaché attachments
**7** Hardly in
**8** Like some poles: Abbr.
**9** Kind of scanner
**10** Female companion in "Doctor Who"
**11** Draws
**12** Politicians take them
**13** Square
**18** Papas of "Zorba the Greek"
**21** One on it may be out of it
**23** Sonora snack
**24** "The Good Earth" mother
**25** Wise one
**27** Board with a couple of seats
**29** Villainess in "The Little Mermaid"
**33** 1961 Elvis hit "___ Latest Flame"
**36** Supermodel Cheryl
**37** Draws
**38** Key letter
**39** Harte of fiction
**40** Brontë heroine
**41** Kind of impression
**43** John ___, Doris Day's co-star in "The Pajama Game"
**44** Poinsettia's family
**45** The Tigers of the Southeastern Conference
**46** Draws
**48** Took a twisty path
**50** Emmy winner Christine
**51** It's news in sports
**55** Rules, for short
**57** A Bobbsey twin
**59** Turning point?
**60** When day is done, briefly
**61** This may be sold by the yard

*by Victor Fleming*

★★★

## ACROSS

**1** Releaser of "1921" in 1969
**7** Author of the best-selling investment book "You're Fifty ___ Now What?"
**13** Participate in drag?
**14** Thing turned while speaking
**15** Source of the word "avatar"
**16** Words of intimidation
**17** They get many saves
**18** Shout about Paris?
**19** Something below the bar
**20** Diet of Worms concern
**21** Lewis Carroll's birthplace
**23** "___ Growing" (Temptations hit)
**24** One against another
**25** Soeur de la mère
**26** One concerned with entrances and exits
**31** Stalemate
**35** Start of a traditional love story
**36** They rock, sometimes
**39** Far-away connection?
**40** "The Art of Hitting .300" writer Charley
**41** A diva may throw one
**43** Not splurge on a 48-Across, say
**46** Inits. by a dateline
**47** Tony's consigliere on "The Sopranos"
**48** It's often taken down Broadway
**49** Make the rounds?
**51** Completely in the dark
**52** Cell assignment
**53** Sci-fi smuggler
**54** R-rated, say
**55** Mean

## DOWN

**1** Band member with a bent neck
**2** 1946 Literature Nobelist
**3** Tennis's Clijsters and others
**4** Cause of fitful sleep
**5** Sartre's "___ clos"
**6** Target of Durocher's "Nice guys finish last" sentiment
**7** Body in a case
**8** Breaks a bottle on, maybe
**9** It ended in 1806: Abbr.
**10** Capacious closet
**11** Hold
**12** Member of the 27-Down group
**13** Item used for studio mixing
**15** Big break
**18** How a gull might feel
**21** O.K.
**22** What Greece has that Germany doesn't
**24** Means of reaching the stars
**27** Brothers who sang "Stayin' Alive"
**28** Biodiversity setting
**29** Period named for an earth goddess
**30** Option for a hit
**32** Setting for big rigs
**33** "Yep, unfortunately"
**34** Orchestra section
**36** Dairy equipment
**37** Remove, as carpet
**38** A question of introspection
**42** Very hot
**43** Go to a lot
**44** Very upscale?
**45** DuPont discontinued it in 1990
**48** Group sharing a coat of arms
**50** Utah Stars' org.
**51** City with both A.L. and N.L. teams, informally

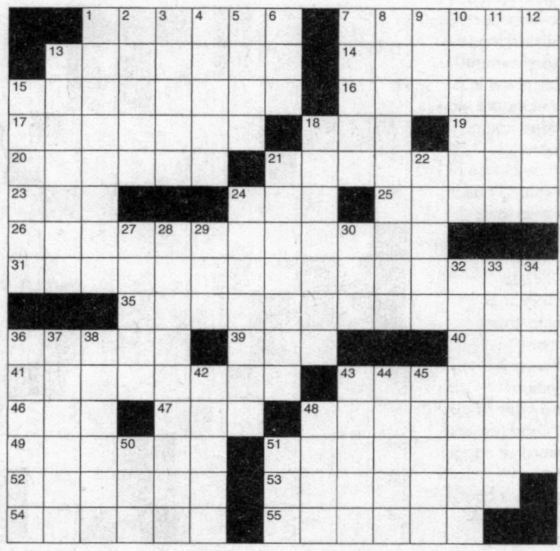

*by Josh Knapp*

# 92

**ACROSS**

**1** Crescendos
**7** Eye-opening things
**13** In the database, say
**15** Not look upon favorably
**16** Brutal force
**17** Nice thing to cut through
**18** It's not hot for long
**19** They're not hot
**21** Lifesaver, briefly
**22** Plains folk
**23** Rankled
**24** Goalkeeper's guarded area
**25** People may be put out if they're not put up
**28** Part of an exchange
**29** Engine sound
**30** Figure seen on the lunar surface
**33** Multitasking, e.g.
**34** Like some cruises
**38** Conceived in a nonstandard way
**39** Badge holder: Abbr.
**40** White House girl
**42** Revolting bunch
**43** Setting for everything
**45** X-ray spec?
**46** ". . . ___ woodchuck could chuck wood?"
**47** Worker in the medium of torn and pasted paper
**49** Will be present?
**50** Sword or dagger
**52** Yaps
**54** Part of a board
**55** Safari jacket feature
**56** Give some relief
**57** Marathoner's concern

**DOWN**

**1** Not just request
**2** Left on a plate
**3** "There!"
**4** It gets replayed
**5** Gunslinger's cry
**6** Quaint photo
**7** Caffeinated?
**8** Tom and Huck, e.g.
**9** "A lie that makes us realize truth," per Picasso
**10** Try to steal a basketball from another player, e.g.
**11** Cartography
**12** "Journal to Eliza" author, 1767
**14** Early flag warning
**15** West Jordan is near it
**20** Semi professionals?
**24** Second of January
**26** They were brought down by Olympians
**27** Move furtively
**29** Members of the genus Troglodytes
**31** Times for wake-up calls, briefly
**32** Longtime power provider: Abbr.
**34** Cruise vehicle
**35** Drumming sound
**36** Arab-___
**37** Like some steaks
**38** Sorrowful
**41** Carol's first word
**43** Stock to hawk
**44** Jobs for plumbers
**47** Roles, figuratively
**48** It has two critical reading sects.
**51** That Mexican?
**53** Charge lead-in

*by Louis Hildebrand*

## ACROSS

1 Eat up
6 Partied hearty
15 Heroine of Exmoor
16 Course in Russian geography?
17 Their points are made bluntly
18 Something passed without hesitation
19 Topic of TV's "This Old House"
21 Royal Crown, once
22 Slow to mix, say
23 Material for many electric guitar bodies
25 Peak's counterpart
27 Attachment used with care?
29 Dedicated literature
31 Sets off
35 ___ before
37 One starting easily?
39 Cry of anticipation
40 Moral obligation
41 Dominican capital
42 Gets under someone's skin?
44 Old imperator
45 Verenigde ___ (America, in Amsterdam)
46 Metropolitan hangover?
48 Indians' home, for short
49 Razor brand word
51 He introduced the symbol "e" for natural logs
53 "The Vengeance of ___" (1968 film sequel)
56 Opposite of very
58 One suspended for a game
61 Worked together
64 First name in rap
65 Debate
66 Was snail-like
67 Hoax
68 "___ trouble!"

## DOWN

1 Schwalm-___ (German district)
2 "Ixnay"
3 Fighter in old strips
4 Magic center, once
5 Admission statement
6 Word from one who isn't following
7 "East of Eden" son
8 In no way new
9 Its letters may be bolted down
10 Like much filet mignon
11 Fried
12 Roles on "Evening Shade" and "Nip/Tuck"
13 Meyers of "Saturday Night Live"
14 Its ruins are a Unesco World Heritage Site
20 Fans sporting a footwear logo
24 Make a comeback
26 Yom Kippur War participant
27 Pays
28 Show respect, in a way
30 They might span generations
32 Tool often used while wearing gloves
33 Like some cavities
34 Chain link?
36 Country singer Akins
38 Rum, to some
43 Wool cover-ups
47 Bug
50 Do intaglio, e.g.
52 Harden: Var.
53 It takes folks in
54 Wedding ring?
55 Mech. master
57 Wedding couple?
59 Something to get caught on
60 Play set
62 Make a case against?
63 2000 Richard Gere title role

by Tim Croce

## 94

**ACROSS**

**1** Land grant, of a sort
**11** "The Praise of Chimney-Sweepers" writer
**15** Person with a shaky story?
**16** Dosage units
**17** Thanksgiving symbol
**18** Drill instructors, e.g.: Abbr.
**19** Viscosity symbols
**20** Joyner joiner?
**22** Bitter herb
**23** Jason of "I Love You, Man"
**25** They change people's profiles
**27** Subject of Article III, Section 3 of the Constitution
**30** They may be charitable
**31** Schaefer alternative
**34** Davis of "Evening Shade"
**35** Fancy follower
**38** Top
**40** Coup de ___ (sudden impulse: Fr.)
**41** Spiral staircase, essentially
**43** One way to travel
**45** "The Way I Am" autobiographer, 2008
**47** Person from Moscow
**51** They hold on to things
**54** Physicist with a unit of distance named after him
**55** ___ stretch
**56** Went around in circles, perhaps
**59** Weakens
**60** Like potpourri, sometimes
**62** Counts
**64** Bluesy James
**65** Spy's device
**66** Be a stinker
**67** 1952 best seller set in California

**DOWN**

**1** Least likely to take command
**2** Hide seeker?
**3** What the fortunate reach
**4** Complain loudly
**5** Author LeShan
**6** Thin
**7** Ending with prefer
**8** Voter registration grp. founded in 1970
**9** Left to the editor?
**10** Companion of Algernon in an Oscar Wilde play
**11** South end?
**12** It was last an official Olympic event in 1908
**13** Skeptical response
**14** Person who's been charged
**21** First name in design
**24** Allied transport, for short
**26** Despite everything
**28** Plata's partner
**29** It just isn't done
**32** Female octopus
**33** Religious mystic
**35** 1994 Michael Keaton film in which real journalists have cameo roles
**36** Main ore of iron
**37** Spanish seaport
**39** Sheller's discard
**42** Gen ___ (demographic group)
**44** Bozo
**46** "You and whose army?!"
**48** Gave out one's address?
**49** A in physics?
**50** Pathfinder producer
**52** Patty Hearst alias
**53** Blows the mind of
**57** Broadcast
**58** Roaring Twenties look
**61** Tibetan wolf's prey
**63** "Battle of Britain" grp.

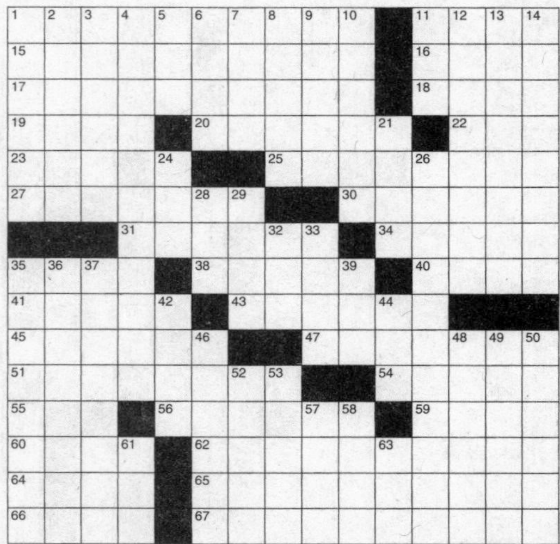

*by Trip Payne*

## ACROSS

**1** Nightclub in the Trump Taj
**7** Like some party prizes
**14** Part of the iris bordering the pupil
**15** Getting there
**16** Famous bodybuilder
**18** "On Golden Pond" wife
**19** "Closer Than Ever," e.g.
**20** Fed. management org.
**21** Zoologist Fossey
**22** Permanent solutions
**23** Resort town on I-70
**24** TV lawyer Stone
**25** Splotchy apparel, familiarly
**26** Often-used word in Matthew 1
**27** Holds over?
**29** Apollonian
**30** In days of knights?
**32** Factors in handwriting analysis
**35** Oldest of a literary quartet
**39** Unwieldy ships
**40** Song from Sondheim's "Into the Woods"
**41** ___ Claire
**42** 11-time N.C.A.A. basketball champs
**43** Racehorse whose 1955 Kentucky Derby win kept Nashua from taking the Triple Crown
**44** Hide
**45** "Laus ___" (words atop the Washington Monument)
**46** New York City's first Jewish mayor
**47** "In Search of Identity" autobiographer
**48** Famous body builder?
**51** All at once
**52** When data's been ___ . . .
**53** . . . you may have to ___ it
**54** Lettuce

## DOWN

**1** Vegetable-oil soap
**2** Old
**3** To look, in Leipzig
**4** Cricketer's action
**5** Mobile home: Abbr.
**6** Disapproving comment
**7** "Speed" star
**8** CD, e.g.?
**9** Priceless?
**10** Bewilderment
**11** Carousel riders?
**12** Summer wind in the Mediterranean
**13** Nickname of Chancellor Konrad Adenauer
**17** Balancing act?
**18** Broadway star Linda who won $100,000 on "Star Search"
**22** Flings
**23** Actress Felton of 1950s TV's "December Bride"
**25** Barrows
**26** Radiant
**28** See 50-Down
**29** Makes binding
**31** Back in business
**32** Some people do it to think
**33** Swiss canton or its capital
**34** 1932 song or 1984 movie
**36** More frail
**37** Gradually quieting, in music
**38** Jabba the ___ of "Star Wars"
**40** Reveille, e.g.
**43** Just know
**44** Michelangelo's country
**46** Cordage fiber
**47** Coveleski of Cooperstown
**49** Governed
**50** With 28-Down, its flag has a lion holding a sword

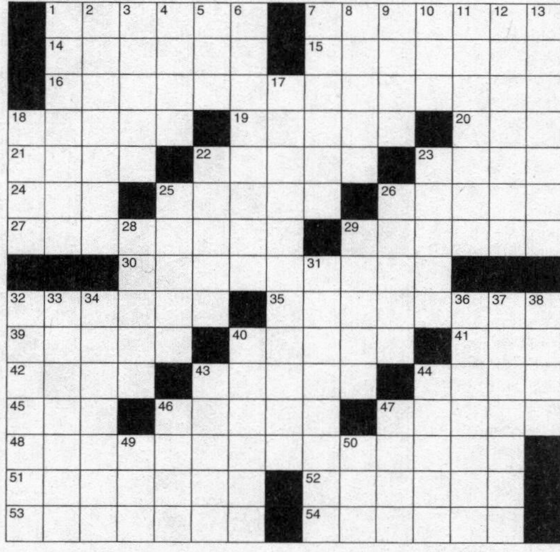

by Henry Hook

# 96

**ACROSS**

**1** Certain fricassee
**9** Around-the-world race
**15** Teetotaler's order
**16** "Would you mind . . . ?"
**17** Special communication
**19** It's not exact: Abbr.
**20** They come to a point while flying
**21** Sacred Buddhist mountain
**22** Dakota relative
**24** Starts occupying
**27** Special communication syst.
**28** On deck
**29** Cause of some shaking, for short
**30** "Pay ___ mind"
**32** King-high games
**34** Deep red
**37** Not even consider
**38** One picking up a lot
**40** Like pirates
**41** Set to go off, as a bomb
**42** Where la Croix-Rouge is headquartered
**44** Radical 1970s grp.
**47** Rumble in the Jungle strategy
**49** Cherry alternative
**51** Become wearisome
**52** Important Indian
**54** It may be exact: Abbr.
**55** One who keeps giving you the business?
**58** Philosophies
**59** Spin out on wheels?
**60** "Funeral Blues" poet and family
**61** In a tight spot financially

**DOWN**

**1** Small part
**2** 1905 revolt setting
**3** Virgin Blue rival
**4** Check information: Abbr.
**5** Gas bill information
**6** Low point
**7** Big Italian daily
**8** Star of the 1998 film version of 45-Down
**9** Get a move on
**10** It increased to 4 cents per oz. in 1958
**11** Home to Seaquarium and MetroZoo
**12** Serve
**13** Diamond dream
**14** Top of the world?
**18** Spillover stopper
**23** Flash
**25** Cut out
**26** Bone: Prefix
**28** Loose
**31** Kind of hat
**33** Biochemical enzyme, briefly
**34** Growl
**35** 1970s–'90s international carrier based in Lima
**36** Went wild
**39** Campbell's competitor
**40** 2004 Best Musical Tony winner
**43** Periods added to harmonize the lunar and solar calendars
**45** 1987 Best Musical Tony winner, informally
**46** Bow
**48** Shake
**49** Greene who wrote "Summer of My German Soldier"
**50** Like some help
**53** "Mi casa ___ casa"
**55** MP3 player maker
**56** One that may balk
**57** Stuff in a bank

*by Alan Olschwang*

## ACROSS

**1** Flower-scented refresher
**11** P.D. personnel
**15** Flimflam's antithesis
**16** Drink in a sippy cup
**17** Longtime battler of the Mongols
**18** Antony's love
**19** It flows through Knottingley
**20** Chicago Sting's org.
**21** Writer who created Shrek
**22** Court figure
**24** Word with pain or treatment
**26** Support at the top?
**27** Pain
**29** They utilize high bands
**31** World leader whose full name included Abdel twice
**33** Catering hall sights
**34** Changing places with swimmers?
**38** Rat
**40** Hit from the 1997 album "Surfacing"
**41** Subs
**43** Gets information from, in a way
**45** Sweetens
**50** Fighting something, say
**51** Like jerky
**53** Sign of availability
**54** Sanctuaries
**56** Second-century year
**58** Locale of the radial notch
**59** Pet problem
**60** Alternative to alternative
**62** "As You Like It" servant
**63** One who used to go clubbing?
**64** Hanna-Barbera productions
**65** Spots

## DOWN

**1** "Original father of harmony," per Beethoven, briefly
**2** Heavenly neighbor of Scutum
**3** Former Ecuadorean money
**4** Production team?
**5** Like some cheap mdse.
**6** It's noble
**7** Guest in a library
**8** Galls
**9** What a priest may say shortly after waking up
**10** Lyricist Dubin and others
**11** Clock
**12** Snipe, e.g.
**13** Some vintage clubs
**14** Floating brown algae
**21** 1970s kidnapping grp.
**23** Group in the Bogart film "Black Legion"
**25** Historical region on the Strait of Dover
**28** One way to take back one's words?
**30** Grayish brown
**32** "Whatever"
**34** Something that's the most luxurious of its kind
**35** Capital on Gulf St. Vincent
**36** Like some thoroughly examined passages
**37** River past Solothurn
**39** "Everybody Loves ___" (Johnny Cash title track)
**42** He wrote "I will show you fear in a handful of dust"
**44** They're often needed to go clubbing
**46** 100 centimes
**47** Where semis aren't typically seen
**48** Opera character who sings "Eri tu"
**49** A bee may be on it
**52** Minor accident results
**55** Phenomena after retiring
**57** It's often volcanic
**60** They're often volcanic: Abbr.
**61** Transformer, e.g.

*by Ned White*

# 98

**ACROSS**

**1** Exude
**7** Family tree abbr.
**11** Backing
**14** Marching ___ (Midwest college band)
**15** Mix
**16** Post-Manhattan Project agcy.
**17** It has a lot of small dishes
**19** Guilty, in a legal phrase
**20** Like many appliances: Abbr.
**21** Forest cover?
**23** Narnian guardian
**25** Security need: Abbr.
**26** Its purpose is frightening
**30** Noted 21-Across dealer
**32** OPEC member: Abbr.
**33** They're checked for life
**35** Connecting, briefly
**36** Climactic musical finales
**38** Like some pulled calves?
**40** "That's ___ one!"
**41** Unload on, in a way
**43** Work containing about 2.5 million quotations: Abbr.
**44** Unsettled sort
**46** "Rumor has it . . ."
**48** Discourage
**50** Tibiae neighbors
**51** Enters
**53** Member of the Hindu trinity
**57** It may lie in a bed
**58** Women who may make people break up?
**60** Place for many belts
**61** ___ about
**62** Some godchildren
**63** Way: Abbr.
**64** Rialto attention-getter
**65** Absorbed

**DOWN**

**1** Graduation, e.g.
**2** Offerer of the Matmid frequent flier club
**3** More
**4** Build-it-yourself wheels
**5** Clandestine maritime org.
**6** Demands of some directors
**7** Company with the stock symbol DPZ
**8** I, for one
**9** Six-Day War setting
**10** "___ Been the One" (2006 Rihanna song)
**11** Pop's condition
**12** Like some projectors
**13** One ___ (kid's game)
**18** More difficult, in slang
**22** They might be smoked out
**24** Reaping time: Abbr.
**26** Longtime human "Sesame Street" role
**27** Crookes tube emission
**28** Measurers of gas properties
**29** Making seven figures, say
**31** Kind of complexion
**34** Gloomy
**37** Nations Unies members
**39** They're often loaded
**42** End of discussion?
**45** Military alert status
**47** Michael with the memoir "Work in Progress"
**49** TV executive Arledge
**51** Doesn't just tear up
**52** Novel with the chapter "Farming in Polynesia"
**54** Old victim of the Spanish
**55** Resident of D.C.'s Observatory Circle
**56** Right hand: Abbr.
**59** "___ weites Feld" (Günter Grass novel)

*by Eric Berlin*

## ACROSS

1 Hearty cuts
7 Response of mock subservience
14 Lid
15 The "thee" in "Get thee to a nunnery"
16 Address location
17 Bad setting
18 1040 subjs.
19 Room in Clue
21 Antibiotic, e.g., briefly
22 Prefix with relation
23 Finds unbearable
25 "Meet Me at the ___"
26 Govt. org. associated with auctions
27 Fencing action
28 Culmination's opposite
29 Blanche DuBois's "I have always depended on the kindness of strangers," e.g.
31 Founder of experimental physiology
32 Bad marks gotten in high school?
33 Lizard Fuel beverage maker
34 Top banana
36 Giant in fashion
40 Cardio option
41 Palate stimulus
42 HVAC measure
43 Not settled
44 Defense attorney's claim
45 Syllables sung by Figaro
46 "Non ___ andrai" (Figaro aria)
47 36-Down, notably
48 Tubes in an oven
49 1886 Alcott sequel
51 Favorite card game of Winston Churchill
54 In the main
55 Musical with the song "Everyone's a Little Bit Racist"
56 Spinner with numbers
57 Boston and Charleston

## DOWN

1 "The Great Railway Bazaar" travel writer
2 Owner of Martini & Rossi, Dewar's and Grey Goose
3 Gets off the fence
4 It separates two names
5 Attention
6 Gloom's opposite
7 Kind of smoothie
8 Pundit pieces
9 Pulitzer winner for "Driving Miss Daisy"
10 Nocturnal cycle occurrence
11 Having gotten the scoop?
12 One standing in the back of an alley
13 Sense of orientation
14 Chestnut
20 Cosmetologist's concern
23 Org. with a handshake in its logo
24 It's alive
25 Biblical scout
28 He played an attendant at Wally's Filling Station in 1960s TV
30 Puss
31 "Our Lips Are Sealed" band
33 2007 hit comedy with a character who dubbed himself McLovin
34 One who might be seen in the offing?
35 Thumbs-down
36 Famously overconfident competitor
37 Indirect
38 Bronzes, maybe
39 Final track on the Rolling Stones' "12×5"
40 Place for extra notes on a piano?
41 Area where the hoax Piltdown man was found
44 Creator of Professor Challenger
47 Obstreperous
48 Calamine component
50 Dawg
52 2006 Bond girl ___ Green
53 Road to enlightenment, for some

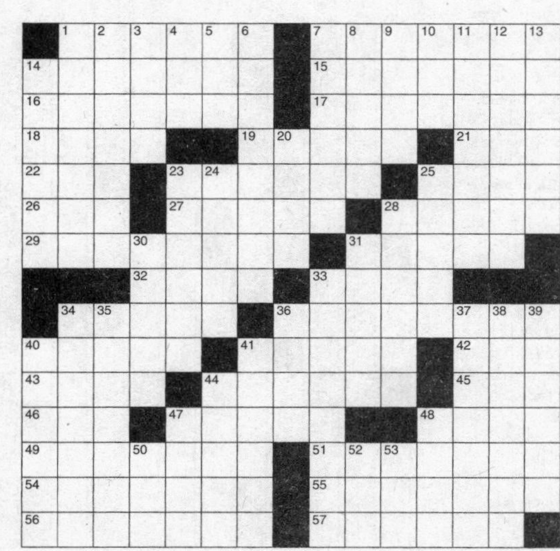

*by Brad Wilber*

# 100

## ACROSS

**1** Inspiration for Björn Again
**5** Bob of stand-up comedy
**10** Waves back?
**14** It has many functions, briefly
**15** Art center since 1819
**16** Risky thing to try in figure skating
**17** Risky thing to try for on "Jeopardy!"
**20** Novel whose title comes from Ecclesiastes
**21** "Doo ___ (That Thing)" (#1 hit for Lauryn Hill)
**22** Nonpro?
**23** Heat unit?
**24** Player of Sethe in "Beloved"
**26** It might go through a filter
**29** Campaign crunch time: Abbr.
**32** Opposite of schadenfreude
**33** Offerer of package plans
**35** Source of jumbo eggs, in brief
**36** Hound
**38** Complicit with
**39** Subject of a Sophocles tragedy
**41** Result of excessive bending
**42** Midgets of the 1960s–'70s, e.g.
**43** Gets charged up?
**45** Hound
**47** Image on Connecticut's state quarter
**48** ___ out a profit
**50** Main role on "My Big Fat Greek Life"
**51** Justice League member
**57** Diamond deception
**58** Drive
**59** Gifted individual?
**60** Fashionista's read, maybe
**61** Like some bets and patients
**62** Bottleneck
**63** Red, e.g., for short

## DOWN

**1** Drama center, often
**2** Lush travel plan?
**3** Detailed outlines
**4** Hotshots
**5** "Apollo 13" actor Joe
**6** 1906 Massenet opera
**7** Brass
**8** Brand with the flavor Fudge Tracks
**9** It might include check boxes
**10** Outfit
**11** Litter lying around a den
**12** Fit
**13** Pablo Neruda's "Elemental ___"
**18** Brunswick, e.g., once
**19** Grad students often dread them
**25** Tours "yours"
**27** Said reflectively
**28** Make like
**29** Debutante who dated J. D. Salinger and Orson Welles
**30** Crushed corn creation
**31** Total hottie
**34** Martinez of the diamond
**35** Clog
**36** Title holders
**37** Disney doe
**40** Driving problem
**41** Ready for retirement
**44** Bear, say
**46** Long
**47** Setting of Hill Air Force Base
**49** Lara's son, in DC Comics
**51** So
**52** Give a name badge, say
**53** Work (in)
**54** Like death's dart, in Shakespeare
**55** Family moniker
**56** Tampico track transport

*by Natan Last*

★★★

**ACROSS**

**1** Not just a mess-up, in modern lingo
**9** Necessary
**15** Alternative to Holiday Inn
**16** First name that's feminine in English and masculine in Italian
**17** Picker-uppers?
**18** Steps taken on a farm?
**19** Ball holders
**20** Nickname since 1959
**22** "___ you!"
**23** Fern feature
**24** Voiceless, in phonetics
**25** National capital on a river of the same name
**27** Dinner ___
**30** Union opponent
**31** Big company located in Times Square
**32** Salesperson who may give you a ring
**34** Knock out, in a way
**36** Film character who lives to be 877
**37** Swiss cheese ingredient
**41** Step on the way to the Olympics, maybe
**45** Old Spanish queen
**46** With 35-Down, something meant to be shaken
**47** Naturally bright
**48** High-school put-down
**50** Drainage area
**52** Big inits. in camping
**53** Musician nicknamed El Rey
**56** Guilt symptom
**57** Support in a stadium
**58** Staple of classic rock, informally
**60** Still
**61** Spread out over time, in a way
**62** Welcome cry for the seasick
**63** Slurs

**DOWN**

**1** Rapture
**2** C.I.A. director under Obama
**3** Battery used to measure brightness?
**4** Providers of tips for improving one's English?
**5** Five bones
**6** "True Blood" actress
**7** ___-Ethiopian War, 1935–36
**8** His #2 was retired in 1997
**9** Org. with the motto "For the benefit of all"
**10** Docs with penlights
**11** Shortens, maybe
**12** Big name in radio advice
**13** Really embarrassed, perhaps
**14** Passed effortlessly
**21** Emotionally tough to take
**23** They're all abuzz
**26** Elaborates
**28** Treat on a stick
**29** Evasive maneuver
**33** Gone flat?
**35** See 46-Across
**37** Key
**38** The tiniest bit
**39** Opposite of pacific
**40** Annual celebration with candles
**42** They're basic
**43** Put on a pedestal
**44** Symbol of chastity
**49** Lavished gifts (on)
**51** Cuts off
**54** Deluxe
**55** "Come ___ these yellow sands": "The Tempest"
**56** Czech-born N.H.L.'er Sykora or Prucha
**59** Lead-in to wash

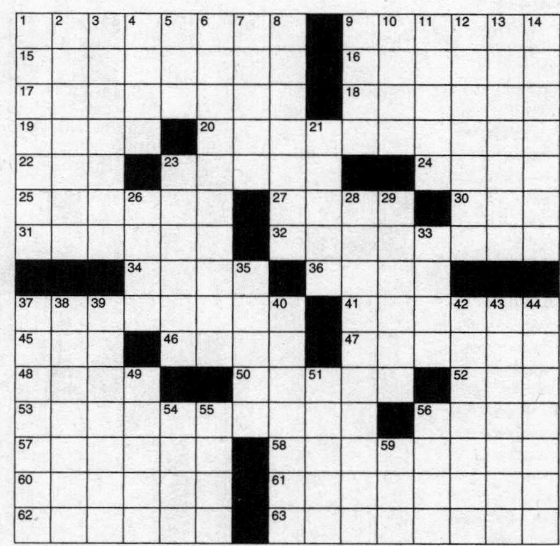

*by Tyler Hinman*

102 

**ACROSS**

**1** Its workers aren't behind closed doors
**9** Thunderstruck
**15** Length of many stands?
**16** Title boy in an old sitcom
**17** Places for some flicks
**18** Wear for some contests
**19** Liberal types
**20** Overly optimistic
**21** Feldshuh of "Yentl"
**22** Brought forth
**23** Gone
**26** Acid head?
**27** Singing group
**29** It was worth three livres
**30** Machine part
**33** Means of catching up with the rest of the class
**34** It occupies 25 pages in the Oxford English Dictionary
**35** "Knock on ___ Door" (Bogart film)
**36** Caesar
**39** Mountainside debris
**41** Lies low
**44** Common hotel bathroom feature
**46** Fuel-efficient transportation
**48** Cry when rubbing it in
**49** Hippodrome competitor
**51** Play an ace?
**52** It's not the road less traveled
**53** Currency that replaced pounds in 1964
**54** Learning environments
**55** ___ Evans, a k a Chubby Checker
**56** Places to store barrels?

**DOWN**

**1** Washing-up place
**2** Like wild horses
**3** Nanny's cry
**4** Catches
**5** Often red item of apparel
**6** Clarifying agent in brewing
**7** "Wide Sargasso Sea" novelist, 1966
**8** Range parts: Abbr.
**9** One giving prior consent?
**10** Mama-san's charges
**11** Olajuwon of the N.B.A.
**12** Zoo sections
**13** Follower of one's convictions
**14** Experimented with
**20** Good spot for a jingle
**22** Kind of marker
**24** Indian bread
**25** 1969 hit for the Doors
**28** "Feather Gown" sculptor
**30** Something you don't get credit for
**31** Cursory cleaning, say
**32** Belly dancer's move
**36** Kills
**37** Family often seen on "The Andy Williams Show"
**38** Underground branch
**40** Crude component
**42** Hours of operation?
**43** Bubblegummer
**45** Take ___ (break)
**47** Word with shoe or shop
**49** Its shell may be soft
**50** Yemeni capital
**52** Start of a Chinese game

*by Barry C. Silk*

## ACROSS

1 Designer known for his "American look"
6 Cruel one
10 It might include hot dogs and baked beans
14 Freeload
15 Wile E. Coyote or the Road Runner
16 "Three Places in New England" composer
17 Go-getter
18 Org. offering college scholarships
19 "Bye-bye!"
20 1916 work by 28-Across
23 Thurman of "Dangerous Liaisons"
24 Greenwich Village campus inits.
25 Blue
28 Subject of this puzzle
34 Writer LeShan
35 When doubled, a book by Gauguin
36 Locale for some Gauguin art
37 Defeat
40 Middle of a patriotic cheer
42 "We didn't do it!"
43 Like some designs
45 Trauma sites, for short
47 Sport ___
48 Title subject of a 28-Across work
52 Cupcake
53 ___-Magnon
54 N.R.C. predecessor
55 Sobriquet for 28-Across
61 Items for Rambos
64 Ames Research Center org.
65 Broadcaster
66 ___ vaccine
67 Anita who sang "Is You Is or Is You Ain't My Baby"
68 Where Hercules slew the lion
69 Mimics mockingly
70 Sugar amts.
71 May gift recipients

## DOWN

1 Austen's Woodhouse
2 Tower
3 It is "resistless in battle," wrote Sophocles
4 Spring river breakup
5 Small fry
6 Barbara Kingsolver's "___ América"
7 Slip
8 Spiral pasta
9 Make secret, in a way
10 Ball catcher
11 "Die Meistersinger" heroine
12 Volleyball need
13 Start of a patriotic cheer
21 Sammy the lyricist
22 Sontag who wrote "In America"
25 Get into uniform
26 Shrewd
27 Ceremonial sites
28 Like some delis
29 Teeth: Prefix
30 Supreme Court justice Stone
31 Chit
32 Beamed intensely
33 "Well, looky here!"
38 Fraternal patriotic org.
39 Former CBS chief
41 Poetica opening
44 Be afraid to
46 Opposite of legato: Abbr.
49 Tent dwellers, maybe
50 Put back on display, in a way
51 More gross
55 Clucking sounds
56 Without dawdling
57 They may be caught on a beach
58 "Garfield" waitress
59 Want
60 Pâté de fois ___
61 End of a patriotic cheer
62 Get rid of
63 Nouvelle-Calédonie, e.g.

*by John Underwood*

104 

## ACROSS

**1** It can be used to get your balance
**8** It's flaky and nutty
**15** Fine trappings
**16** Modem, e.g.
**17** Activity in which stakes may be laid
**18** Suspect eliminator, often
**19** Hatch ___
**20** Big name in Web-based correspondence
**22** Old televangelism letters
**23** Ice
**24** Appropriate
**25** Play to ___
**26** Early Japanese P.M. Hirobumi ___
**27** Old sitcom couple's surname
**28** Reads online
**29** Comparable to a pin?
**31** Buoys
**33** Ranked
**35** Square
**36** So-called "Texas White House," once
**40** Natives of Umm Qasr
**44** Minor's opposite
**45** Back ___
**47** Stay-at-home worker?
**48** Beep, say
**49** Date preceder
**50** Gifford's replacement as Philbin's co-host
**51** Barrister's deg.
**52** Cloudiness
**53** Charming person?
**54** Very hot
**56** Ascii alternative
**58** Argue
**59** Degree divisions
**60** Holds out
**61** Doctor's order

## DOWN

**1** Peaceful place
**2** Ones left holding the bag?
**3** Hollywood icon since 1924
**4** Stuffed and roasted entree
**5** Put down
**6** Abbr. after Sen. Richard Lugar's name
**7** It has a sticking point
**8** Impress, and then some
**9** Tony winner between "A Chorus Line" and "Ain't Misbehavin'"
**10** Heat meas.
**11** Studio site
**12** Having a knack for
**13** Shadow
**14** Natural
**21** Tiny bit
**24** Not likely to be dissuaded from
**25** Microwave option
**27** Safin who won the 2005 Australian Open
**28** Word on a prescription label
**30** ___ Wheeler, 1964–70 chairman of the Joint Chiefs of Staff
**32** Whence the song "The Lady's Got Potential"
**34** He said "I am free of all prejudice. I hate everyone equally"
**36** "Mécanique Céleste" astronomer
**37** Barnes & Noble acquired it in 1987
**38** It might include a washboard
**39** Ring after exchanging rings?
**41** Extravagant romantic
**42** Bars
**43** Least copious
**46** Fritz the Cat's creator
**49** Singer profiled in "Sweet Dreams," 1985
**50** Come and go
**52** Great Trek figure
**53** Kind of leg
**55** Heat meas.
**57** When German pigs fly?

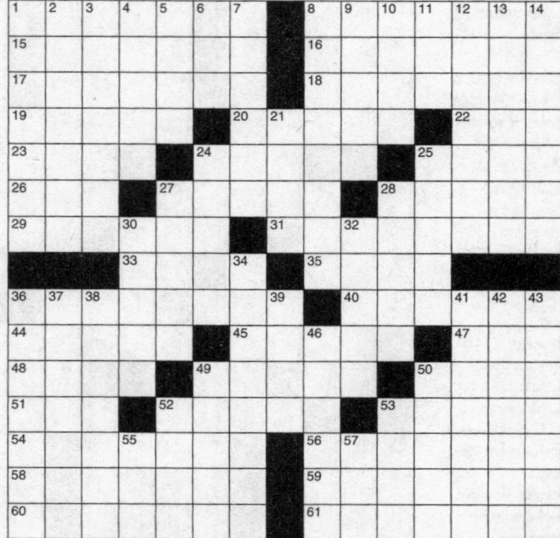

by Barry C. Silk

## ACROSS

**1** Music lovers flip for it
**8** Turndown?
**14** Way off
**16** Determined response
**17** It helps you sleep at night
**19** Tie up a line, perhaps
**20** 17-Across disrupter
**21** Unoccupied
**22** Rage inducers
**23** Antoinette after whom the Tony Awards are named
**25** String ___
**28** Goes after
**30** Avouch
**31** Some dolls can do it
**33** Private modes of transportation?
**35** Teased
**37** Enzyme's end
**38** Chorus "instrument" in Verdi's "Il Trovatore"
**39** "Pokémon" genre
**40** Hard to find, in old 13-Down
**42** Like some '39 New York World's Fair buildings
**43** How some roads ascend a mountain
**45** Presidential portrait site?
**47** T-bar or Z-bar
**48** Sister of Lazarus, in the Bible
**49** Mideast leaders
**51** Belief that all things are made of a single substance
**53** Redwood National Park sight
**56** "Unfortunately . . ."
**59** Some charity events
**60** Denied
**61** Unshaded
**62** Replies to irritably

## DOWN

**1** Pres. appointee
**2** Showy flower of the iris family
**3** Benedict of "The A-Team"
**4** "You get the idea": Abbr.
**5** Emperor before Hadrian
**6** Began energetically
**7** Passes over
**8** "Just a Closer Walk with Thee" and others
**9** Glaswegian "Gee!"
**10** Inclusive, as some resorts
**11** Like many low-paying jobs
**12** New York stadium name
**13** See 40-Across
**15** Familiar
**18** Onetime foe of the recording industry
**22** Person with a burning resentment?
**24** Indian chief
**25** Popular Mexican tourist destination
**26** "Molly ___ Can't Say That, Can She?" (1990s best seller)
**27** "Diner" co-star, 1982
**28** Evaluate
**29** Jazz (up)
**32** English jurisdiction
**34** Section of a hockey rink in front of the goal
**36** Prefix meaning "10": Var.
**41** Completely overrun by
**44** Closest to the center
**46** Force commanded by the Duke of Medina Sidonia
**48** Biotite and lepidolite
**49** Boosts, with "up"
**50** Whiz
**52** Grover Cleveland was once its gov.
**53** Offspring of Chaos, to Hesiod
**54** Rock guitarist Ford
**55** Speed unit
**57** "I didn't need to know that," informally
**58** Econ. class topic

*by Mike Nothnagel*

# 106

**ACROSS**

**1** Spell
**7** Crams
**15** Continue the journey
**16** In Dutch
**17** Least hospitable
**18** How some are offended
**19** Cobbler, at times
**20** Practice
**21** ___-majesté
**22** Turkey's dewlap
**23** Tribulations
**25** Baseball's Belinsky and Jackson
**26** Prickly area of a prickly pear
**27** Sue Grafton's "N"
**29** "Should ___ shouldn't . . ."
**30** Visitors
**35** Cousin of a woodcock
**38** Britton who wrote "The President's Daughter," 1927
**39** Fifth-century pope, the first to receive the title "the Great"
**40** Ones with read faces?
**43** Mac
**44** Got by
**45** Rebelled
**48** "Calvin and Hobbes" bully
**51** Part of the N.C.A.A.'s purview: Abbr.
**52** Look daggers
**53** Start of a "Name That Tune" bid
**55** Text te-hee
**56** "Your children are not your children" poet
**57** Bank of America Stadium team
**59** Attire
**60** Inclusive words, fittingly?
**61** They may be lined up at the bar
**62** Weed
**63** Herbs of the mint family

**DOWN**

**1** Goal of middle management?
**2** Quaker Oats product
**3** Acting
**4** Must
**5** TV announcer who played himself in "Bananas"
**6** Some specials
**7** Rolling Stones hit just before "Honky Tonk Women"
**8** Ill-fated NASA effort
**9** Jazz pianist/composer Williams
**10** Tax fig.
**11** Landlocked ___ Sea
**12** One with a high Q score
**13** Five-time Horse of the Year, 1960–64
**14** Celtic canines
**24** Former union members: Abbr.
**28** Apnea specialist, for short
**31** Some court contests
**32** Shortage in a rush-hour subway
**33** Not intended for just a single application: Var.
**34** Dry state
**36** Walker, quickly
**37** Grand
**41** Put on a pedestal
**42** Intimate
**46** Base of support
**47** Legendary MacGregor
**48** Child prodigy of "Heroes"
**49** Florida's ___ National Forest
**50** Lords of London
**54** Have a little something
**58** Invention that's not thought highly of

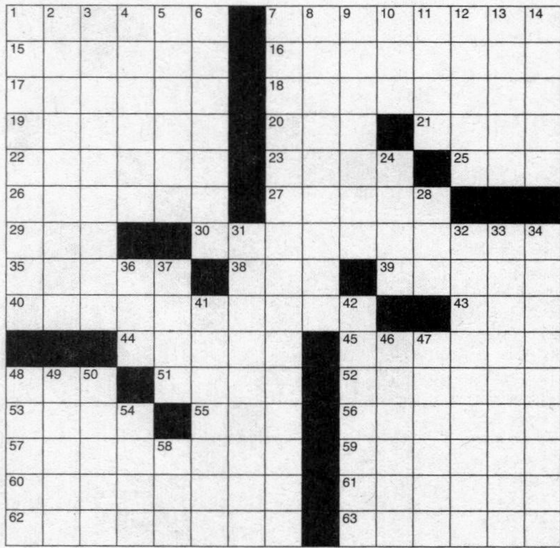

*by John Farmer*

## ACROSS

**1** Mover of merchandise
**9** Deadens
**14** Like singing in a shower
**16** Ship sinker
**17** Unwilling to get organized
**18** Divine
**19** Showing extreme embarrassment
**20** ___ War ("Charge of the Light Brigade" conflict)
**22** Fictional parrot type featured in Monty Python's "dead parrot sketch"
**24** 7 and 11
**26** Some swings in a ring
**27** Threw a tantrum
**28** Reach in total
**29** Inner ear?
**32** "Draft Dodger Rag" singer
**33** Athletic schedule list
**34** Ordering option
**35** Spaying customer?
**36** South-of-the-border homes
**37** Pack animal
**38** Pack animal?
**39** 1970s American Motors car
**40** They often make a splash
**44** Where to find free spirits
**45** While traveling
**48** Lieutenant of Capone
**49** Having trouble delivering the eulogy, say
**51** Labor activist Silkwood
**52** 1860 campaign nickname
**53** Catch
**54** Survivor of many battles

## DOWN

**1** "Born from jets" company
**2** It might make you red in the face
**3** Around the witching hour
**4** Archetypes
**5** Drove
**6** Extends, as a lease
**7** Choose not to say?
**8** Mideast grp.
**9** Tackled energetically
**10** W.W. II enders, for short
**11** Architect's starting point
**12** Micronesian nation that hosted the 10th season of "Survivor"
**13** "Diamonds Are a Girl's Best Friend" composer
**15** Plato and Aristotle, e.g.
**21** A lot
**23** Elmer's product
**24** Play thing
**25** Competition
**28** Bookwork, e.g.
**29** Dextrose
**30** Big brute
**31** Wellington, e.g.
**33** Tree-dwelling snake
**34** Enter, as a cross street
**36** The M-1, for one
**37** Impolite
**38** Snapper, of a sort
**39** Nose, slangily
**40** Eggheaded experts
**41** Dealing with honey makers
**42** Prefix with chloride
**43** Singer Lewis with the 2008 #1 hit "Bleeding Love"
**46** Slow-moving ships
**47** Sword: Fr.
**50** ___-to

*by Patrick Berry*

108

## ACROSS

**1** Many a stuntman's sequence
**6** TV series featuring a robotic dog named K-9
**15** Revived
**16** Something to chew on
**17** Completely lose it
**18** Waiting for the starting gun, say
**19** Gondolier, e.g.
**20** Very
**21** Seasonal sound
**22** Pump alternative
**24** Kitchen gizmo
**27** Termagant
**30** Sold all one's stock?
**33** Bouncing off the walls
**37** Title castle town of book and film
**38** Catching a few z's
**39** Jed's first chief of staff on "The West Wing"
**40** Soup pastas
**41** Jackknifed, e.g.
**42** Causes of some breakouts
**44** Cause of fatigue
**46** Not get involved
**47** Paving stones
**49** Out
**53 & 55** With 55-Across, campus hangout
**58** Surface
**59** 1985 Golden Globe–nominated role for Eddie Murphy
**62** Drop shots
**63** Without assistance in a fight
**64** Split up
**65** Not applied neatly
**66** One side in an informal game

## DOWN

**1** Proceeded with caution
**2** Alternatives to wraps
**3** Ticket category
**4** Hit 2004 Morgan Spurlock documentary
**5** It might turn a B into an A
**6** U.K. decorations
**7** 1998 biography subtitled "Living in the Shadows"
**8** Not tread lightly
**9** Conductor's bane
**10** Dedicated lines
**11** 1960s atty. gen.
**12** Got beaten by two people?
**13** Crop cropper
**14** The Szczecin Lagoon is an extension of its mouth
**23** Food often described using the number of fingers it takes to eat it
**25** Cutting-edge technology?
**26** Jolt, e.g.
**28** 1970 hit with the lyric "Girls will be boys and boys will be girls"
**29** Old-fashioned argument enders
**31** Soup pasta
**32** News source beginning in 1925
**33** Early pop?
**34** ___ chief (publ. honcho)
**35** Shoot with steam?
**36** Helpless performances?
**43** Historical war zone: Abbr.
**45** In
**48** Introductory course?
**50** "Thug" and "loot" derive from it
**51** Make an opening offer?
**52** Some cricket matches
**53** Ones going head to head?
**54** It might be required for entrance
**56** "You're not famous until my mother has heard of you" quipper
**57** Mary who founded Mount Holyoke College
**60** "Mahalo nui ___" ("Thank you very much," in Hilo)
**61** Considerably

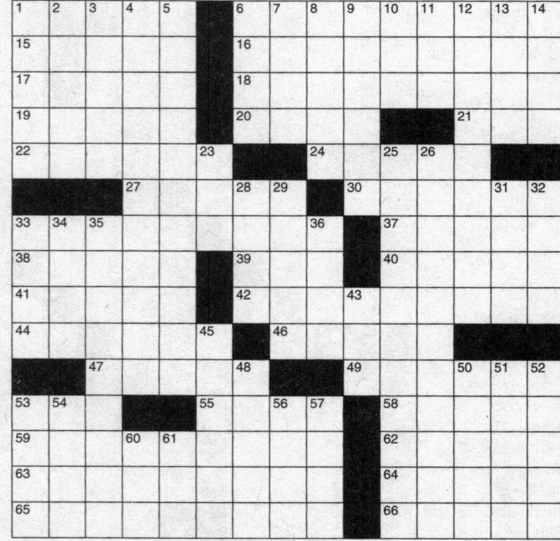

*by Mike Nothnagel*

## ACROSS

**1** Chutzpah
**6** Block boundaries: Abbr.
**9** Self-defense, e.g.
**13** Detector of some potentially dangerous waves
**17** Question of concern after someone has had a bad experience
**18** Mauna ___
**19** Row in a garden
**20** Corps groups
**21** "Children of Men" star Clive
**22** Bosox nickname
**23** Toyota sedan
**26** Words before an attempt
**31** Tide, at times
**32** Arizona's ___ Peak National Observatory
**33** Juvenile development
**34** Rapidly increasing pace
**37** Younger brother of George W. and Jeb
**38** Lids around lochs
**39** Alvin of the American Dance Theater
**40** Over
**42** Michael who played Cochise on TV
**43** Young or wee follower
**44** 1923 A.L. M.V.P.
**45** Japanese pilgrimage destination
**49** Put out
**50** Far Eastern affirmative
**53** Where moles might be found
**56** Creator of big suits?
**57** Have a little something
**58** A famous one begins "How sleep the brave . . ."
**59** Very dark

## DOWN

**1** Rail part
**2** Like a perfect game
**3** See 8-Down
**4** Big mess
**5** Like clichés
**6** Arab League member
**7** Town near the D. H. Lawrence Ranch
**8** With 3-Down, slopes
**9** Don't tread lightly
**10** It has a large bed
**11** "Sicut ___ in principio" (doxology phrase)
**12** Sondheim's "Multitudes of ___"
**14** Powerful piece
**15** Wikipedia alternative
**16** Like curious onlookers
**21** Enthusiastic cry of support
**22** Mysterious sightings
**23** "Thy servants ___ spies": Genesis 42:11
**24** Soap staple
**25** Food glaze
**26** You don't say it when you stand
**27** Loud
**28** City just NE of Citrus County
**29** Word said upon arrival
**30** Words said upon departure
**32** Lumber features
**35** Ian Fleming or James Bond
**36** Power outage backups
**41** Woman of La Mancha
**42** Distinctive qualities
**44** Compact material
**45** Big name in footwear
**46** He broke with Stalin in 1948
**47** Domino, e.g.
**48** "This doesn't look good"
**49** Wallpaper meas.
**50** Kind of garden
**51** Asia's ___ Sea
**52** Dot in a 10-Down
**54** "___ vindice" (Confederacy motto)
**55** Society affair

*by Barry C. Silk*

# 110

## ACROSS

**1** It has 33 letters
**16** All-Star Game, e.g.
**17** Optionally
**18** High seats
**19** "Lucia di Lammermoor" lord and namesakes
**20** Oscar nominee for "My Man Godfrey"
**21** Storms
**23** Field with bases
**24** Wandered from the direct course
**26** Actress Berger
**27** Skid's cause, maybe
**28** Protected by law
**29** Four-year sch. of higher learning in Providence
**32** Condomless vis-à-vis protected
**34** Tacoma-to-Walla Walla dir.
**35** Shows one's feelings
**37** Rio ___, multinational coal-mining giant
**39** ___ Verdes Estates, Calif.
**40** Chaotic place
**44** Classic 1974 role for Marty Feldman
**45** Middle: Prefix
**46** Inner opening?
**47** Gun, to Guillermo
**49** Ham, e.g.
**51** Pro at protection
**53** Health form field
**54** "An Inconvenient Truth" topic

## DOWN

**1** Neck ties?
**2** Open
**3** Burlesque-goer, typically
**4** Mantilla wearers
**5** Setting of the 2007 animated film "Persepolis"
**6** They might make you tear up
**7** Store figure
**8** New Guinea port
**9** "You're absolutely right"
**10** Ex-senator Sam of Georgia and others
**11** Duds
**12** When computers are working
**13** Spanish city and province on the Mediterranean
**14** Baroque dances
**15** Freebie on some airplane flights
**22** Lie in the sun
**25** Sticks
**26** Some Rockefeller Center murals
**28** Time-honored
**29** Plumber's job, maybe
**30** Idea person
**31** Ancient city to which Paul wrote an Epistle
**33** Angels are sometimes seen over them
**36** "Love is reciprocal ___": Marcel Proust
**38** At all
**40** Treating badly
**41** Japanese mushrooms
**42** Pack in a ship's hold
**43** Baseball's Joe and others
**45** Battle
**48** ___ Ishii, character in "Kill Bill"
**50** Men might dress in this
**52** High-quality vineyard

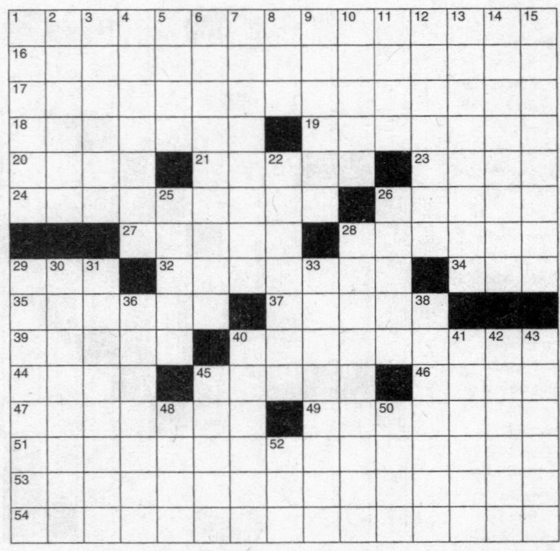

*by Kevin G. Der*

## ACROSS

1 Building blocks
5 Way around in comic books
14 Bandar ___ Begawan (capital of Brunei)
15 Succumbs to interrogation, perhaps
16 "Varsity Blues" actor Scott
17 Annual college event since 1935
18 Exceedingly rare infant
20 Gravitate
21 S. E. Hinton classic
24 Purely physical
25 Prefix with glottal
26 Wave function symbol
29 Light construction material
30 Third-degree, in math
32 Group from a very distant place
33 Like
34 Looking forward to being docked?
36 Nail holder
37 Breed
38 Words after an iffy statement
39 Rod
41 K'ung Fu-___ (Confucius)
42 Org. at the center of the 2007 memoir "At the Center of the Storm"
43 Like Ibsen, to his countrymen
44 Providers of many openings?
48 Director and star of the 1958 Best Foreign Language Film
50 One whose motto is "The only easy day was yesterday"
51 "No way, no how"
54 No gentle giant
55 Like some nonvoters
56 Ancient dweller in present-day Kurdistan
57 Sorry souls
58 "Step the meek fowls where ___ they ranged": Emerson

## DOWN

1 Component of morning dress
2 They're blown up and thrown up
3 Image on Oregon's state quarter
4 Making waves?
5 Shows
6 Treasured instrument
7 Real good-looker
8 Where the N.Y. Liberty play
9 Person who's talented but not versatile
10 Contents of some arms
11 "That's my cue!"
12 More than spicy
13 Many an ex-pat takes it
15 "Mulholland Falls" actor, 1996
19 "That's enough out of you!"
22 Payment option
23 It might have a lot of extras
26 Protest music pioneer
27 Where many heads are put together
28 Listener's acknowledgment
29 Provoke
30 See 35-Down
31 Tour grp.
35 With 30-Down, locale of lots of locks
40 Trying
43 Rice product
44 Brand with Ohranj and Razberi varieties, briefly
45 Pass
46 ___ Bulba (literary Cossack)
47 Driving hazard
48 Go for a few rounds?
49 Swarms
51 Go out for a bit?
52 Absorbed
53 Big blast

by Mike Nothnagel

112 

## ACROSS

**1** Lewis with 12 Emmys
**6** Medium size in a lingerie shop
**10** Ireland's Hill of ___
**14** Result of tribesmen putting their heads together?
**15** Unthinking state
**17** "Toodles!"
**18** Dewy-eyed
**19** "Nightswimming" band
**20** Those along the Ebro?
**22** Slightly amused reaction
**23** Adept at apery
**25** Peak on the eastern edge of Yosemite Natl. Park
**26** Quarter
**27** Parisian possessive
**29** 14th-century Russian ruler called "the Moneybag"
**30** Butterfly with black-and-white eyespots
**35** Go to work on
**37** OPEC member
**38** Get spooked, maybe
**40** Like lions and leopards
**41** One of seven in the film "Se7en"
**42** Light bites
**43** Ancient text
**47** Weak excuse for missing homework
**49** Biblical patriarch
**50** AOL alternative
**51** Supportive of
**53** Whiff
**55** Boot
**57** Hogwash
**58** Went after some shocking things?
**59** One may get kinky
**60** Beagle in the funnies
**61** Juice extractor

## DOWN

**1** Show signs of life
**2** One often seen at a family reunion
**3** Explosive time in history?
**4** Fairness determiner
**5** Phrase on a Google search button
**6** Things with sticking points
**7** Ingredient in a Long Island iced tea
**8** Relatives of the Shoshones
**9** Cacao plant feature
**10** Like some counters
**11** 17-Across, Polynesian-style
**12** Hundred Years' War siege site
**13** Not knowing what to do
**16** Boring the pants off
**21** Paris's ___-Chapelle church
**24** Obsession
**25** ___ operandi
**26** Seal creators, sometimes
**28** Wyo. neighbor
**30** Goes after, in a way
**31** You may get a rise out of it
**32** Noted shopper scolder
**33** Pitch sources
**34** Kansas' Fort ___ State University
**36** Sound after dropping off?
**39** Action preceders
**42** "___ insist!"
**43** Former CBS C.E.O.
**44** Introduction to biology?
**45** Singer Fabian and others
**46** Pale yellow
**48** Applesauce-topped treat
**50** Poke
**52** Super 88, of the 1950s and '60s
**54** W.W. II inits.
**56** "MTV generation" member

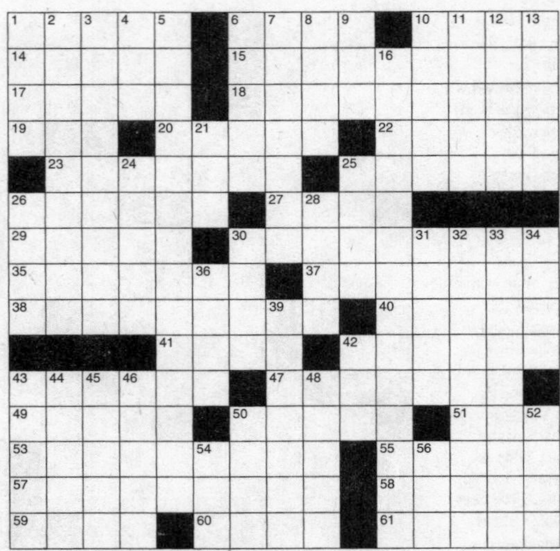

*by Kevin G. Der*

☆☆☆

## ACROSS

**1** Dance that simulates the drama of a bullfight
**10** Chuck wagon fare
**14** 1978 Bob Marley hit whose title words are sung four times before ". . . that I'm feelin' "
**16** Faux Japanese reply
**17** One needing kisses, say
**18** Jazz duo?
**19** Nooks for books, maybe
**20** Furry folivores
**22** It may be set with music
**24** Cudgel
**25** Believers' comments
**27** Escaped
**31** Sound at an auto race
**32** It holds the line
**33** Foot of the Appian Way?
**34** Trouble, in a way
**35** Locale of some mirrors
**36** Letter-shaped girder
**38** Lord John Boyd ___, winner of the 1949 Nobel Peace Prize
**39** Study, say
**41** Winston Churchill's Rufus, for one
**42** They know the drill
**44** Turned up
**45** Child's play, perhaps
**46** Snitch
**47** Company that makes Aunt Jemima syrup
**51** Area next to an ambulatory
**55** Letter-shaped fastener
**56** Daydreaming
**58** Days of old
**59** Worked the docks
**60** Waste of Congress?
**61** "You got it!"

## DOWN

**1** Early Inverness resident
**2** Cadaverous
**3** Ticklee's cry
**4** "You have got to be kidding!"
**5** The Divine, to da Vinci
**6** City at the mouth of the Fox River
**7** Shade of red
**8** "She was ___ in slacks" (part of an opening soliloquy by Humbert Humbert)
**9** Baddie
**10** Shady spot in a 52-Down
**11** Cousin of a cassowary
**12** ___ fee
**13** One with fire power?
**15** Trick-taking game
**21** March instrument?
**23** Out
**25** Au courant
**26** Keen
**27** Nutrition units
**28** Some essays
**29** "A Lonely Rage" autobiographer Bobby
**30** The farmer's wife in "Babe"
**31** Did a farrier's work
**35** Start to like
**37** Energetic 1960s dance with swiveling and shuffling
**40** God of life, death and fertility who underwent resurrection
**41** Pattern sometimes called "Persian pickles"
**43** "I'm very disappointed in you"
**46** Song verse
**47** Canal cleaner
**48** Menu option
**49** Teacher of Heifetz
**50** Fashion model Wek
**52** See 10-Down
**53** Ko-Ko's dagger in "The Mikado"
**54** Current happening?
**57** Kick in

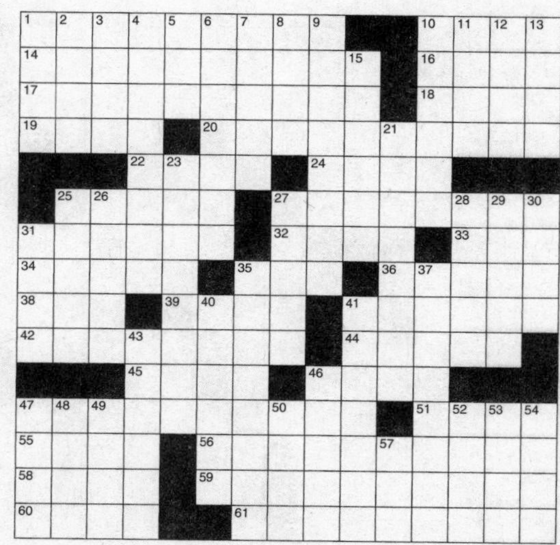

*by Natan Last*

# 114

## ACROSS

1 Source of troubles
12 ___ of God
15 "Later!"
16 What the 1939 50,000-word novel "Gadsby" completely lacks
17 Bank offerings
18 "Uh-huh"
19 Turns down
20 Spirit
21 ___ leaf
22 Irritation suffix
23 Irritated, after "in"
25 Like most music
26 Persian, e.g.
27 Not yet delivered, after "in"
28 W.W. II air ace who lent his name to an airport
29 Wee hour
30 Meyerbeer output
31 ___ Day (September 19)
35 How some dares are done
36 Outline
37 Bar tenders?: Abbr.
38 Places for dust to collect
39 Assn.
42 Apparently is
43 Insurance providers, for short
44 "Super Trouper" group, 1980
45 Kind of delay
46 Poke
47 Packers QB whose #15 jersey is retired
48 LAX datum
49 One end of the Welland Canal
52 Hi-___
53 At someone's mercy
54 Ones needing career counseling, maybe: Abbr.
55 Shell locations

## DOWN

1 Eat out?
2 Hindu drink of the gods
3 Play with the line "Hell is other people"
4 Guys
5 Revolutionary patriot James
6 Start to smell, maybe
7 Union inits. starting in 1886
8 "Well, I'll be!," as it might be said on September 19
9 ___ Santiago, 1987 N.L. Rookie of the Year
10 City near Provo
11 Scratches, with "out"
12 "Later!"
13 200 milligrams
14 Like soldiers known as Gurkhas
21 Stick
23 Wiped out, slangily
24 Top
25 What debaters debate
27 Hedge word
29 "That's fine"
30 Pendant adornments
31 Some diner equipment
32 It has a long tongue
33 Student excuser
34 Live folk album of 1968
38 D.T.'s
39 Italian restaurant chain
40 TV newswoman Soledad
41 Doorstep numbers?
44 ___ 2600 (hit product of the 1970s–'80s)
46 Joe
47 "This instant!"
49 Record
50 Bit of chicken feed
51 Org. with the annual Eddie Gottlieb Trophy

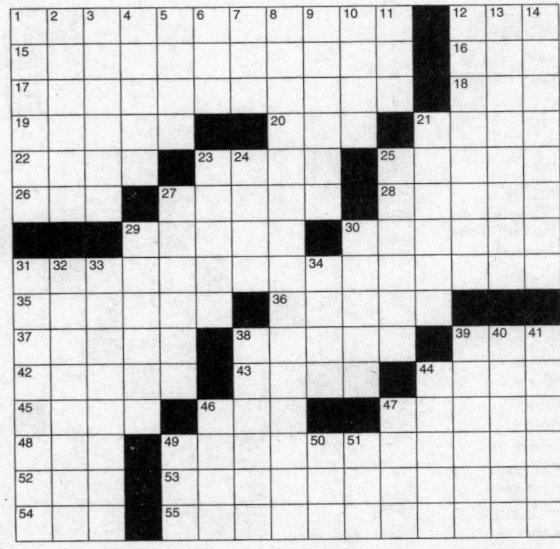

by Alex Boisvert

## ACROSS

**1** Reversion to an earlier type
**8** Shout after a knock
**15** King's honor
**17** Where moles may try to dig?
**18** Hamburger's course?
**19** Xbox 360 competitor
**20** Attempt to make out
**21** Actress Suvari
**23** Den ___, Nederland
**24** Ones at home on the range?
**27** Victory celebration, of sorts
**31** Integrated
**32** Muralist José María ___
**33** Understanding responses
**34** An artificial satellite may have one
**38** Before, briefly
**39** Modulate
**40** Yield
**41** "Friends" who aren't really being helpful
**44** Basis of some discrimination
**45** Exceptional
**46** Bits
**47** Stout
**50** Halo tarnisher?
**51** Follow
**55** Film about an aristocrat captured by the Sioux
**58** Dish named for the queen consort of Italy's Umberto I
**59** Ready for the bad news
**60** It's a square

## DOWN

**1** Clear conclusion?
**2** Sweat
**3** Like many of Shakespeare's rhymes
**4** Very strong
**5** Ithaque, e.g.
**6** Generates
**7** ___ circus
**8** People in this are watched closely: Abbr.
**9** Occasion to serve light refreshments
**10** Roll top?
**11** Katherine ___, 1983–89 Treasurer of the United States
**12** Place for loading and unloading
**13** Book concerned with the end of the Babylonian captivity
**14** Kite flying destination?
**16** Smog stat.
**22** "A special laurel ___ go": Whitman
**23** Plague
**24** Beat badly
**25** John of "Freaky Friday"
**26** Sluggish tree-dweller
**27** Models
**28** Passing remark
**29** Vichyssoise garnish
**30** Vegetable oil, e.g.
**32** Game stopper?
**35** Mastered
**36** Was shy
**37** Was shy
**42** Like the Colossus of Rhodes
**43** Flock-related
**44** Leader who said "There is no god higher than truth"
**46** Model who wrote "The Way to Natural Beauty"
**47** Occurrences
**48** Release
**49** Deconstruct?
**50** Shooting option, briefly
**52** War of 1812 siege site
**53** City SW of Padua
**54** One doing school work?
**56** Sprout
**57** Curse

*by Barry Silk*

# 116

## ACROSS

1 Unforgettable edible
16 Concern of a certain federal commissioner
17 Fission boat?
18 Capital on the Rimac River
19 Plays
20 1040 amt.
21 Nero's buyer
23 Vehicle for an annual round-the-world trip
26 Ingredient in plastics
27 Mention casually
30 Her theme song was a 1966 hit
31 Opium product
33 Pan
34 Clash sharply
37 Be in the red for black and tans?
39 Registration agcy.
40 His chariot was drawn by four fire-breathing horses
42 Neighbor of Sunnyside in New York
44 Indication that one is just teasing
45 Occurrence after the first and third quarters of the moon
46 Nirvana
50 Mad specialty
52 Take-out meal?
53 Large copier
54 Tropical fruit, in Toledo
57 See 58-Down
58 On account (of)
62 Not so much
63 They're usually even on one side

## DOWN

1 One entering a number
2 One day
3 Defeats decisively
4 Of blood
5 Good day?: Abbr.
6 Rack up
7 Old name in news
8 Drawing device
9 Regal symbols
10 Occurrence after retiring
11 Advantage
12 They cover the ears
13 You might exchange words with them
14 Order member
15 "I don't know" lead-in
22 ___ around (close to)
23 Shoot in the garden
24 Fat, to François
25 Many skit actors
27 Not very sharp
28 Western costume accessory
29 Leading
32 N.F.L. cornerback Starks
34 Head pieces
35 Unlikely number for a rock concert
36 National service
38 Actress Andersson of "Persona"
41 One stuck in the snow
43 19th-century literary family in Massachusetts
47 They're below some chests
48 2002 Al Pacino film
49 Trackers' aids
51 Longtime "Days of Our Lives" actress Jones
52 One stripping on a kitchen counter
54 City noted for its campanile
55 Fingered
56 Square
58 With 57-Across, welcome words when the check arrives
59 Kidder's word
60 Historic barrier breaker
61 Hacker's aid

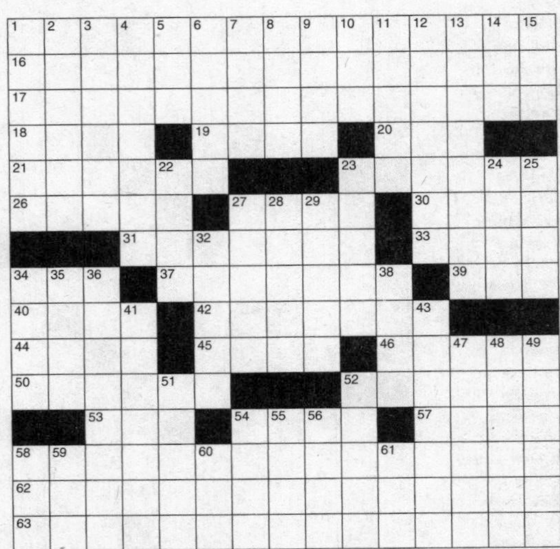

*by Harvey Estes*

★★★

## ACROSS

1 Beach nos.
5 Scorer of a record 158 goals
9 Certain dry cell, briefly
14 Bucket of bolts
15 Target of a 1989 E.P.A. investigation
16 Language related to Winnebago
17 Weapon for un soldat
18 Game in which players barely bet?
20 Makeshift
22 Drives in the country
23 Place
24 Yupik relative
26 Amateurs
28 Emphatic response during a drill
32 TV biz figure
33 Preceder of what should have been said
34 2008 French Open champion ___ Ivanovic
35 Horizon happening
37 Dealmaker's delight
39 Club ___
40 Rope fiber source
42 Beneficial thing to release
43 Gator rival
45 Having a headline?
46 Pulitzer-winning writer Sheehan and others
47 Came up with an invention
48 They don't take many tricks
50 Needs for 8-Downs
54 Much of high society
56 Knowledge of body?: Abbr.
57 Childish comeback
58 Many a team booster
59 Torch site
60 Up
61 Certified letters?
62 "Pardon the Interruption" airer

## DOWN

1 Three-time M.V.P. of the N.B.A. finals, familiarly
2 Indiana town where Cole Porter was born and buried
3 TV station?
4 Lab subject
5 Parties, say
6 Some singers
7 School concerned with classes?
8 Hand pic, perhaps
9 Macho credo
10 Knows the plans of
11 Stick together
12 Forever
13 Overseas article
19 Like apples and oranges
21 Monitors
25 Salome, to Herod Antipas
26 Spelunking aids
27 Dig deeply
29 Burial site for many French kings
30 It doesn't come out of the stomach
31 Spread unchecked
33 Above ___
36 Solipsistic sort
38 Fraternity activity
41 Pitchers, e.g.
44 Real
45 Kind of TV
48 Pop singer DeSario
49 Ways: Abbr.
51 "Rats!"
52 Way up
53 Gun of old
54 Funerary receptacle
55 ___ lepton

by Kyle Mahowald

# 118

**ACROSS**

**1** What boosters boost
**7** Coffin nail
**13** Oil-rich peninsula
**14** Ready to go, you might say
**15** Ancient Romans
**16** Sherlock Holmes story not by Conan Doyle, e.g.
**17** About whom Churchill purportedly said "A modest man who has much to be modest about"
**18** Took the offensive
**19** Of the north wind
**20** In the buff
**21** Curaçao flavoring
**22** Joust participants
**23** They offer rates for automobiles
**25** Things that talk in sch.?
**26** Isn't strict enough, say
**35** Bitingly sarcastic
**36** Splits with one's beloved
**38** Skin soother
**39** Attend to, as a loose shoe
**40** Veteran
**41** Plant family that includes the hibiscus
**42** Special announcer
**43** Not behind the defenders
**44** Topmost optic in a microscope
**45** Nickname for a cheater in the Oklahoma land rush of 1889
**46** Most valuable, possibly
**47** James in many westerns

**DOWN**

**1** Equatorial Guinea's capital
**2** Delivery professionals?
**3** It deserves to be condemned
**4** Town that Wild Bill Hickok was marshal of
**5** Pedigree
**6** Like paintings in progress
**7** Integration that exceeds the sum of its parts
**8** Semitic fertility goddess
**9** Price holder
**10** Winner over the Patriots in Super Bowl XXXI
**11** Organic compounds used as solvents
**12** Swamp flora
**14** Showing the most wear and tear
**16** People of much experience
**24** Candor
**26** Servant in a cause
**27** Meaningless talk
**28** Thinks the world of
**29** Closet hangings
**30** Los Angeles County's ___ Beach
**31** ___ of Aquitaine, Henry II's wife
**32** Passes, as time
**33** Milky and iridescent
**34** Uses a key, perhaps
**35** Singapore lies just off its tip
**37** Offbeat Parisian tourist sites
**38** Behave cravenly

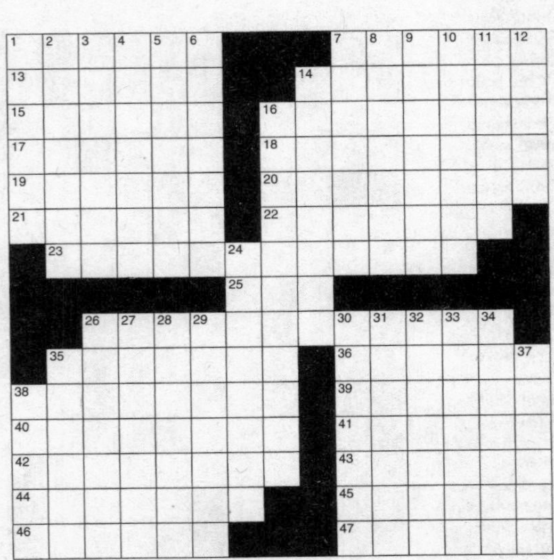

*by Patrick Berry*

★★★

## ACROSS

**1** Subject of the 1989 musical monologue "Bon Appétit!"
**11** Gimbel contemporary
**15** Old torturer
**16** Latin trio member
**17** Country whose capital is Palikir
**18** Union member of the future: Abbr.
**19** Start to court
**20** Company that developed NutraSweet
**22** Worker that never gets tired
**26** Jung's feminine side
**27** Big name in oil
**31** Postpones
**33** Spying aid
**34** Yellow primrose
**36** Oscar winner after "Rocky"
**38** Tops
**40** We
**41** Does some macramé work
**43** Guys who make people look good
**44** View from the Arlberg Pass
**45** Applied, as paint
**47** Bit of biblical graffiti
**48** Novelist Binchy
**50** "Married . . . With Children" actress Sagal
**52** Record listing
**54** Mass stack
**59** Genève and others
**60** It's easy to burn
**64** Target of un coup
**65** Twin
**66** Evening for Evangelo
**67** Thing to swing from

## DOWN

**1** Chichi-___ (largest of Japan's Bonin Islands)
**2** "O'Hara's Choice" novelist, 2003
**3** Sure winner
**4** Obi accessory
**5** Reason for a tryst
**6** One whose lead is followed in the service
**7** Rush
**8** Some bracelets
**9** Strand on an island?
**10** Strands of biology
**11** Bad lover?
**12** 1992 film directed by and starring Edward James Olmos
**13** Warden player in "Birdman of Alcatraz"
**14** Simplify
**21** Fall off
**23** Unconventional sort
**24** Every, in prescriptions
**25** One taking a first step
**27** Sexy numbers
**28** Send
**29** Berth place
**30** Young rivals, often
**32** Cancún kinsman
**35** Family of 18th- and 19th-century painters
**37** Vitiate
**39** Calypso relative
**42** Seraglio section
**46** Home of the University of Delaware
**49** Third-largest asteroid
**51** Supporter of the mascot Handsome Dan
**53** High-end shoe and handbag maker
**55** Sitcom guy with a frequently upturned thumb, with "the"
**56** Sum lead-in
**57** Zip around France?
**58** Sun-damaged
**61** It's attached to a hoop
**62** A hoop may be attached to it
**63** Century-beginning year

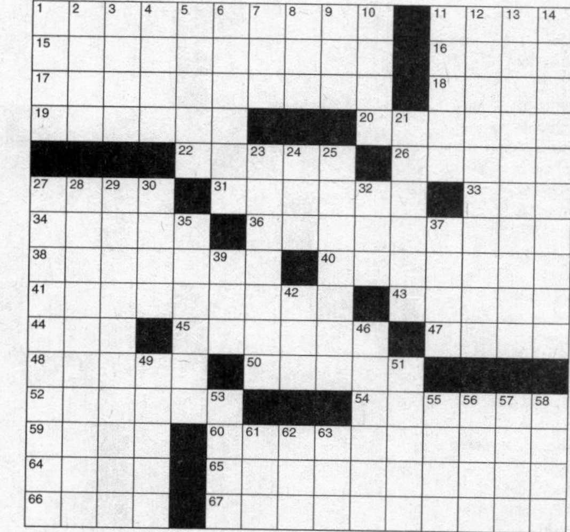

*by Frederick J. Healy*

120

## ACROSS

**1** Take in
**6** Unenthusiastic response
**14** Companion of Hearst at San Simeon castle
**16** Like friendship bracelets
**17** Dualistic deity
**18** Club restriction
**19** Ordinary human being
**21** Z preceder
**22** Signs of disuse
**23** Big exporter of diamonds: Abbr.
**24** Black Forest resort
**26** Maestro ___ de Waart
**27** "___ It Grand, Boys" (Irish standard)
**29** See 35-Down
**30** Hostess's ___ Balls
**31** Little something
**32** Equal
**33** "Easy does it!"
**39** Grp. for counselors
**40** Capital of the Apulia region
**41** Not much at all
**42** "Good Guys Wear Black" star, 1978
**45** Golfer Aoki
**46** Blood
**47** Not worth ___
**48** Private instructor: Abbr.
**49** Drink with a straw
**50** Box: Abbr.
**51** Strength of character
**54** Literally, "sheltered harbor"
**57** Mean
**58** Does some body work?
**59** Some porters
**60** Far from macho
**61** Cultural doings in Cádiz

## DOWN

**1** Actor voicing the mayor on "Family Guy"
**2** Aussie with purple hair and ornate glasses
**3** Be too reserved?
**4** Languishes
**5** Stretch in a seat
**6** "Easy does it!"
**7** Sammy nicknamed "The Red Rocker"
**8** 1977 memoir set at Harvard
**9** Year Marcian became emperor
**10** Bud abroad
**11** Open-sided porch
**12** Made a long story short?
**13** Sisters of Charity founder and family
**15** ___ Jorge (Azores island)
**20** ___ cycle
**24** Chicago's Little Village, e.g.
**25** Out of harm's way, in a way
**27** Presently
**28** Ballpark concessionaire's offerings
**29** Nazareth native, e.g.
**34** Win
**35** With 29-Across, picnic dishes
**36** Try to get dirt on, say
**37** Process of grooming and dressing oneself
**38** Artemis or Atalanta
**42** Some chips
**43** They have many suction cups
**44** Capital of the Brittany region
**48** Ones underfoot?
**49** Hardly worth mentioning
**51** Longtime La Scala music director
**52** Church with elders: Abbr.
**53** Topping on Mediterranean pizza
**55** Connecting words in logic
**56** Spend, with "out"

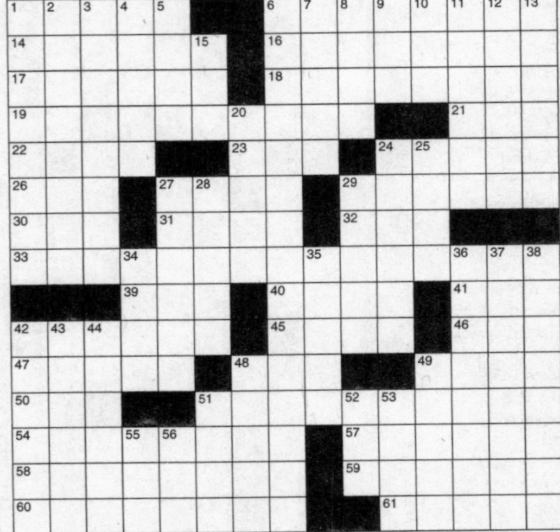

*by Jim Page*

★★★ 121

## ACROSS

**1** Big-time kudos
**9** Film about the Statue of Liberty?
**15** Exasperated cry
**16** Response to a good dig
**17** Hidden danger
**18** Preparatory stage
**19** Subject of the biography "King of the World"
**20** Bright spot in architecture?
**22** Saison de septembre, mostly
**23** Deal killers
**25** Sets right
**26** Honoree on the third Friday of Sept.
**27** Like many old series, now
**29** Grammy-winning Gnarls Barkley, e.g.
**30** Bats are smaller than normal in it
**32** Disco or swing follower
**34** Mascot that's a shell of a man?
**36** Slinky and stealthy
**40** What's-his-face
**41** Demi Moore was in it
**43** ___ factor
**44** Springtime arrival
**45** College football coach Miles
**47** Wiesbaden's state
**51** Application datum: Abbr.
**52** It's under the Host
**54** Torpedo
**55** Eponymous general
**56** Be cut down to size
**58** Mute neighbor, maybe: Abbr.
**59** Dot-com with an asterisk in its name
**61** Words at the outset
**63** Picture receiver
**64** Moved out?
**65** Official's helper
**66** Opening used before opening a door

## DOWN

**1** Lombardia's capital
**2** "Operation Bikini" co-star, 1963
**3** Robbed of
**4** Goal of some candidates
**5** Means of forced entry
**6** Bad blood
**7** Immobilized, in a way
**8** What sticks to your ribs?
**9** Tops of golf courses?
**10** Subtle warning sound
**11** It goes through lots of luggage: Abbr.
**12** Hot
**13** Captain Nemo's final resting place
**14** Beseech
**21** Things that disappear in the shower?
**24** Modelesque
**28** Namby-pambies
**30** Do school work
**31** One concerned with checks and balances
**33** Street name lead-in
**35** One side of Hawaii
**36** Common toy go-with
**37** One being printed at a station
**38** Customize for
**39** Kudos
**42** Dog's coat?
**46** Still
**48** Definitely gonna
**49** Film critic Joel
**50** Protect, in a way
**52** Triumphant song
**53** Like some mythology
**56** "Laverne & Shirley" landlady
**57** Emulate Niobe
**60** "Ready" follower
**62** Crib note?

*by Patrick John Duggan*

# 122

**ACROSS**

**1** They're highly reflective
**8** Misses
**15** Ned Buntline dime novel subject
**17** Signs of unavailability
**18** The Iron Horse
**19** Composer Janácek
**20** It. was part of it
**21** San Francisco street or theater
**23** Skeleton part, in Padua
**24** Defensive end Antwan
**28** Ski resort forecast
**30** Crude, slangily
**32** Paternal relative
**36** Beckerman who wrote "Love, Loss and What I Wore"
**37** Poe title character
**39** "The Hoosier Folk-Child" poet
**40** Screen setting
**42** "Easy now . . ."
**44** Farmwork
**46** #1 honor
**47** Where lederhosen are worn
**50** Woolly
**52** Many a Playbill paragraph
**53** Not baring one's sole?
**54** Least sound
**59** Costs of admissions?
**62** Alaska area almost half the size of Rhode Island
**63** License
**64** Sequoias, e.g.

**DOWN**

**1** "___ of you . . ."
**2** Sight near a lagoon
**3** What I will follow
**4** One way to travel
**5** Tricks
**6** Opposite of coarse
**7** What a person goes by in Paris
**8** Relatives of flies
**9** City near Horseshoe Curve
**10** Shooters for pros
**11** High school dept.
**12** Actress Skye and others
**13** Nips
**14** Food service Fortune 500 company
**16** Private consultant to the federal government, in slang
**22** Go out very slowly
**23** Totally dominating
**24** ___ suspension (ear medication)
**25** Supermarket work station
**26** Some team members
**27** Certain portraits of Zola, Chabrier and Mallarmé
**29** One may put a damsel in distress
**31** Formal introduction?
**33** It's high in the Sierras
**34** Sing
**35** Took in
**38** Bit or hit lead-in
**41** Cry of respect
**43** Don
**45** Ancient philosopher whose name means "old master"
**47** Brook
**48** Like some shirts
**49** "What's your ___?"
**51** "Viva ___!"
**53** What may accumulate in the mouth
**55** Slimming option, briefly
**56** One of 31 in Mexique
**57** Some medicines
**58** Shows disapproval
**60** Red sushi fish
**61** Stable particle

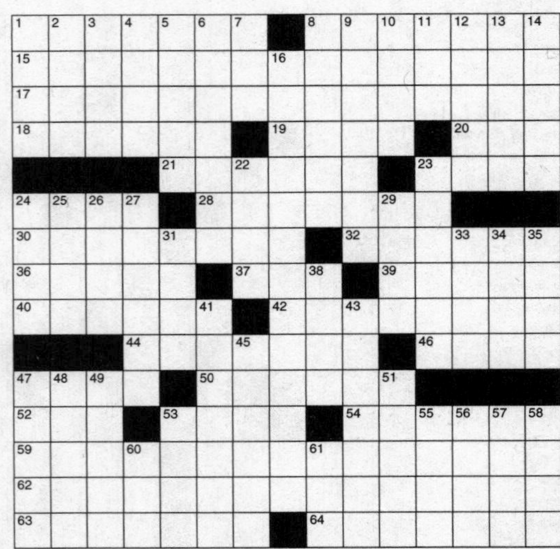

*by Barry Silk*

## ACROSS

**1** Debut Olympian of 2008
**6** Dish served with Roquefort cheese
**15** Tropical vine
**16** Treasure State's motto, aptly
**17** Andy Warhol subject
**18** Easily past
**19** Had trouble with, as icy roads
**21** What wavy lines often represent
**22** "Let's ___"
**23** Film director Anderson
**25** Fell hard, with "it"
**26** It might be physical: Abbr.
**29** Shaker's cry
**31** They're often seen on scoreboards, for short
**33** "The Sirens of ___," Kurt Vonnegut novel
**35** Alcohol, it's said
**38** Hepburn and Tracy shared one
**39** Aromatic plant native to the Pyrenees
**40** Kind of pudding
**41** Ab ___ (absent: Lat.)
**42** "___ There Was You" (1997 film)
**43** Flier with delta wings
**44** Arm supporters, for short
**46** They often get rings: Abbr.
**48** Brand follower?
**50** Refrain from singing when you're happy?
**52** Tea originally wrapped in foil
**54** Plato and others
**58** Ulexite is rich in it
**59** Pope when the Visigoths seized Rome
**60** Poker player's declaration
**61** Title IX concern
**62** Ones with bewitching eyes?

## DOWN

**1** Smile on
**2** Game with hazards, safeties and remedies
**3** Entertainer who was the first man to be married at Caesars Palace
**4** Personification of purity, in literature
**5** Make seedier?
**6** Make chicken
**7** It has 12 flowers on each side
**8** Overly confident
**9** One way to break ties
**10** Result of a break
**11** Garments covered by amices
**12** Language written with no spaces between words
**13** Mud bogger's purchase, briefly
**14** "Lost" actor Daniel ___ Kim
**20** Air Force base near Las Vegas
**24** Holistic medicine topic
**26** Line up
**27** Simplified, in a way
**28** Start to change?
**30** Cambodian cash
**32** They often have seconds
**34** Turndown from the overcommitted
**35** Salsa ingredients?
**36** Vulcans, e.g.
**37** NASA's Spirit and Opportunity
**45** Michelin, for one
**47** Albert with a National Medal of Science
**49** List in a wish list
**50** Put shoes on?
**51** They're found within minutes
**53** Capital on the Gulf of Guinea
**54** Foreign Mr.
**55** The same partner?
**56** "American Morning" home
**57** Spoonful, maybe

*by Tyler Hinman and Byron Walden*

# 124

**ACROSS**

**1** To boot
**7** Big impression
**13** Worked up
**15** Photons, e.g.
**16** Made unbearable?
**18** Writing style of old Latin manuscripts
**19** Like 1-Down
**20** Rare battery varieties
**21** Options for thinning
**22** Harsh-sounding bird that immobilizes its prey by impalement
**23** Like part of a foot
**24** 1995 Literature Nobelist
**25** Lonely
**27** Limerick neighbor
**31** Jerks
**32** Had a prior link with
**34** Some imposing museum displays, briefly
**35** Place for many a shot
**42** Outfit for a new voyage, say
**43** Ogled
**44** Explosive stuff
**45** "Sure thing!"
**46** Cathedral candle
**47** Events with marching bands?
**48** People taking les examens
**49** Heroin and the like
**50** Ties don't have them
**51** Eye muscles attach to it

**DOWN**

**1** Stealthy fighters
**2** Like Edward Albee's first five plays
**3** 1984 Best New Artist Grammy winner
**4** One taken care of by a caretaker
**5** Attendees at some biz meetings
**6** Speeders' dreads
**7** Ends abruptly
**8** Pugilists . . . or stationery store items
**9** Tear
**10** Compounds that smell of rotting fish
**11** Didn't just follow around
**12** Vice admiral on the U.S.S. Enterprise
**14** Fixed some greens
**17** Since: Sp.
**26** Glorified gatekeeper, in Goiás
**27** Burns up
**28** Feen-a-mint was one
**29** Certain full house, in poker lingo
**30** Always moving
**32** Mandolin effect
**33** White item in a 1944 Matisse painting
**34** Job requirement, often
**36** He was served to the Olympians as food
**37** More than suggestive
**38** Leak
**39** Noel opener
**40** Certain cat or dog
**41** It's S. of the Vale of Tempe

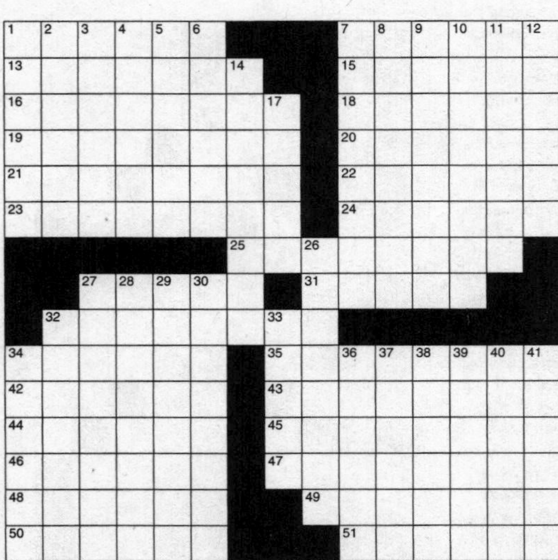

*by Joe Krozel*

**ACROSS**

**1** Massive
**10** "Hairspray" mom and others
**15** Versatile
**16** One to hang with
**17** Faded
**18** Blackmore heroine
**19** Cry after failing
**20** Ezio Pinza's "Mr. Imperium" co-star
**22** Medical research org.
**23** Easy tots to baby-sit
**24** Perfect
**28** Donatello sculpture subject
**29** Outcast
**30** Integrated with
**33** More of the same, in research papers
**34** Capital on the Buriganga River, old-style
**35** Avant-garde saxophonist John
**36** Tiny irritations
**38** The Pink Panther, e.g.
**39** Old means of public humiliation
**40** Subject of the 1997 biography "Woman in the Mists"
**41** They're made by origami artists
**43** Temporary downturn
**44** Be the charming type?
**46** Chicken
**50** "Pinky" Best Actress nominee Jeanne
**51** Italy, once
**53** With 31-Down, its products are often squeezed
**54** Hitchcock trademark
**55** "The Faerie Queene" character
**56** Occasion to break glass?

**DOWN**

**1** Kind of ball
**2** Massive star
**3** Launcher launched in 1958
**4** Takes, with "for"
**5** They're listed in a bill: Abbr.
**6** Youngest Best Actress Oscar winner, 1986
**7** Magic practiced by native Guianans
**8** ___ Hot (city in Inner Mongolia)
**9** Linguist's concern
**10** Reach
**11** Attendance incentives
**12** "It's anybody's guess"
**13** Actor who won comedy and drama Emmys for the same role
**14** Some card readers
**21** Motown's original name
**22** "___ the soles of her shoe?": Hamlet
**24** Fall preceder
**25** Foot part?
**26** Getting in line?
**27** "I can resist everything except ___": Oscar Wilde
**28** Leeches
**30** Move to your previous place
**31** See 53-Across
**32** Exclusive
**34** Shoots craps, e.g.
**37** 1982 Grammy-winning song by Toto
**38** Nudge
**40** Less natural
**41** Last full year of St. Julius I's papacy
**42** Not so easy to get one's hands on
**43** Odious type
**45** Hospital administration?
**46** Eroded
**47** Gloating cry
**48** Sporty Spice of the Spice Girls
**49** Part of a food chain
**52** Faddish disk of the 1990s

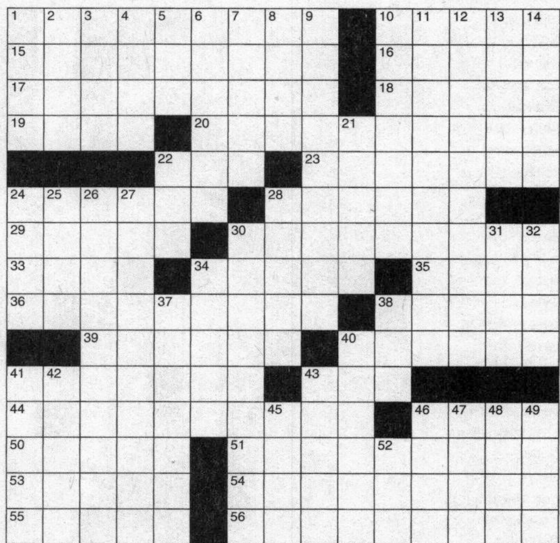

*by Samuel A. Donaldson*

126 

## ACROSS

1 Apparently floored
11 Like some fraternities nowadays
15 Baby's mind, e.g.
16 It spins its wheels
17 When "you're gonna want me for your girl," in a 1963 hit
18 Longtime "The Price Is Right" model Parkinson
19 Chief Powhatan's son-in-law
20 Like some Ger. nouns
21 Clean rags?
22 Much like
23 Pleased
25 Ziti alternative
27 Bat mitzvah, e.g.
29 Nut's offspring
31 Kind of state in the East
32 Transfuses
34 Neighbors of Indians
36 "Mr. Hulot's Holiday" Oscar nominee
38 Plaza-to-plaza stretch: Abbr.
39 Putting to rest
43 Response to "Are you awake?"
47 Freud's "Totem ___ Tabu"
48 Attempt to bypass opposition
50 Sun-baked
51 Many 31-Across practitioners
53 Bit of rootless flora
55 Org. in which people get belted
56 Any member of the Safavid dynasty
57 Shut up
59 Christian apologist who wrote "The Four Loves"
61 Last name of twin gymnasts in the 2004 Olympics
62 Crush
64 1957 Tony winner Adams
65 It might have red herrings
66 What's often pounded out
67 Pieces of surprising news

## DOWN

1 An unused item may be placed in it
2 Ointment base
3 "Sic et Non" theologian
4 Copper bracelet?
5 Star light?
6 Half of a popular 1960s singing duo
7 Places where stands have been made
8 Attacked energetically
9 The Bible's "cunning hunter"
10 Vacationing very briefly
11 General starting point?
12 Go from aluminum to alumina, say
13 Bistro seen in "Manhattan"
14 It's under a canine's coat
24 Show featuring the scheming Dr. Zachary Smith
26 Japanese for "large hill"
28 One with a long neck and a rounded body
30 Out of practice?: Abbr.
33 Like items that have been put away
35 NASA's Falcon and Intrepid
37 Poll abbr.
39 Put to rest
40 Expose to light
41 "Raid on Entebbe" role
42 Family member
44 Avant-garde
45 NASA vehicle
46 Sly sorts
49 Last, to Luigi
52 Record producer Ertegun in the Rock and Roll Hall of Fame
54 Coat cut
58 Eliza's mentor, to Eliza
60 Piedmont university
63 Tuned in

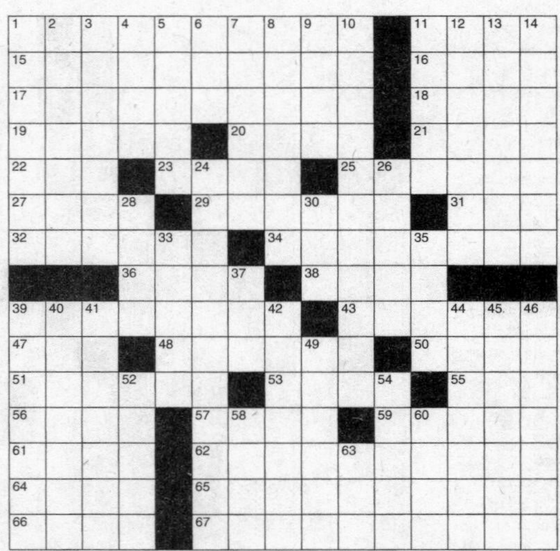

*by Peter A. Collins and Joe Krozel*

## ACROSS

**1** Big wheel's overseer
**9** Driving dances
**15** Pool exhibition
**16** Homes on the range?
**17** Hieronymus Bosch, for one
**18** Harsh critic
**19** One landing with a turned-up face
**20** Dark force
**21** San Diego County beach town
**22** Chemical endings
**24** Suitor's surprise
**26** Activity book staples
**28** Dance move
**30** Dance move
**32** Bridge builder's grp.
**33** Closing statement?
**35** Inside protector
**36** "That's more like it!"
**40** Zero, e.g.
**41** Big name in auto parts
**42** Reptilian toy in "Toy Story"
**43** Brand discontinued by Keebler
**44** Some taters
**48** Show featuring an alien from the planet Gallifrey
**50** Prince in Baum's "Rinkitink in Oz"
**52** Palooka
**53** Without exception
**55** Lee of Hollywood
**57** Domain of the Normandy campaign: Abbr.
**58** Large numbers
**59** Giant in photography
**61** Kind of cartridge
**62** What prolonged crowing may indicate
**63** 1957 Oscar nominee for "A Farewell to Arms"
**64** Safari sights

## DOWN

**1** Like some résumés
**2** Time's 1986 Woman of the Year
**3** They're not taught together
**4** Fox's relative
**5** Hurting
**6** Acid jazz band with the 1996 hit "Virtual Insanity"
**7** Major Joppolo's town
**8** Boy toy surnamed Carson
**9** Jewelry box?
**10** "Spill it!"
**11** Slangy event suffix
**12** Japanese tourist city on Kyushu
**13** 25-Down someone, say
**14** Bygone union member: Abbr.
**21** Cut
**23** Delphic figure
**25** Surveilled
**27** Emulated a rat
**29** "___ Juvante" (Monaco's motto)
**31** Classic caper film, with "The"
**34** Guttersnipe
**35** "Prosit!" relative
**36** Toward l'Arctique
**37** Nuance
**38** Those prone to meltdowns?
**39** Screen abbr.
**43** High-school class, informally
**45** Turning up on the farm?
**46** Extend
**47** Plant pores
**49** Certain pilgrim
**51** Get a sense for
**54** Skippy's most famous role
**56** Hitch
**58** Wasn't a seeker?
**59** Sprinkling
**60** Org. concerned with touchdowns

by Kevin G. Der

# 128

**ACROSS**

**1** Industrial time units
**10** House manager
**15** Really bugged
**16** Slide presentation?
**17** Breaks from the pack, say
**19** "Snow Falling on Cedars" star, 1999
**20** Straight
**21** Withdrawal fig.
**22** Shooter who co-created the zone system
**26** Not under
**28** Bolt
**29** Art of manipulation?
**32** Candy man
**34** Like some arms and legs
**35** Some neckwear
**37** They have large basins
**38** Rave review
**39** Game show purchase
**40** Isn't blocked, as a signal
**42** 1970 Tony winner for Best Play
**45** P.R. is found in it
**48** More susceptible to burning
**49** "Meet John Doe" director, 1941
**51** Bit of parental diversion
**55** Calling
**56** Strip in a bar
**57** They're entered legally
**58** Many bloggers

**DOWN**

**1** "Three Sisters" sister
**2** First string
**3** Packers' stat.
**4** It may be right in front of your eyes
**5** Shakespearean lament
**6** Indian restaurant serving
**7** Mast-to-tackle rope on a ship
**8** Is part of the decision-making process
**9** Ostentatious accessories
**10** Fall cuisine?
**11** Hyped up
**12** Coming right up
**13** First string?
**14** ___ Axton, co-composer of "Heartbreak Hotel"
**18** Flag
**22** Old Hamburger?
**23** One who might celebrate Pi Day
**24** El ___ (Peruvian volcano)
**25** Biblical spot?
**26** Place for some relics
**27** Jamie Lee Curtis's "Freaky Friday" role
**29** Where many students click
**30** Heavens: Prefix
**31** You'll get nothing out of a good one
**32** First name in raga performance
**33** Tie up
**35** Fatally poisoned royal, for short
**36** Looking up
**38** Stains
**40** Raleigh suburb
**41** Reinforced ring support?
**43** Mitchell of "Step by Step"
**44** Little ___ (big toy company)
**45** Orchard pest
**46** It flows through Gainsborough
**47** Pads
**49** Rabbit fur
**50** Longfellow's bell town
**51** It has a domestic counterpart: Abbr.
**52** Joint application
**53** Suite composition: Abbr.
**54** Bygone bird

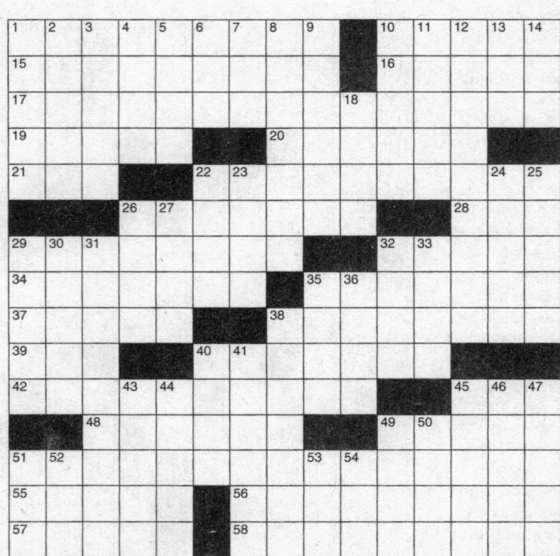

*by Tim Croce*

## ACROSS

**1** "Alas"
**10** Is successfully interrogated
**15** Summer salon service, for some
**16** One of Ariel's sisters in "The Little Mermaid"
**17** Directly
**18** Swindle
**19** Title role in a 1983 black-and-white film
**20** Keenly observant
**22** Annex: Abbr.
**23** "___ End" (1971 Barbra Streisand hit)
**25** Org. with the motto "Start With Trust"
**26** Lugs
**28** Biblical preceder of 27-Down
**29** One with an ear and a small mouth
**32** What an idea comes to
**33** Broadway's "Never ___ Dance"
**34** Makeup lessons?
**36** Wet bottoms
**38** Quietly tells a tale
**39** Misery
**40** One with delta wings, briefly
**41** Wing: Prefix
**42** Not mixing well
**45** Well-said
**46** Decides one will
**47** Author Robert ___ Butler
**51** Target of some leg-pulling
**53** In ___ diagnosis
**54** U.S.-born Japanese educated in Japan
**55** Violent outburst
**58** Brilliant effect
**59** At a loss
**60** Thinks
**61** Saves

## DOWN

**1** One of the Pine Islands
**2** Like some harrows
**3** Viking poet
**4** Rifle range activity
**5** Make out, to Harry Potter
**6** Exclamation at a lineup
**7** Something to gaze in
**8** Virility
**9** Not lost
**10** In poor shape
**11** Hydrocortisone additive
**12** Person prone to proneness?
**13** Ups and downs of exercise?
**14** Remove graffiti from, in a way
**21** Wide receiver Welker
**23** Fat, as a chance
**24** What "1776" got in 1969
**27** Biblical follower of 28-Across
**28** Something to land
**29** Very full
**30** Sales statistic
**31** Play furniture?
**33** Festive
**35** Thrice, to a pharmacist
**36** Friends, e.g.
**37** Chacon of the 1962 Mets
**39** Inimical
**42** Mad about, with "over"
**43** Gets help for
**44** Means of quick wealth
**46** Passes by
**48** Leader who died 27 days after his election
**49** Was faulty?
**50** ___ guerre
**52** Appear elated
**53** Black Knights' home: Abbr.
**56** Progress preventer
**57** Rescue inits.

by Thomas Heilman

130

## ACROSS

**1** Good-for-nothing
**10** Transmission repair chain
**15** Light seeker's question
**16** Eponym of an annual award for best left-handed pitcher
**17** Word
**18** Ancient neighbor of Lydia
**19** Legis. period
**20** Like many Miami Beach buildings
**21** Vice president Barkley
**22** Populist power couple of the 1940s–'50s
**24** Ornamental pond fish
**25** It may be radioactive
**29** Piece of cake
**31** Airport alternative to JFK or LGA
**32** Code broken by Joe Valachi
**34** Picasso's "private muse"
**36** Some Musée d'Orsay hangings
**38** Adversary of Rocky
**39** Mufflers and such
**41** Wimbledon's borough
**42** Pou ___ (vantage point)
**43** He said "Most editors are failed writers—but so are most writers"
**45** Fix, as some bald spots
**46** Stick with it
**48** Smart
**50** Alternative
**52** Beggar in Sir Walter Scott's "The Antiquary"
**53** K.P. unit
**57** Cologne is found on it
**58** It can't travel in a vacuum
**60** Great, to Gaius
**61** Gets some words in edgewise?
**62** Antiknock fluid
**63** What many text messages are full of

## DOWN

**1** They often take a beating
**2** Sourpuss's look
**3** Grps. concerned with class struggle?
**4** Hold hands?
**5** Sumac with a wide range
**6** Earl ___, 1930 Triple Crown-winning jockey
**7** Spits out
**8** Opposite of torrid
**9** Its news network won a 2008 Peabody Award
**10** Polo setting
**11** Olympic speed skater Ohno
**12** Unmacho features
**13** Cleveland Indians mascot
**14** Picking up the dry cleaning, e.g.
**22** Diminutive
**23** Bolt
**25** Response of approval
**26** Response of approval
**27** It doesn't include the lower classes
**28** Go at a clip
**30** Bite site
**33** Botanical casings
**35** One that may 28-Down
**37** Attacks pettily
**40** "Clever!"
**44** Like Brahma, Vishnu and Shiva
**47** "South Park" parka wearer
**49** Dovetail, e.g.
**51** Not fantastic
**53** Quid pro quo
**54** It may have a bald spot
**55** Ciliary body locale
**56** Word after foreign or city
**59** Lush development?

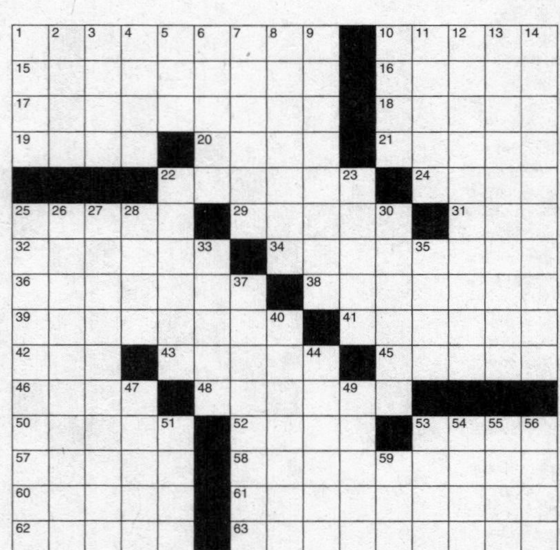

*by Paula Gamache*

**ACROSS**

**1** Where some diggers dig
**8** Chuck Yeager, e.g., in brief
**15** Kreplach cousin
**16** Purina partner replaced by Nestlé
**17** Before
**18** Home of the Great Geysir
**19** Toadlike
**20** See 5-Down
**22** "Socrate" composer
**23** Self-titled platinum album of 1988
**24** Red flannel hash ingredients
**26** Isinglass
**27** Dir. from Asheville to Winston-Salem
**28** Like Miró's "The Tilled Field"
**30** Blemish
**31** Counter measures?
**34** Make a silk purse out of a sow's ear, e.g.?
**35** They keep airliners aloft
**41** "So is that ___?"
**42** Adds to the staff
**43** Sleeping aid
**44** ___ tide
**46** Like some punches
**47** Elvis Presley's "___ Liked the Roses"
**48** Takes several courses
**50** Words from M.L.K. Jr.
**51** "I've ___!"
**52** Crime scene clue
**54** "In my mind . . ."
**56** Common blog link
**57** Unable to get much worse
**58** Lays away for good
**59** Supply

**DOWN**

**1** Night ___
**2** Maui locale that was once the capital of the kingdom of Hawaii
**3** Fended off
**4** Roadster that debuted in 1989
**5** With 20-Across, natural energy source
**6** Grp. with the 1977 album "Out of the Blue"
**7** What food courts aim to satisfy
**8** Books and such
**9** Fem. force
**10** France's ___ d'Hyères
**11** "The straight path"
**12** Together
**13** Like a volcano
**14** Charms
**21** One industry above the rest?
**24** Fuel derivable from biomass
**25** Tipped one's hat to
**28** Lethal compound
**29** Neighbors of Belarusians
**32** "___ better be good!"
**33** Notch, e.g.
**35** Produce batik
**36** Driving club
**37** Give for a while
**38** Colts' former home
**39** Token
**40** Like Buckingham Palace
**45** Rumbly tummy soother
**47** Dame of whodunits
**49** Trenchtown, for one
**51** Wilhelm of Cooperstown
**53** "Chicago" lyricist
**55** Org. in "The Sting"

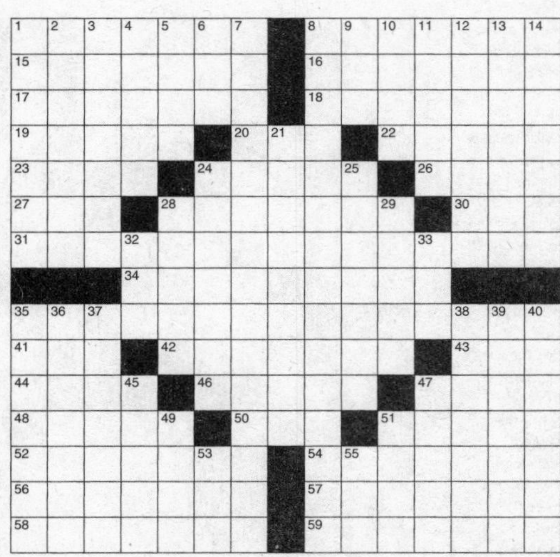

*by Mark Diehl*

# 132

**ACROSS**

**1** Mimeographs, e.g.
**12** Breathless wonder
**15** Paperless reading materials
**16** Dentiform : tooth :: pisiform : ___
**17** 1970s woe
**18** Resident ignored by census takers
**19** Alliterative pro team name
**21** Shake, say
**22** Actress Balsam who was once married to George Clooney
**23** Western wear
**27** "___ vile" (epithet for Falstaff)
**28** Van Gogh's "Portrait of ___ Tanguy"
**29** Nielsen count
**31** Inserts, often
**32** Like arugula's flavor
**33** "You ___!"
**36** Possible causes of sleep apnea
**37** Runner's place
**38** Makes excessively large
**41** Song involving an 8-Down, in part
**43** Stock-buying venue
**44** Place for pick-ups
**45** Writer who doesn't need an agent
**52** Receiver of contributions, for short
**53** "You needn't worry about that"
**54** Party staple
**55** Had people over
**56** Ascertain
**57** Ingredients in everything bagels

**DOWN**

**1** "After whom ___ thou pursue?": 1 Samuel
**2** Green
**3** Snack brand
**4** Low-grade coal
**5** Concludes
**6** Locations for Pluto, sometimes
**7** Part of a famous conjugation
**8** Something plucked in 41-Across
**9** Slobbery cartoon character
**10** Fray
**11** Clean
**12** Scandalize
**13** Twerp
**14** Gradually destroys
**20** Clippers' skippers, e.g.
**23** Mineral ___
**24** Raw foodists don't need them
**25** Edges
**26** Alternative to grayscale
**27** It's left in a book
**30** Fit
**32** Results of road fatigue
**33** Item in Commissioner Gordon's office
**34** Favored
**35** Simple top
**36** Dash part
**37** Epithet for the mouse in "To a Mouse"
**38** Do lines?
**39** Jo's suitor in "Little Women"
**40** Available as evidence, maybe
**42** Quarterback nicknamed the Golden Arm
**46** ___ Fonck, top Allied fighter ace of W.W. I
**47** Consoles, in a way
**48** Optic layer
**49** Earthen embankment
**50** Cigarette label word
**51** "Chariots of Fire" beat it for Best Picture

*by Trip Payne & Patrick Berry*

## ACROSS

**1** Spanish 101 conjugation part
**6** Further
**10** Staunch
**14** Greek port
**15** Opal alternative
**17** Lemony Snicket's count and one of Snoopy's brothers
**18** Supposed tools of the devil
**19** Serbian provincial capital on the Danube
**21** Supermarket suppliers
**22** Pulitzer-winning critic Richard
**23** Dawdling
**24** 1999 comedy featuring aliens called Thermians
**27** "Glengarry Glen Ross" Tony winner Schreiber
**28** Zimbalist's violin teacher
**29** One of the Obama girls
**34** Pope during the reign of Charlemagne
**36** Stole
**38** Clipper trio
**39** Hua succeeded him
**41** "Morning Dance" band Spyro ___
**42** Duo first seen in "Puss Gets the Boot," 1940
**45** Portable power tool
**49** Much-repeated part of binary code
**50** Father figures?
**51** Earlike organ
**54** Morning cry
**56** Puffy hat wearer
**57** Less than upstanding
**58** A stroke might indicate it
**59** "Right"
**60** Shared-bath accommodations, briefly
**61** Opel model

## DOWN

**1** Monopoly subj.
**2** Stand-out performance
**3** Big name in insurance
**4** Court evidence, at times
**5** Domestic chicken breed
**6** In
**7** City near Ben-Gurion airport
**8** Perseveres
**9** Father-and-daughter actors
**10** Possible result of a gunshot
**11** Fool in "Pagliacci"
**12** Bitter-___
**13** Unpleasant
**16** Acupuncture alternative
**20** Nordic
**23** Exactly
**24** Rock type
**25** 2000 musical that won four Tonys
**26** One who asks a lot?
**30** Modern dwellers in ancient Numidia
**31** Zoom
**32** Foreign address
**33** Diurnally
**35** On both sides of
**37** Invasive Japanese import
**40** Oxcart driver's shout
**43** Honors for top scorers?
**44** Leaping desert rodent
**45** Italian apology
**46** Rhône-___ (French region)
**47** 1970s Big Apple mayor
**48** Keebler's chief elf
**51** Acct. numbers
**52** "A Book of Nonsense" author, 1846
**53** First name in humor
**55** Prefix with tour

*by Karen M. Tracey*

# 134

**ACROSS**

**1** 911 pest, e.g.
**12** V.P. between Wallace and Barkley
**15** D. H. Lawrence novel made into a 1969 film
**16** Time for Tours tourists?
**17** Many a first course
**18** Dull finish?
**19** Hit with a heavy blow
**20** Had sum problems
**22** 30-day winter month
**25** Flip
**26** 1999 Clorox acquisition
**29** "A penny saved is a penny earned," e.g.
**31** Fed. accident investigator
**32** Makes a big hit
**34** Home of the Museum of International Folk Art
**36** Quinn who played Annie in film
**37** Land at a Spanish airport?
**38** Be down, apparently
**40** Clown
**41** Idaho motto starter
**42** Least likely to crack
**44** Parisian possessive
**45** Ones with shovellike forefeet
**47** What a virtuous woman is worth more than, according to Proverbs 31:10
**49** Aromatic herbal quaff
**51** ___ Dove (the constellation Columba)
**55** Follow closely (along)
**56** Restaurant parties, often
**59** Archaic ending
**60** Fruit with a pit, to a Brit
**61** Got into the swing, say
**62** Clandestine classroom communicators

**DOWN**

**1** 100-lb. units
**2** Study, e.g.
**3** Childish retort
**4** Flight destinations
**5** Desk features
**6** Enemy of the Moors, with "the"
**7** True, at times: Abbr.
**8** Cud chewers
**9** Alluring adolescents
**10** NASA spacewalks
**11** "Yet do thy cheeks look ___ Titan's face": Shak.
**12** Track edges
**13** Unpressured
**14** Comforters on kids' beds
**21** "The Count of Monte Cristo" hero
**23** "Uncle Vanya" wife and others
**24** What directors sit on: Abbr.
**26** Play halters
**27** Any one of Handel's Op. 2 pieces
**28** Longtime flame?
**30** Mashed potato alternative
**33** Sri Lanka exports
**35** They're hooked up to some TV's
**39** Be more than reluctant to
**40** American Heart Mo.
**43** Shade
**46** French city that shares its name with a car
**48** Bars that gradually get smaller
**50** It can stop the show
**52** Exactly, after "to"
**53** Catch, in a way
**54** Bygone grp. of 15
**57** "To Helen" writer's inits.
**58** Salt std., e.g.

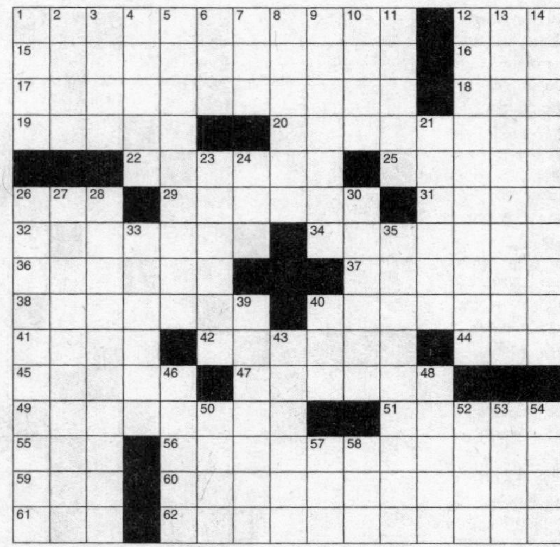

*by Myles Callum*

## ACROSS

**1** Thrill
**9** Recording studio sound shields
**14** Cause of some tan lines
**16** Avoid extinction, say
**17** Hero/giant created by Rabelais
**18** Shiftless sort
**19** Merkel of moviedom
**20** Wrinkle-resistant fabric
**22** ___ sequence
**23** Foul
**26** Some pinball targets
**27** Mature tadpole, of a sort
**28** Sugarhouse stuff
**30** Dot follower, often
**31** Selective service registrant
**32** National champions in 2002, 2004 and 2005
**35** Grandson of Noah
**36** Suffered defeat
**38** Way up or way down
**39** Menacing
**40** Eco-friendly commuters, for short
**41** Operatic tenor Vickers
**42** Smokestack output
**43** Maria's love in the 1996 Tony-winning play "Master Class"
**44** Olympic blade
**46** Owner of the Flickr Web site
**50** "AC360°" channel
**51** Marshall Plan signer
**53** TV tuner input option: Abbr.
**54** Its logo features a globe on a table
**56** Language group including Hebrew
**59** Stretches
**60** Snowy locale of song
**61** Pole position?
**62** Navigation figure

## DOWN

**1** Plinking weapon
**2** Jungle obstacle
**3** Five-sided pods
**4** Disguise part
**5** Actress Ortiz of "Ugly Betty"
**6** Make tired
**7** Rosa damascena product
**8** Words of consolation
**9** Results of bull markets
**10** Eyebrow-raising
**11** Quarter image
**12** Debate format
**13** Game with 40 pieces per side
**15** Kraft offering in a can
**21** Go (for)
**24** Braking maneuvers for skaters
**25** Lies along the waterfront?
**29** Tin contents
**31** First name in homemaking hints
**32** Pianist leader of the Philly Pops
**33** Took evening courses?
**34** Trattoria offering
**35** Poorly organized
**36** Arcade star of the '80s
**37** Woman at a reunión
**41** Rattle
**44** Drug store?
**45** Joe ___, ex-Royals third baseman known as the Joker
**47** One-stanza poem
**48** Exposed
**49** Common daisy
**52** Creator of 1867's "Grand Caricaturama"
**55** Had an uneventful day
**57** Soirée invitee
**58** "___ even!"

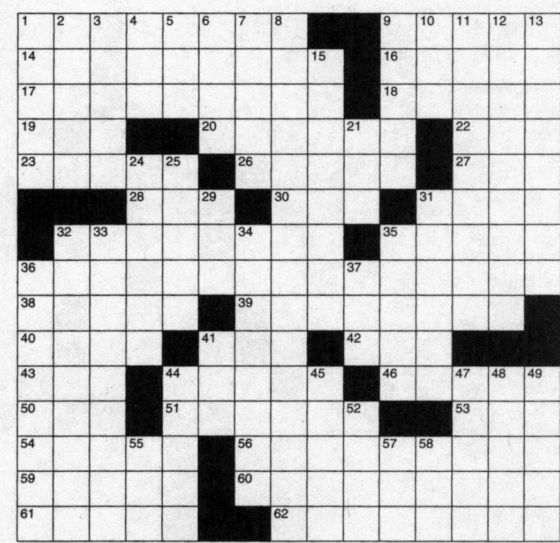

*by Todd McClary*

# 136

## ACROSS

**1** Conductor of many TV experiments
**9** Many people get 100 on it
**15** Words of solace
**16** Like some palms
**17** Hunter of fish
**18** Get intense
**19** Scottish: Mac:: Arabic: ___
**20** Where Charles de Gaulle was born
**22** Goo
**23** Advent number
**25** Like some old lamps
**27** "Frank TV" airer
**28** Home of minor-league baseball's Aeros
**30** They don't respond favorably
**31** Obstinate type
**32** Children
**33** Snack for a dragonfly
**34** Miffed, after "in"
**35** Many servers
**37** Bite
**39** Things associated with pits and spits, briefly
**42** "Let ___"
**44** Haven
**48** Unhappy face
**49** U.S.-born Jordanian queen
**50** Direct
**51** Small note
**52** Ventura County's most populous city
**54** Second biggest city in Russia's Orenburg region
**55** The Guinness book once dubbed her "television's most frequent clapper"
**57** Mount Saint ___ (Alaskan/Canadian peak)
**59** The Engineers of N.Y.'s Liberty League
**60** Completely
**62** "Nothing to get upset about"
**64** Periodicals with unturnable pages
**65** 1966 Pulitzer-winning poet Richard
**66** Touched the least
**67** Heartbeat halves

## DOWN

**1** High point of the O.T.
**2** Cousins of oribis and dik-diks
**3** Stockbreeding devices
**4** Cause of an explosion
**5** Antithesis of apathy
**6** Hospital procedure, for short
**7** Drifter
**8** Refuse to let go of
**9** Book end?
**10** Big telecom company
**11** Pond denizen
**12** Fall for something hook, line and sinker
**13** Err
**14** Ready to be put to bed
**21** Title woman of song who "lives in a dream"
**24** New York congresswoman Slaughter
**26** What a colon may mean
**29** Home of Creighton U.
**31** Oahu "thank you"
**36** Coquette
**38** Melodramatic outburst
**39** They may have just one or two stars
**40** Ore galore
**41** San ___ (Western pen)
**43** Players with saving accounts?
**45** Fantastic
**46** Motivate
**47** Columbus discovery of 1493
**52** She won the 1970 National Book Award for Fiction
**53** About 5.5 million Europeans
**56** Survey choice, at times
**58** Stripe
**61** Right turn from Nord
**63** P

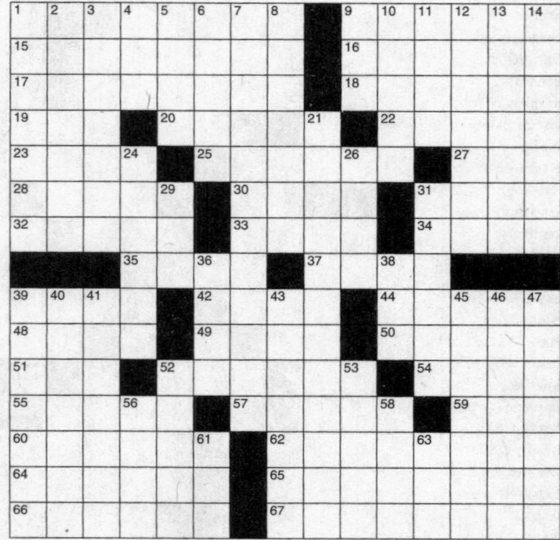

*by Barry C. Silk*

★★★

## ACROSS

**1** Prussia annexed it in 1802
**6** Means of execution for favored criminals in antiquity
**9** Guru
**14** Beak
**16** It may come in waves
**17** Condition
**18** Fore's opposite
**19** Senatorial support
**20** It comes between Shaban and Shawwal
**22** Bad thing to break
**23** Member of the first family
**25** Dwellers along a tributary of the Little Colorado River
**26** One of a pair of fictional roommates
**27** No-votes?
**30** Promised one
**33** Some crystal
**35** Spaced
**36** Brand with a three-leaf logo
**37** Like most recorded music nowadays
**39** Like a Romeo's adventures
**40** Lose credibility
**42** State reps., of sorts
**43** Sending out signals?
**44** Many a blog post
**48** It contains a dash
**49** Left Bank frequenter
**51** West Bank grp.
**52** Flip-flop
**54** It tells you how much you've 56-Across
**56** See 54-Across
**57** Common addition to a tank
**58** Possible reaction to dander
**59** ___ Robbins, co-lyricist of the #1 "Rocky" theme song "Gonna Fly Now"
**60** Smidge

## DOWN

**1** Annual sports awards since 1993
**2** Cliffside detritus
**3** Piglet
**4** Posted item: Abbr.
**5** Dark picture
**6** Reading from a surveyor's compass
**7** Title role in a Joe Orton play
**8** Undecided
**9** Name on a shoe
**10** Trading specialist, briefly
**11** Setting of Fellini's "La Dolce Vita"
**12** Creator of Mr. Fielding and Prof. Godbole
**13** It doesn't include the packaging: Abbr.
**15** She opined "Macho does not prove mucho"
**21** Ride for 007
**24** Rages
**26** Support
**28** That's life
**29** Structural support
**30** Day or night lead-in
**31** Tough to crack
**32** State flower of Nevada
**34** Not just think
**38** Perennial herb with florets sometimes called "ham and eggs"
**39** Co-star of "Friends" and "Friends with Money"
**41** Dan ___, 1948 Best Actor nominee for "When My Baby Smiles at Me"
**42** Legend, e.g.
**45** Probably will, after "is"
**46** D-backs, e.g.
**47** Numbers place
**49** Word on a monument
**50** Rescue team, briefly
**53** Automobile pioneer, initially
**55** Reaction upon seeing something squeak by?

by Karen M. Tracey

# 138

## ACROSS

**1** One looking for a kiss
**11** Heap of hay
**15** Stabilized
**16** Knowing firsthand
**17** Setting for a 1979 horror film
**18** Often winded part
**19** Rips
**20** Stack buildup
**21** Tied up in knots
**22** Spring's opposite
**24** Nation once called Île de France
**26** Spot for a rock band's logo
**28** Year in the reign of Macbeth, in Scottish history
**29** [I told you so!]
**31** Not touching
**33** Blow apart
**35** Thins out
**36** "Voilà!"
**38** "Luck and Pluck" author
**39** Military asst.
**40** Nixed
**42** O, in Morse code
**44** Element of Times Square
**47** ___ Hunt, Tom Cruise's character in "Mission: Impossible" films
**48** Double-bonded compound
**50** Latin 101 verb
**52** P. Diddy's first name
**53** Chocolate source
**55** Crew members
**56** Sibyl's forte
**57** At leisure
**58** One of the 1960s Rams' Fearsome Foursome

## DOWN

**1** Big to-do
**2** Provide with new staff
**3** Like Dolly or her clones
**4** Has some luck fishing
**5** Practice
**6** Amps up
**7** They're seldom taken literally
**8** Parts of some portfolios, informally
**9** Man-made
**10** French quarter?
**11** Transfix
**12** Like a rock
**13** Chiromancer client, e.g.
**14** Under-the-table action
**21** Voice of Buzz Lightyear, in "Toy Story"
**23** Rooter
**25** Indonesian capital
**27** First rendering, say
**29** More than mist up
**30** Tea drinker of fiction
**32** Certain bazaar merchant
**33** Like
**34** Part of Western Sahara
**37** Plate appearances
**41** Cull
**43** Étoile's element
**45** Gulf state resident
**46** "Eraserhead" star Jack
**49** Like cobwebs
**51** Team follower?
**53** Some chest-pounding, for short
**54** Metal mold, as from a blast furnace

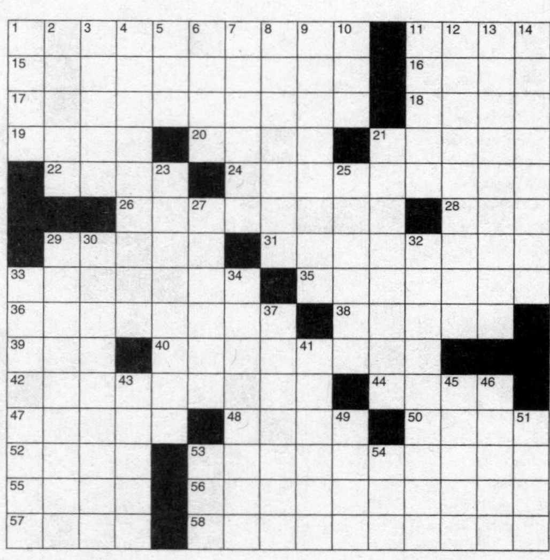

*by Mark Diehl*

## ACROSS

**1** Pacer pacer?
**10** It began with the slogan "It's time to get connected"
**15** Like some college appointments
**16** Old Olds
**17** Park it
**18** Frankincense or myrrh
**19** "Breakfast at Tiffany's" actor
**20** One in a line of 36
**22** Winston Smith's greatest fear, in "1984"
**23** Recording artist?
**25** Something from one's bag of tricks
**26** Uris hero
**27** ___ Island, birthplace and longtime home of Cornelius Vanderbilt
**28** 45-Across and others: Abbr.
**29** Reed ___, Mr. Fantastic of Marvel Comics
**31** Part of a U.S. embassy address
**33** Drift Prairie sharers
**34** See 46-Across
**38** Serve without consequence
**39** Protection for someone on the run?
**40** Grayish
**43** Western terminus of the Northern Pacific Railroad
**45** Arizona pol Jon
**46** With 34-Across, protests peacefully, in a way
**47** City of 2½ million at the mouth of the Yodo River
**48** Small two- master
**49** With 58-Across, violinists' productions
**51** "The View from Castle Rock" author
**52** Mail
**53** James Birdseye ___, Union general in the Civil War
**56** Vampire hunter's aid
**57** Columbus's flagship?
**58** See 49-Across
**59** Fancy entrees?

## DOWN

**1** Patron of pregnant women
**2** Mint preserves?
**3** Like corn dogs
**4** Rigatoni, e.g.
**5** Prefix in many juice names
**6** ___ Tres Marías (Mexican islands)
**7** U.K. honour
**8** Some reds
**9** Compound used to stabilize perfumes
**10** Accent, e.g.
**11** Company retirement asset?
**12** Spoon, say
**13** Lion and unicorn wearer
**14** Corn dog alternatives
**21** Spiritedly, on scores
**23** "Silver Spoons" family name
**24** Minor amounts
**27** Stuff
**30** "Yikes!"
**32** P, in a phonetic alphabet
**34** Relenting assent
**35** Hope can always be found here
**36** Used lofty words?
**37** Hoisted quaffs
**39** Greta of "The Player"
**40** Consternated
**41** Attain on the wing
**42** Jerry who wrote "Hello, Dolly!"
**44** "Pebble in the Sky" author
**48** Mongolian dwellings
**50** Groundbreaking discoveries?
**51** Costa ___
**54** Doozy
**55** "Happy Days" event

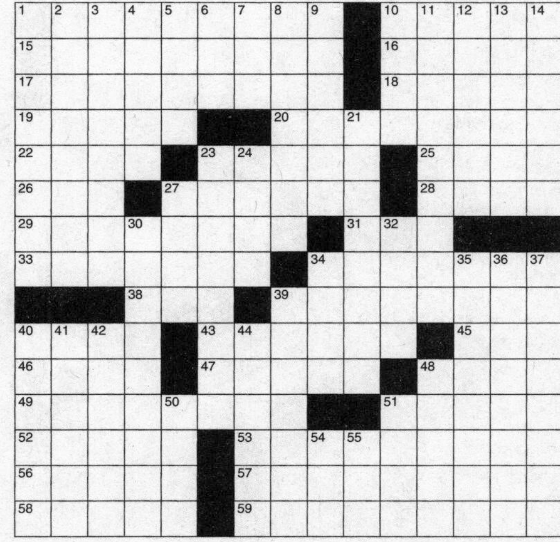

*by Byron Walden*

## 140

**ACROSS**

**1** Oil-based paste mentioned in the lyrics to "Lucy in the Sky with Diamonds"
**11** Script meaning "God is great" appears on its flag
**15** Get inspired
**16** Do or die
**17** Late news?
**18** Thanksgiving dishes
**19** Thanksgiving dishes
**20** Buildings often have them
**22** Delivery possibility
**23** "___ say, Rise up and walk?": Luke 5:23
**24** Headmaster of literature
**26** G.P.S. abbr.
**27** "Tais-___!" (French "Shut up!")
**28** Hiiumaa Island belongs to it
**29** What a priest may prepare for
**31** Minor modification
**32** "Dick Tracy" character Catchem
**35** Lead-in to "I really should get going"
**38** Inits. associated with Hyde
**39** Turkey tender?
**41** Always effective
**42** Small, narrow bays
**45** 1999 best-selling memoir
**46** Fix
**49** Underhanded change, slangily
**51** Bats
**52** Este día
**53** Soldier's 1000
**54** Bars without other people?
**55** It's read virtually, briefly
**57** Existential musing
**59** Burning state
**60** Folkies' do
**61** Pique
**62** Opposite of simplicity

**DOWN**

**1** Moon of Mars
**2** Breaks one's back
**3** Play an ace?
**4** Begin
**5** Unstable leptons
**6** Preceder of 46-, 59- or 61-Across
**7** Motherboard array
**8** Translator's challenge
**9** Required
**10** Conference room props
**11** What often grows attached?
**12** Human as opposed to an animal, notably
**13** Of heraldry
**14** Plays after some snaps, in brief
**21** Parlor pieces
**24** Prodder's cry
**25** Average guy?
**27** Divide, in a way
**30** Raised lines
**32** Cutting-edge cinema?
**33** Her idea may be taking off
**34** Film character who says "I promise teach karate. That my part. You promise learn"
**36** They work by themselves
**37** The Ghostbusters, e.g.
**40** Space neighbor?
**43** Preceder of Jefferson Airplane at Woodstock
**44** Man of Rio
**46** #1 country hit for Dolly Parton
**47** Food for jays
**48** Moves with no urgency
**50** Silk alternative
**51** Star of "Herbie: Fully Loaded," 2005
**54** 0, for 180 degrees
**56** Come by
**58** Sat

*by Natan Last*

★★★

## ACROSS

**1** Bum
**7** Florist's container
**15** Burning
**16** Former senator with the memoir "Power, Pasta and Politics"
**17** Carrier of fatty acids
**19** Part of a deg.
**20** Fix, as sails
**21** Cartoon cat with an exclamation mark in his name
**22** Play makers?
**24** Health claim on a food label
**26** 2004 N.B.A. All-Star Michael
**29** Western deal since 1994: Abbr.
**31** Kind of support
**33** Kia model
**34** ___ Island, discovery of Sunday, April 5, 1722
**36** Rake
**38** Common restaurant offering that was Julia Child's last meal
**41** Silent's opposite
**42** Undisturbed
**43** Teeny "tiny"
**44** Singer of sewing machine fame
**46** Like "m" or "n," to linguists
**49** It's barely noticeable
**51** Knighted English composer
**53** Auctioned property, maybe
**54** Crucial
**56** Oil, e.g.
**58** Brawl
**59** Name associated with spirits
**63** Anodyne
**64** Ace, say
**65** Cirque du Soleil troupe, e.g.
**66** "Ratatouille" rat and namesakes

## DOWN

**1** 1970s–'80s prime-time soap star
**2** Symphony inspired by Napoleon
**3** Unenthusiastic response to an offer
**4** Songwriter Washington
**5** Elevation: Abbr.
**6** One of the Barrymores
**7** 1965 hit parodied by the Beatles' "Back in the U.S.S.R."
**8** Sour condiment
**9** Spinning circles?
**10** Not like
**11** Arab commander
**12** Bakery item folded in half
**13** Plains native
**14** "My mama done ___ me"
**18** Start of a cry by Juliet
**23** Exhibited signs of spoilage
**25** Brass guardian of Crete, in myth
**27** Word in many French family mottoes
**28** Hamlet
**30** Computer acronym
**32** "What Is to Be Done?" writer
**35** "___ Dreams," 1986 #1 hit
**37** Cool red giant
**38** Work unit abbr.
**39** Bitterly complain
**40** With emphasis, as text
**45** Mutated gene
**47** Peak
**48** Brings down
**50** Old Finnish coin
**52** Like un millionnaire
**55** Slangy assents
**57** Oil holder
**59** Abbr. in car ads
**60** Setting of many jokes
**61** Accutane target, slangily
**62** ". . . ___ will die"

by Michael Shteyman

# 142

**ACROSS**

**1** Westinghouse/Intel award winner, e.g.
**8** Stateliness
**15** Place for a skating edge
**16** Fox's cousin
**17** Librarian, at times
**18** They come out in the spring
**19** "Notorious" company
**20** Where inside info is revealed?
**22** Where Japanese trade shares: Abbr.
**23** "The King and I" film director
**25** Sluggard
**26** One of the Coreys on "The Two Coreys"
**27** Far from soft
**29** Princeton Review subj.
**30** Seeming
**31** Marveled aloud
**33** "Phooey!"
**34** Sounded like a bufflehead
**37** Discounted
**38** Show to the public
**39** Name in cosmetics since 1931
**40** Luxury Hyundai sedan
**41** Egg head?
**42** Plays a trump card
**46** Insubstantial
**47** Their feet don't walk
**49** It turns up in a field
**50** Records that may be broken
**51** Improvisatory composition
**53** Suffix in linguistics
**54** Seeing the sun rise, say
**56** Ran off, in a way
**58** Home to Hitsville U.S.A.
**59** Satan, with "the"
**60** Ancient Negev dweller
**61** Comeuppance

**DOWN**

**1** Reels
**2** Alert while driving
**3** "No more for me"
**4** One of a jazz duo?
**5** Aptly named Philadelphia indoor soccer team
**6** Some players in penalty boxes
**7** Sick
**8** Losing pitcher in the 1956 World Series perfect game
**9** "___ Nice Clambake" ("Carousel" tune)
**10** Threshold adjoiner
**11** Prefix with cycle
**12** Orange County seat
**13** "Here we go!"
**14** Half Dome's home
**21** Prison part
**24** Checkers' place
**26** Shout to a 25-Across
**28** Cell choice
**30** Land on a peninsula
**32** Daughter of Loki
**33** "___ spiro, spero" (motto of South Carolina)
**34** It's a downer
**35** Open, as a jacket
**36** Not at all excited by
**37** Reached the peak
**39** ___ raison (sensible: Fr.)
**41** An egg develops from it
**43** Biceps, e.g.
**44** Stir up
**45** Dwellers on Lake Vänern
**47** Like many parties: Abbr.
**48** Jobs in technology?
**51** Counselor on "Star Trek: T.N.G."
**52** Onassis and others
**55** Trunk attachment
**57** Root word?

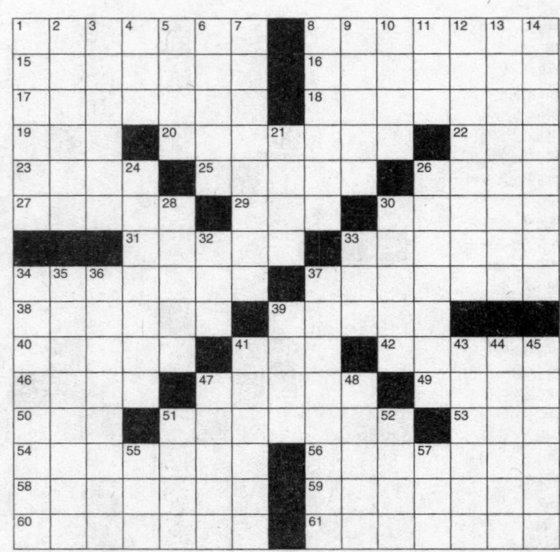

*by Barry C. Silk*

## ACROSS

**1** Place to buy a smoothie
**9** Electrum and others
**15** Author born Howard Allen O'Brien
**16** Little show-off's cry
**17** You shouldn't go through with it
**18** "The Great Escape" setting
**19** Went belly up
**20** Subject of some amateur videos
**22** World Wind developer
**23** Plays for a fool
**24** Crams, maybe
**26** Symptom for a car mechanic
**27** ___ Arcs, French ski resort
**28** Chicago-based magazine with one-million-plus circulation
**30** Trailer
**32** An inset might depict one
**33** 10-time Gold Glove winner of the 1990s and 2000s
**34** Film in which Olga Kurylenko plays the Bond girl
**38** Person of great interest?
**39** Suggest
**40** Girl's name that sounds like two letters of the French alphabet
**41** Resting place
**42** Cooler
**45** Genre of rock's Fall Out Boy
**46** Jazz great seen in the 1967 film "Hotel"
**48** Staff lines?
**49** Cuffs
**51** @ follower, sometimes
**52** Balzac's "___ Bette"
**54** Cat calls
**56** Little music maker
**58** Loosen, as a bra
**59** Trunk item
**60** Candy brand
**61** Beginning of time?

## DOWN

**1** Peanut butter quantity
**2** Fidgetiness
**3** East or West area
**4** Biologists' study
**5** Lake ___, home of the Bass Islands
**6** Cowboys' home, informally
**7** "___ was!" (German exclamation)
**8** Stop daydreaming
**9** Journalist Joseph
**10** Studio part
**11** Advance
**12** Musical that won a 1944 Pulitzer
**13** Singer famous for her wide vocal range
**14** Long Island's ___ Hill National Historic Site
**21** Elflike
**24** Rhapsody, e.g.
**25** Bathtub sound
**28** Treasure
**29** Result of a long exposure, often
**31** Iago, for one
**32** 48-Across starter
**33** "___ happens . . ."
**34** The late Elizabeth Bowes-Lyon, familiarly
**35** Ship with a memorial in New York City's Central Park
**36** Main route?
**37** Ride, maybe
**41** Pal
**42** Italian writer Pavese
**43** Key of Beethoven's "Für Elise"
**44** "You're doing it all wrong!"
**47** Port containers
**48** Frankie of "Malcolm in the Middle"
**50** Symbol of blackness
**52** "The Last of the Mohicans" girl
**53** Wroclaw's river
**55** Try hard to win
**57** Trivial Pursuit goal

*by Will Nediger*

144 

**ACROSS**

**1** Agreed
**6** "Only bad witches are ugly" speaker
**12** Drama queen
**14** They might be weaving
**16** "You ___!"
**17** Asian range, with "the"
**18** Break by hitting
**19** Prompts
**20** Apt to turn out badly
**21** Trademark relatives
**22** Something taken before swinging
**23** Lame excuse
**24** Opening and closing facilitator
**25** Soon enough
**26** Loafer attachment
**28** Common household pest
**33** "Sweet!"
**35** Sports equipment wired for scoring
**37** Bit of regalia
**41** Mixed with something else
**42** Separator of light and dark
**43** "Les Mains Sales" playwright, 1948
**44** Delivered by a third person, perhaps
**45** Snow-covered cover-up
**46** It contains the three-fifths clause
**47** It's typically easier to give than take
**48** Setting one back the most
**49** Comparatively shrewd
**50** Ecclesiastical districts
**51** Trivial stuff

**DOWN**

**1** Founder of the Foundation for Florida's Future
**2** "That wasn't a joke!"
**3** Its capital is Gaborone
**4** Artistic impressions?
**5** Bursts open, as legume seedpods
**6** Set piece?
**7** Ballerina, often
**8** Inactivity
**9** By
**10** Least exciting
**11** Politico Hutchinson and others
**13** Asian royal
**14** Send from abroad
**15** Blouse coverer
**25** Heirs, legally
**27** Licenses
**29** Said while pounding the fist, say
**30** One signing off
**31** It's free of charge
**32** Apartment adjuncts
**34** It needs to be built up when it's bad
**36** Participants in a kids' game
**37** Like some nights and eyes
**38** Deliver by truck
**39** Lucia's brother in "Lucia di Lammermoor"
**40** Opposite of turbulent
**41** Singer of the 1991 hit "Wicked Game"
**44** Refreshing things

*by Joe Krozel*

**ACROSS**

**1** Third Servile War leader
**10** 1970s R&B trio in the Rock and Roll Hall of Fame, with "the"
**15** Driving ambition?
**16** Hero
**17** How a towpath proceeds vis-à-vis a canal
**18** Indication of time passing
**19** Credit card come-on
**20** Gaming debut of 1985, briefly
**21** Certain blowup
**22** Fatty acid, e.g.
**23** Bring up
**25** Jam
**27** Got a 15-Across on
**31** Whence the expression "mum's the word"
**35** "Hogan's Heroes" figure
**36** Med. supplier?
**37** Chocoholic's dessert
**39** Christchurch native
**40** Green patch
**44** 1999 film satirizing media ruthlessness
**45** Half-sister of King Arthur
**46** Assuaging agents
**48** Black tea from India
**53** Ninth, e.g.
**56** Young vixen
**57** First lady of the 1980s
**58** Shower accessory
**59** Courage
**61** Former congresswoman nicknamed Mother Courage
**62** Louis Armstrong's "Weather Bird" collaborator
**63** David who played Bosley on TV's "Charlie's Angels"
**64** Not willful?

**DOWN**

**1** Oscar-nominated western
**2** Golf attire
**3** Not grounded?
**4** Richards with a racket
**5** Den delivery
**6** FAQs bit: Abbr.
**7** Part of a pinball machine
**8** Endure
**9** Stays until the end of
**10** ___ disk (blind spot)
**11** Unite (with)
**12** Early instruction
**13** One placed on a team
**14** Part of 20-Across: Abbr.
**24** Ancestors from long, long ago
**26** Vassals
**28** Creator of Earthquake McGoon and Moonbeam McSwine
**29** "The Silence of the Hams" director Greggio
**30** Become less of a person?
**31** Bank manager?
**32** One of his lost works is "Medea"
**33** Container abbr.
**34** Supply of arrows
**38** Turns up
**41** Soviet premier Kosygin
**42** New Brunswick's river
**43** Skew
**47** Sometime sampler stitching
**49** Municipal dept.
**50** Touristy Tuscany town
**51** Thing worth keeping
**52** Tricky shot
**53** Outfitted
**54** Great Depression figure
**55** Like slime
**60** Cousin of -let

*by Karen M. Tracey*

# 146

**ACROSS**
**1** "Sweet!"
**6** "Dial ___ Murder"
**10** Mini, e.g.
**14** Inherently
**15** Europe's third-largest island
**16** Rover's watcher
**17** Rover's reward
**18** Self-absorbed individual
**20** Start of an Einstein quote that holds true when solving clever crosswords
**22** Doesn't fall short
**23** Chicken choice
**26** R.S.V.P., e.g.: Abbr.
**27** R.S.V.P. facilitator: Abbr.
**29** Thought about Paris?
**30** Gas usage units
**33** North Dakota Fighting ___
**34** Middle of the quote
**37** Guardian spirits
**38** Type A problem
**39** Most ready
**41** Far Eastern capital
**42** Scented, medicinal plant
**45** Originator of the phrase "Pandora's box"
**47** Something often read from
**50** End of the quote
**52** Unpleasant rules to be under
**54** Check box choice
**55** Antony's love
**56** Trix alternative?
**57** Treat unjustly
**58** Unable to part?
**59** Scene of W.W.I fighting
**60** Smart

**DOWN**
**1** Bests
**2** "Hello, Dolly!" composer
**3** Pool openings
**4** County in Kansas, Missouri or Oklahoma
**5** Some unsubstantiated sightings
**6** Knights, e.g.
**7** Order
**8** Hatch in Washington
**9** Get back
**10** Parts of many military uniforms
**11** Relays
**12** Pac-10's Beavers: Abbr.
**13** Zeitung article
**19** Gets down
**21** Some W.W. II internees
**24** Ger.
**25** Questionnaire info
**28** Drain
**30** Strains
**31** Big honor for a college athlete
**32** One might refuse to shake hands
**34** Head of state who resigned in 1974
**35** Making the rounds
**36** Esquire's plea?
**37** M.A. hopeful's hurdle
**40** Writer of "A Man Must Fight," 1932
**42** Burning
**43** Burning
**44** It can be conserved
**46** Some kitchen waste
**48** Performer with a big mouth?
**49** Fourfront?
**51** Bogotá baby
**52** Indexing aid
**53** Singer who appeared with Charlton in "Secret of the Incas"

*by Matt Ginsberg*

# 147

**ACROSS**
**1** Routines
**8** Who said "A man's kiss is his signature"
**15** End up
**16** Source of much talk
**17** Play or movie starring William H. Macy
**18** The Green City in the Sun
**19** Winner of eight consecutive M.V.P. awards
**21** Outsides of sandwiches?
**22** See 49-Down
**23** It was made to fall in 2001
**26** Southwestern resort community
**27** Dr Pepper Museum locale
**28** One of only two women on Rolling Stone's list of "100 Greatest Guitarists of All Time"
**33** Salt baths
**35** Singer with the 2000 #1 hit "Be With You"
**37** Anne Rice's Brat Prince
**38** Active Ecuadorean volcano
**39** Where you might be among Hmong
**40** Swing-set set
**41** Every, to a pharmacist
**42** Roll up
**44** Two-time NOW president Eleanor
**49** Garlicky dish
**51** Bachelorette party attendees
**54** Ago
**55** "Don't you believe it!"
**56** Where Arabic and Tigrinya are spoken
**57** Booty
**58** Reversible silk fabrics

**DOWN`**
**1** 19th-century abolitionist
**2** Shakes in the grass?
**3** Small diamonds, say
**4** Puerile
**5** Ben & Jerry's stock
**6** "___ Pow! Enter the Fist" (2002 spoof film)
**7** Detail in a captain's log
**8** Cousin of a cockroach
**9** Stagger
**10** Ballet dancer Bruhn and others
**11** Gun-shy
**12** Old Far Eastern capital
**13** Person in a tree, briefly
**14** Parisian pronoun
**20** Steaminess
**23** Rage
**24** Scaling tool
**25** Martini's partner
**26** German: Abbr.
**27** Thin fragment
**28** It may still be moving when you eat it
**29** Late late hour
**30** Bad ignition?
**31** Small carps
**32** First three-letter White House monogram
**33** They're made in short order
**34** Runabout or Royale
**36** Success
**40** Kind of roll
**42** Take ___ look at
**43** 1957 hit for the Bobbettes
**44** Drop on a stage
**45** It's north of Libya
**46** Foreign dignitaries
**47** Sneak ___
**48** Former capital of Italy
**49** With 22-Across, prepares to put on the line
**50** Old-time actress Haden
**51** Country stat.
**52** Choice for chat
**53** Sch. whose teams play at the Pete Maravich Assembly Center

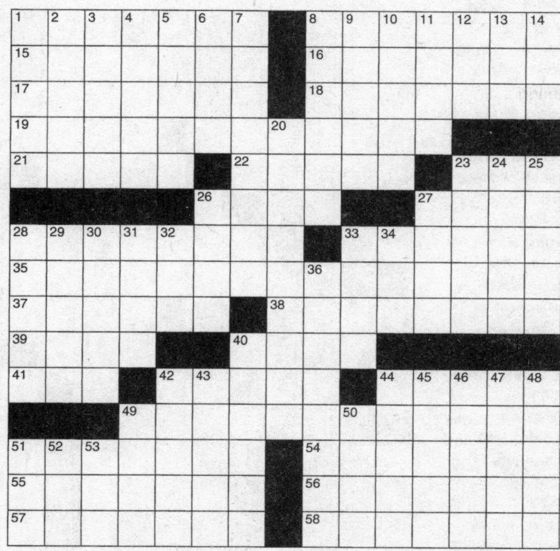

*by Pete Mitchell*

# 148

**ACROSS**

**1** Like Delftware
**8** Robert B. Parker's private eye
**15** Court slam dunk
**17** Seriously deteriorate
**18** Projects
**19** Rubs the wrong way
**20** Gathered dust
**21** Rewards for good dives
**22** It's in the cards
**23** "The Right Stuff" subj.
**24** Stucco ingredients?
**25** Dotty
**26** Precursor of Pascal
**27** Things to rush for: Abbr.
**28** It builds up in bars
**29** Designing women
**30** Use a metal detector, maybe
**32** Bolts
**35** Sound system parts?
**36** Baseball positions: Abbr.
**39** Wolf who wrote "The Beauty Myth"
**40** Life-or-death
**41** Fashion
**42** 2006 Grammy-winning blues singer ___ Thomas
**43** Fall shade
**44** See 46-Across
**45** Sch. figure
**46** With 44-Across, 1940 Laurel and Hardy film
**47** Chemical relative
**48** Writing that mixes reportage and fiction
**51** It's not a total knockout
**52** Writer of pieces in passing?
**53** Wagner opera title role

**DOWN**

**1** Persuasiveness
**2** Glued, in a way
**3** Makes grand adjustments?
**4** Magnetron parts
**5** Some nags
**6** Much may come after it
**7** Quarantining org.
**8** Corporation allocation
**9** Very slow-burning, as a fire
**10** Waiting area announcements, briefly
**11** Big A.T.M. maker
**12** It may be chain-linked
**13** Star QB for the 1980s–'90s Bengals
**14** Many tuxes
**16** Equivocate
**22** Creator of a bathroom cloud
**23** Collective bargaining watchdog org.
**25** Pollster's concern
**26** Points
**28** Important match
**29** Irritated
**30** Southeastern Conference team, for short
**31** Online shopping icon
**32** Fish by thrusting a baited hook into holes
**33** Auto-rotating system
**34** Bookstore section
**36** Philosophical studier of the universe
**37** Cousin of a crocus
**38** DC Comics superhero
**40** Spandex source
**41** Choir robe accessories
**43** Asian nobles
**44** Brew from Tokyo
**46** Star turns
**47** Preface: Abbr.
**49** Turn back
**50** Letter run

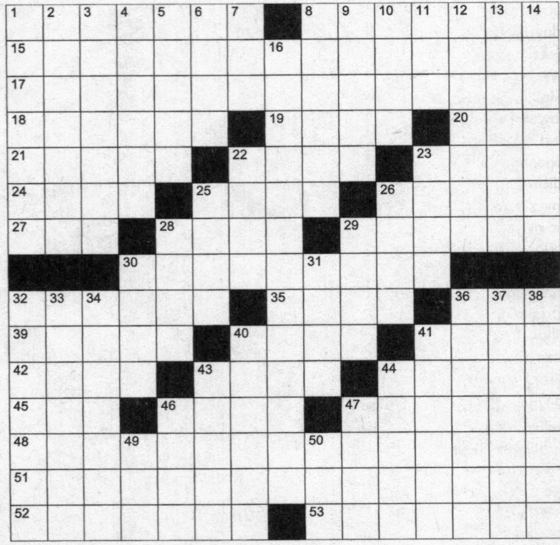

*by Brad Wilber*

## ACROSS

**1** Spread choice
**5** Captor of Han Solo
**10** ___ 1000, annual Mexican off-road race
**14** Opera singer created by Arthur Conan Doyle
**16** Well out of range
**17** Bypass
**18** Twisted
**19** Player of Danni Sullivan on "Scrubs"
**20** Cords, e.g.
**22** They may cover rocks
**24** Princess in Mozart's "Idomeneo"
**25** College Park player, briefly
**28** Park in Ranger Smith's charge
**31** Trucial States, today: Abbr.
**32** Decks
**33** Cone holders
**34** Religious house
**36** They lack details
**37** Exert some pull
**39** Generational indicator in some names
**40** "Ad majorem ___ gloriam" (Jesuit motto)
**41** "Guerrilla Warfare" author, 1961
**43** Jazzman ___ Allison
**44** Many Mexicanas: Abbr.
**45** Not too rocky, say
**47** Paris's House of ___
**49** Brunswick stew ingredient
**53** Bank opening?
**54** Conspirator's cautious conversation starter
**56** French "some," with "les"
**57** Home of Our Lady of the Lake University
**58** Starling, e.g.
**59** He-Man's twin sister
**60** Striplings

## DOWN

**1** Roman's foe of yore
**2** 24-Across's "Zeffiretti lusinghieri," e.g.
**3** Apt. amenity
**4** Bivouac
**5** Writer of the 1918 play "Exiles"
**6** Steers
**7** "Gilmore Girls" co-star Alexis
**8** Big ___
**9** They may be patronized
**10** Like some lava
**11** Buff
**12** Whippersnapper
**13** Refuges
**15** Overseas capital
**21** Obey
**23** Professional shooter, briefly
**25** First name in rap
**26** Faint illumination of the moon's dark side
**27** Hammers away at
**29** Trailing evergreen related to savory
**30** Davis who played Maggie in two "Matrix" movies
**32** "Six Feet Under" star Peter
**35** One may play at a ballpark
**38** Knoxville-based org.
**39** Tony Blair advocated it
**42** Sherlock's French counterpart
**43** Red choice
**46** Joe's love interest in "South Pacific"
**47** Measure of support?
**48** Sweetheart
**50** First name in Hollywood gossip
**51** Vance Air Force Base locale
**52** Bill Clinton and Arnold Schwarzenegger, to the stars?
**55** Sound from a bowl

by Karen M. Tracey

# 150

## ACROSS

**1** It's often laid on someone else
**6** Gun-cleaning aid
**9** Indian honorific
**14** High-altitude home
**15** Motel freebie
**16** Take on
**17** Detours
**20** Its slogan was once "More bounce to the ounce"
**21** Espouse
**22** Panama, e.g.
**23** Site for a bite
**25** Calyx component
**27** Béret holder
**28** Onetime ring master
**29** Some blemishes
**30** Showed again
**31** Court order
**33** Decathlete Johnson
**35** Many thoroughfares . . . or what this puzzle's Across answers consist of?
**39** Illegal match play?
**40** Infernal
**42** Aid in avoiding the draft?
**45** Mass communication?
**47** World Cup cry
**48** In case
**49** Stepping-off point
**50** Sailboat stopper
**51** Stowe girl
**52** Square on un calendario
**53** Cousin of a hyacinth
**55** Possible result of an appeal
**60** Rhone feeder
**61** Rio producer
**62** Crackerjack
**63** Spring Air competitor
**64** Org. that may call for a recall
**65** City in North Rhine-Westphalia

## DOWN

**1** Comic actress ___ Lillie
**2** Start of many rappers' stage names
**3** Dig discovery
**4** Predecessor of Thornburgh in the cabinet
**5** Marshal played by Fonda, Costner and Lancaster
**6** Person who's combining
**7** 10/: Abbr.
**8** Ebbed
**9** Pack
**10** Seller of Squishees on "The Simpsons"
**11** Like Venus vis-à-vis Mercury
**12** Come up with something
**13** Critic and then some
**18** Cranes constructing homes, e.g.
**19** Minister's area: Abbr.
**23** "Le ___" (Jules Massenet opera)
**24** Intoxicating round
**26** Member of the carrot family
**27** Fool's place
**29** 27-Down users, e.g.
**30** ___ post (railing supporter)
**32** Not keep a poker face
**34** One who's more than devoted
**36** Unable to hit pitches?
**37** Total alternative
**38** Determine
**41** CD follower
**42** Some pyrotechnics
**43** Make a shrine to, say
**44** "Yours" alternative
**46** Seat of Shawnee County
**49** Talk trash about
**50** Canine features
**52** High-culture strains
**54** Not so rich, informally
**56** It's somewhere in the neighborhood: Abbr.
**57** Impersonated
**58** Stanzaic salute
**59** Staple of Indian cuisine

by Donald K. Willing

# Answers

# 1

ALEC FARSI AMPS
MAYO OLEOS NOAH
OVEN OLDHICKORY
NEWCALEDONIA
GREETS TROVE
SNARE TSE RADIO
TERN GHETTO DAN
SOMETHING
ASS RAMONE ESAI
PAPUA ENO SMELL
EGYPT DISMAL
BORROWEDTIME
BLUERIBBON ONEG
ROSA PILOT NADA
ABET ASALE ELAL


# 2

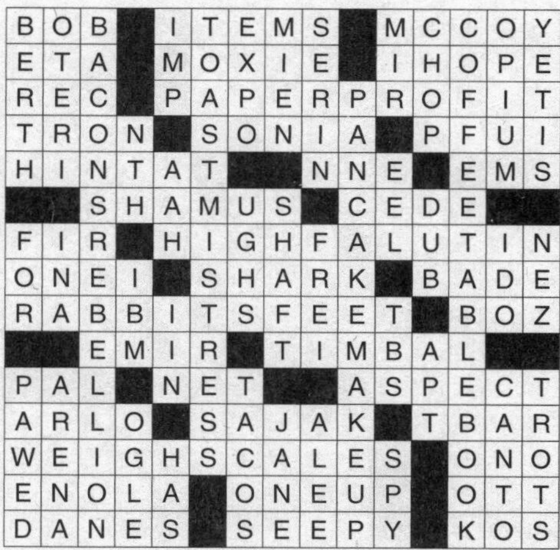

BOB ITEMS MCCOY
ETA MOXIE IHOPE
REC PAPERPROFIT
TRON SONIA PFUI
HINTAT NNE EMS
SHAMUS CEDE
FIR HIGHFALUTIN
ONEI SHARK BADE
RABBITSFEET BOZ
EMIR TIMBAL
PAL NET ASPECT
ARLO SAJAK TBAR
WEIGHSCALES ONO
ENOLA ONEUP OTT
DANES SEEPY KOS

## 3

## 4

## 5

DDE ROGET MUDDY
REX ABASH ANISE
OVERHILLANDDALE
VIRUS TOROS
ETTE GIRLIE POT
SOS ERROL BORE
ALAMO SORREL
LETSMAKEADEAL
SAMIAM INFER
IDBE SEDER KIT
PEA SENSOR PACE
RHONE KAREN
TAKEOVERTHELEAD
SHEET REVEL EGO
PADDY SCAMP MEN

## 6

SCRUB STP REMAP
FLAME TRA IVANA
POMPADOUR BANGS
DDS RIPEST DELT
EDNA NEMESES
ALOT ATTIRED
SAUCY RPMS DWI
INTHECROSSHAIRS
ADS SEEM YEMEN
SODAPOP RENT
APPAREL RELO
MELT DIABLO TAU
BRAID SPITCURLS
LOIRE TET KNIFE
ENTER SDS SOBAD

# 7

ALLIN BEARD CFO
LOOIE ARTOO ARR
TOWNANDGOWN RIB
APPS IGOR ANDES
SHIITE ILIED
STARSANDBARS
SPITS HMO LIP
ION YOKOONO ECO
NOT MAE BERET
GLOOMANDDOOM
TOWIN OREIDA
FADED NOTA TUBA
ABE WEARANDTEAR
ILE ALTAR DELTA
REP YIELD EDSEL


# 8

ERGO DOLED EWOK
DEAN EBOLA MAGE
IMTERRIBLYSORRY
TIEGAMES LATTES
AVAS JIVE
LENTIL WAGE GPS
ATEIN SASH SALT
IHAVENTGOTACLUE
ROLE ARON DRAMA
SSE TMAN WEASEL
BREW RASP
VETOED PASTIMES
ITSWORTHTHERISK
ETAL ORDIE OCTA
WARS PESOS NEAT

## 9

MACAW TWAS GLEE
PLUTO YORE MARX
HAROLDROME AMAT
FROZE ACASE
SONOMA YELL ZEN
PROPANE ATTEST
ELLENGLASGOW
DYAN ONA ECHO
IRVINGBERLIN
ICETEA SAPPORO
NOL STOA SISTER
ALIST BROIL
RACE JACKLONDON
ODIN AMER GUIDE
WATT NADA STEED

## 10

HOPI SCOT FLAW
OVALS EONS ROSA
SINEW PACKLIGHT
END ANISE ONSET
DEADHEAT HUG
BAIT MODELTS
SPELL OARS YOU
PLAYINGWITHFIRE
CAR ILLS AUNTS
ATSTAKE OLEG
ICE OLDFLAME
SPADE KNEED WAX
HOLYSMOKE AMANA
URDU COED YOKEL
LEAP SKYS BEST

# 11

DREAM SLUMS TEX
EARLY HANOI WAR
FIRSTSTRING IRA
YDS HEED GNARLY
JILT POODLES
MUSICALSCORE
ARUBA PBS SOLD
ZIP LORISES RIO
ESSO UAR CRIES
MOTHERTONGUE
STRAUSS EROS
HEARTH EMIT DWI
ENS FITTOBETIED
BOP INSET RAVEL
ANY TEASE SNAKY

# 12

BORAT MOATS CBS
ODORS EATIT OAT
BENCHWARMER UTA
IONS CATCHY
IMSORRY CLICHES
ROTATE CHATUP
KOOKS BLESS OPS
ENOS BLEEP ATOM
DSL CLARK MEARA
PODUNK CORTEZ
MAITRED PAPOOSE
EGGSAC PERP
RAE CHAIRPERSON
IPO KIOSK TOILE
TEN SPLAY SETAT

## 13

## 14

**15**

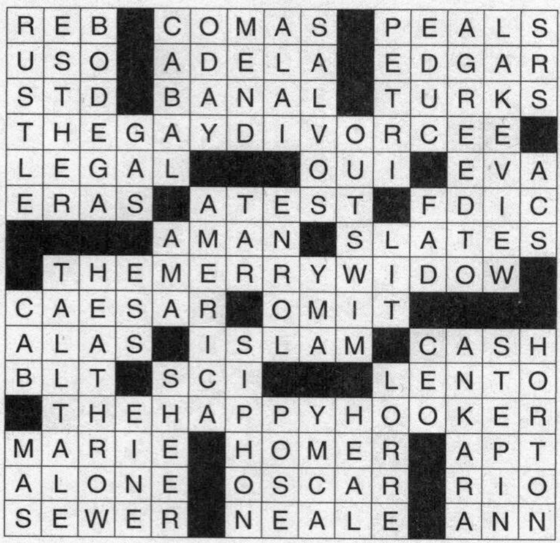

**16**

## 17

## 18

## 19

ROTC TVS ASONE
ITAL HIE CLIMAX
BODYHEAT ATBEST
SHADOW ALVA GAO
ETAL AIRBALL
BTU EVE SASE
LASTLETTER VIDA
EXPOS MER MERRY
WISP CENTERLINE
AMAS ACT SOS
ENDZONE GOOP
NOR UVEA CASTLE
JOANNA DEADHEAD
ONMEDS APR ACNE
YEATS MAS WHEN

## 20

ANTI SHIN AFAR
MEAN STINT LALA
PACKAPUNCH BRIT
SRO LINDA PEEVE
PECKINGORDER
POLICE ONT
OMAN LAPAZ STP
PICKOFTHELITTER
STY CEDAR OLEO
STA AARONS
POCKETCHANGE
UNLIT HESSE ADO
TEAM PUCKEREDUP
TARP ETHEL RANT
SLAY NEED AMES

## 21

## 22

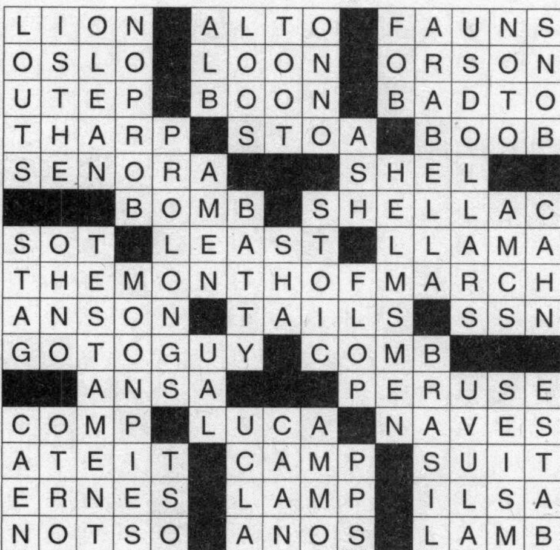

# 23

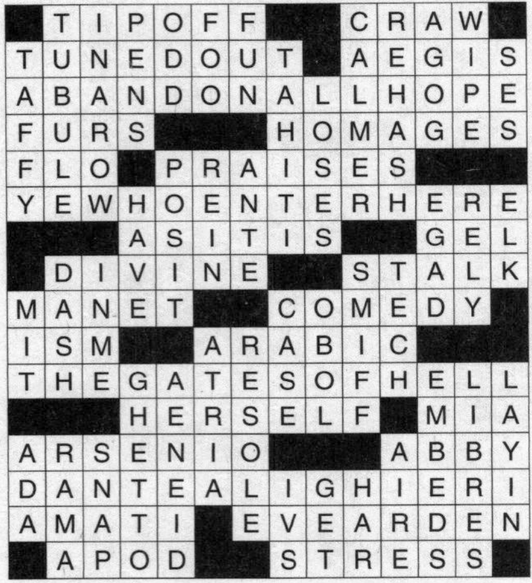

# 24

## 25

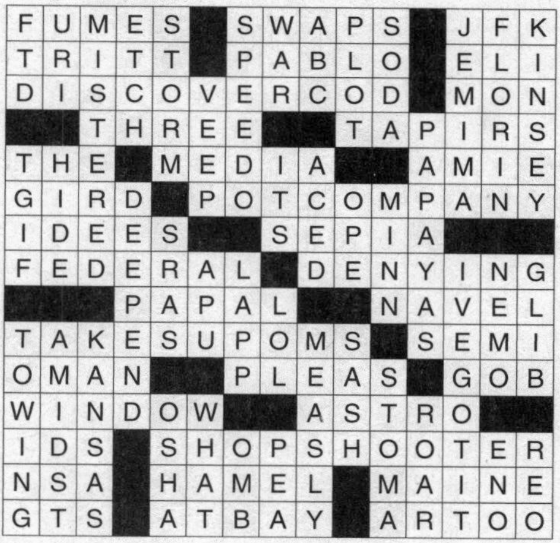

## 26

## 27

## 28

# 29

ALASKA AMSO PTS
TARTUP SAYS ROW
CHARLEMAGNE IMA
ORBIT OHIO SVEN
PUBLICDOMAIN
ROSERED SWAT
ESP DIMS ORECK
CHICKENCHOWMEIN
DACHA GMEN YAO
EATS PEUGEOT
AUGUSTAMAINE
GRID AGAR ATPAR
AGR BRAIDEDMANE
TEL AVID COARSE
ESS TENS UNDEAD

# 30

ATOMIC ACTV CDS
RIVERA BORE HEN
CAINANDABEL ERA
NOR BEDLAMP
OBI PAL STOPIT
HANDLEBAR SOSO
SCREEN MEGS
HEATEDBLANKET
AROD REININ
ICED BALDEAGLE
GAMEON SAE RED
ENABLED INA
TOI SWITCHBLADE
ILL OLGA OCELOT
TAS NYSE ESTATE

# 31

# 32

# 33

AVILA TELE RDAS
VIDAL AXEL AERO
ARESTINGOFFICER
STAT DAIS ELK
TULSAOK EBBETS
BLARED IDYL
HIHO IVY ROPY
ACOUNTPASTDUE
ELEM ESO ASTA
ROSE SONICS
ASHPIT TAKEAIM
ELL PECS ELOI
APEALTOTHECROWD
MATT ADUE SINAI
POSE PSIS TEENS

# 34

GED GABS EDSEL
POUR AURA DOUSE
AIRJORDAN INBED
STA FBI STOP
HEIRTOTHETHRONE
ARLO SONY SEER
ALT NOLO NOR
EREISAWELBA
IQS WAHL SEA
RUTS RUES EZRA
AIREDALETERRIER
AXIS ALB NCO
MONTE AERLINGUS
ARGOT DOVE SESE
COENS ONES ARE

## 35

RAGA VOILA FAZE
ERAS ARRAU ONIT
PERK MEANS RAPS
ONCEUPONATIME
SAIDHI IRS RAI
ESA URIS IMCOLD
WHENIWASABOY
ALSO IKE REEL
BACKINTHEDAY
CRISTO SPEC UTA
SAM SSW IRONON
INYEARSGONEBY
JETE ORION EVAH
AGAR UNCLE LEGO
WORD TSKED SNOW

## 36

MEOWS THEDA SAD
ATRIA DUNES CRY
CHANT SNACKRACE
ATTIC MOSUL
SNORELOSER SPAM
TORY EVIL THETA
SLY IRIS DEEDED
SNIDELINE
ZIPLOC NEAT RPM
ELLEN LOAD AERO
ELIA TURKEYSNUB
AZTEC METED
BABYSNITS AUGER
OWL ASTER STENO
WEE REEDS TESTY

## 37

## 38

## 39

## 40

## 41

## 42

## 43

## 44

## 45

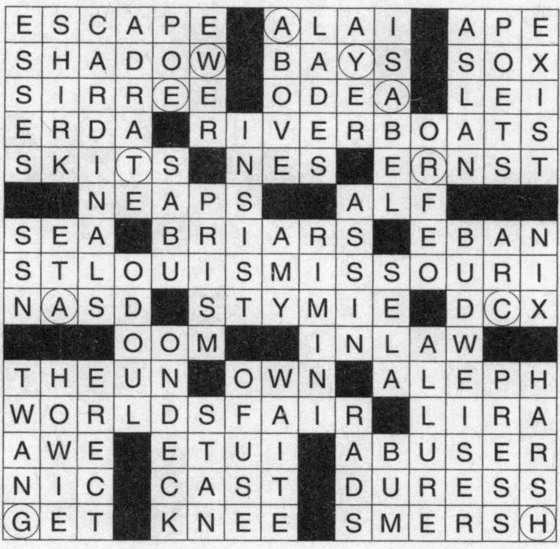

## 46

## 47

EQUI JAMB SLEPT
BURT ALOU PODIA
BIDE CLAM ICING
PUMPKINPIRATE
RAN NIL
GERBIL LIFT SHE
ALOUD WOKE AMID
SUPREMEBERATING
EDEN ELBA GORGE
SER LADY TANKER
PEN SET
ERRATICTHERED
BLOOD SOAR AMOR
ABOVE TATA GIZA
YEMEN OXEN STET


## 48

GESSO SRTA NOHO
ELIAS HOOD INON
NEARTOONESHEART
EMMA NUIT ACDC
SEENBUTNOTHEARD
INS ASS TIS RUE
STEER WON SEXY
NORTHEAST
OTTO OHO PAILS
PRO SUE KIA COL
PARTHENONFRIEZE
LEIA WHOA PRED
EARTHSHATTERING
ALOU TART LANGE
TASS STAY SYKES

## 49

## 50

## 51

## 52

# 53

# 54

## 55

## 56

## 57

## 58

# 59

DINTS FLEX IDED
INOUT GONE DUNE
ACTRESSCARLISLE
LITTLE OMOO TAJ
SALARY EXOTICA
POKERTABLEMONEY
ERE ARE DEN
ASNER NIT DEPOT
REG GUY RNA
GUNSMOKEBARKEEP
IMITATE SHEAFS
APA ITRY OPRAHS
NICKNAMEFORACAT
TRIO GIST OTERI
SENS OTIS SEDER


# 60

ADHOC ADEPT MTV
BRIAR NACRE AGO
LIFTINGTOOL LIL
EPI MESA BEREFT
WEST FACED
TOPHAT MATADORS
OSLO SHOVES NEY
THUMB ANO TOKEN
EEG USHERS DEVO
MAINSTAY OBEYED
NUDES FRED
MOSTEL BOER JOE
AXE PLAYINGCARD
MER OASES EMCEE
ANT TRUST NIKON

## 61

OMEN GLIB SSGTS
FOCI ROLL LEONE
FOOTLOOSE UNION
PAWPAWPRINTS
ESKIMO APOGEE
CANCANOPENER
LEAKS RANGE SPA
ANCY ROLOS SOON
TSK HAUER LOCKE
TOMTOMTURKEY
ELAYNE ENCORE
BONBONVOYAGE
BRIAR INAMERICA
ECOLE ECRU EDNA
DANTE WEEP RONA

## 62

STOWE SEAT BINS
TACOS PILE UNIT
ACERS EGER TCBY
ITAL BEHEMOTH
RIND EDT SHEENA
CORNDOGS ORDER
EEL OAT FUSE
MICHAELPHELPS
HERO MED ELY
SNORE EMBOSSES
TUNDRA EUR TROD
STATEDLY ROLE
ELOI ELAL SODOI
BAUM ISLE SKEET
BYTE NEST TEDDY

**63**

**64**

# 65

BIMBO ALAMO HOW
AMOUR NAVAL ODE
HUMMINGBIRD LID
SAMOA SAM RYES
ELMS ROBOT
ITSREALLYTIMEHE
MRIS TOE BARED
PAR HEADS RAG
EDGAR PAL FORE
LEARNEDTHEWORDS
LIANA LEER
JOAD DYE VESTA
OOH GEORGEBURNS
WPA MANIA IRATE
LSD TREKS TEPEE

# 66

STINGER GRATIN IMAC
AGAME UELE CASH
ILIAD IMAS ERIE
LETITSNOW OUTINGS
LAKE UNPINS
DOG PEASANT
UGLIER ASSORTED
CRETIN RINTINTIN URSA
TENACITY TINSMITH
FTDODGE GAL
DISTINCT OLLA
ROCKS OLDYELLER
AWOL SLID CLARA
KALE IDLE TINYTIM
ENDS TINEAR GEEKS

## 67

## 68

## 69

## 70

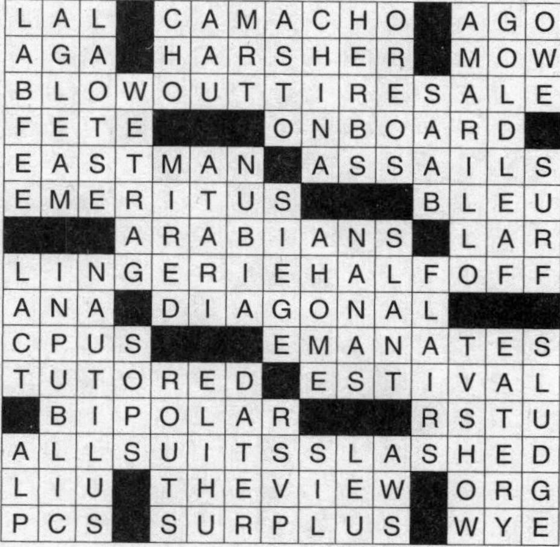

## 71

CHATS PECS OMAR
PUGET AGUA ROBE
REARRANGED IVAN
MIXES DIGEST
INFIDEL DECADES
SILTED CINEMA
ALIEN PAVE IRAE
ALP TORNADO OCS
CAFE POTS POUTS
LAPELS MINNIE
TWOTONE DINEDIN
RAPIER SOFIA
ESPN OUTOFORDER
VIET AFAR NTEST
INDO DOGS SHAPE

## 72

BRILLIG GIMBLE
LINEARA FORAGED
ALCOHOL READING
SEASON GYRE RYE
RECAP CLAD
BANDERSNATCH
OREO IGNORAMUS
DIEOUT MYSORE
YARDSALES ETAL
LEWISCARROLL
CAKE SNIDE
HUH WABE JAILED
ARAPAHO SULTANA
TAKESON ORIENTS
SLITHY BEAMISH

## 73

| S | T | U | D |  | D | A | Z | E | D |  | S | O | P | H |
|---|---|---|---|---|---|---|---|---|---|---|---|---|---|---|
| A | R | N | O |  | E | C | O | N | O |  | A | R | I | A |
| T | A | I | G | A | W | O | O | D | S |  | M | I | L | L |
|  | N | O | I | S | E | R |  |  |  | J | O | N | E | S |
| M | S | N |  | M | Y | N | A | H | L | E | A | G | U | E |
| A | F | R | O | S |  |  | R | E | S | T |  | S | P | Y |
| K | I | E | V |  | S | A | T | I | A | T | E |  |  |  |
| E | X | P | E | R | I | M | E | N | T | A | L | E | R | A |
|  |  |  | R | A | D | A | M | E | S |  | E | M | I | R |
| S | T | S |  | J | E | N | I |  |  | A | M | I | G | A |
| W | I | C | C | A | B | A | S | K | E | T |  | N | H | L |
| O | P | R | A | H |  |  |  | A | V | O | C | E | T |  |
| O | T | I | S |  | W | A | Y | N | E | M | A | N | N | A |
| S | O | B | E |  | A | L | I | G | N |  | I | C | O | N |
| H | E | E | D |  | R | A | N | A | T |  | N | E | W | T |

## 74

| D | A | T | E | D |  | H | A | I | R |  | T | S | P | S |
|---|---|---|---|---|---|---|---|---|---|---|---|---|---|---|
| E | L | A | T | E |  | A | M | M | O |  | R | H | E | E |
| L | A | B | O | R |  | J | O | H | N | N | Y | O | N | X |
| U | R | L |  | E | P | I | S | O | D | E |  | E | D | D |
| X | M | A | R | K | S |  |  |  | O | V | U | L | A | R |
| E | S | S | E |  | Y | A | R | D | S |  | R | A | N | I |
|  |  |  | M | A | C | R | A | E |  | A | B | C | T | V |
| L | I | L |  | T | H | E | S | P | O | T |  | E | S | E |
| O | B | A | M | A |  | A | T | O | N | E | S |  |  |  |
| O | E | D | S |  | O | R | A | T | E |  | O | M | O | O |
| K | E | Y | S | I | N |  |  |  | P | U | T | O | N | X |
| A | N | G |  | S | T | R | E | A | M | S |  | Z | E | E |
| T | H | A | T | H | I | T | S | X |  | R | E | A | D | Y |
| M | A | G | I |  | M | E | T | E |  | D | I | R | G | E |
| E | D | A | M |  | E | S | A | S |  | A | N | T | E | S |

## 75

DODOS MST DEBUG
ERECT ISA ERASE
EACHANSWERHASAN
ORNOT KEY AGE
JAMESII WADDLES
ESP WORRY
SWOOP ZENMASTER
TASSO ODD TOOTH
SNEAKINTO ENTRY
GECKO HEM
VALERIE APPEASE
ERE BED TOAST
NUMBEROFLETTERS
UBOAT UTA HENNA
SANDS TDS SEDAN

## 76

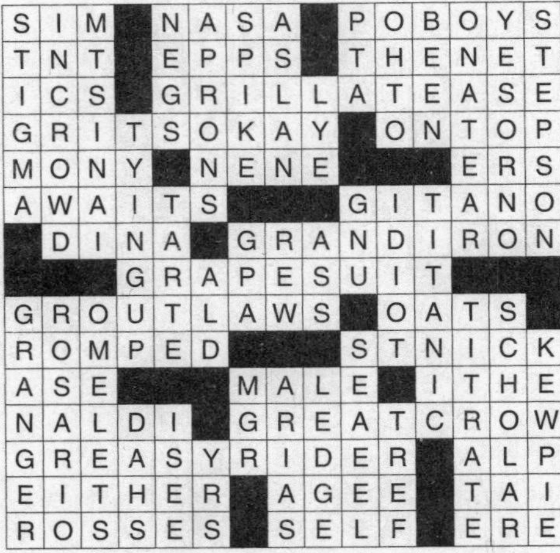
SIM NASA POBOYS
TNT EPPS THENET
ICS GRILLATEASE
GRITSOKAY ONTOP
MONY NENE ERS
AWAITS GITANO
DINA GRANDIRON
GRAPESUIT
GROUTLAWS OATS
ROMPED STNICK
ASE MALE ITHE
NALDI GREATCROW
GREASYRIDER ALP
EITHER AGEE TAI
ROSSES SELF ERE

## 77

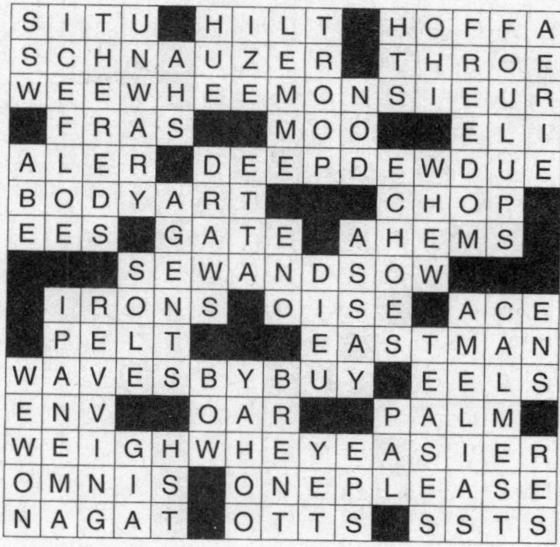

## 78

## 79

## 80

# 81

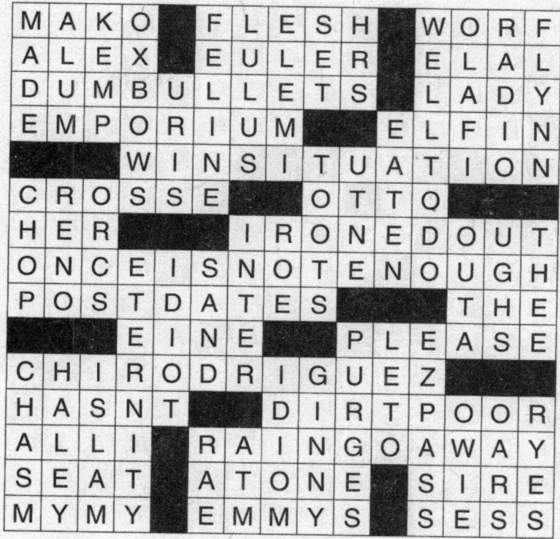
MAKO FLESH WORF
ALEX EULER ELAL
DUMBULLETS LADY
EMPORIUM ELFIN
WINSITUATION
CROSSE OTTO
HER IRONEDOUT
ONCEISNOTENOUGH
POSTDATES THE
EINE PLEASE
CHIRODRIGUEZ
HASNT DIRTPOOR
ALLI RAINGOAWAY
SEAT ATONE SIRE
MYMY EMMYS SESS

# 82

WORSHIP TAMALES
BROCADE EMINENT
CROONER CANTATA
TOOMUCHHEAVEN
MUFTI OIL INT
OTO FIFE MOTTO
WEREWOLF AUSTEN
RAREEARTH
STMARK EPITAPHS
ARISE SPED HAI
CAN MAO SCAMP
HIGHWAYTOHELL
ENLARGE RADIATE
TEENIER CHANNEL
SEDATES ANNEXES

# 83

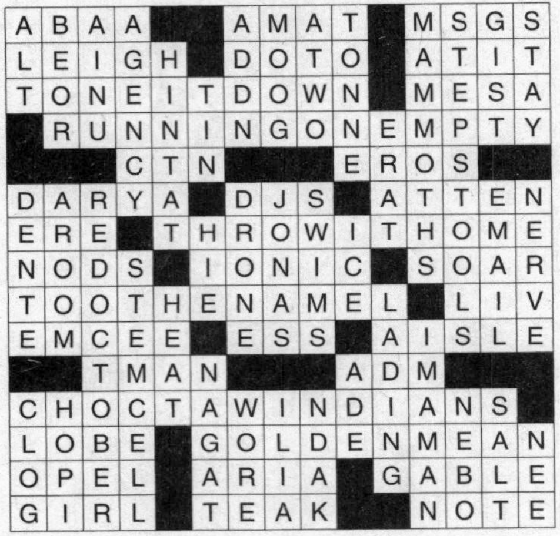

ABAA AMAT MSGS
LEIGH DOTO ATIT
TONEITDOWN MESA
RUNNINGONEMPTY
CTN EROS
DARYA DJS ATTEN
ERE THROWITHOME
NODS IONIC SOAR
TOOTHENAMEL LIV
EMCEE ESS AISLE
TMAN ADM
CHOCTAWINDIANS
LOBE GOLDENMEAN
OPEL ARIA GABLE
GIRL TEAK NOTE


# 84

THOR JOEY SCALD
SINE ARLO EULER
KEEP CUMULATIVE
LEAK RIC MEA
EMIGRATE SOMBER
MENSCLUB LAI
ETE SNO ESKERS
NORSE ANG TENET
DOSING IOS TSU
TSO COMPLAIN
ROTUND SPOILING
ICH ABA LEAL
PROGRESSED NIKE
EERIE HERE ONIT
RANTS YEAR SGTS

## 85

## 86

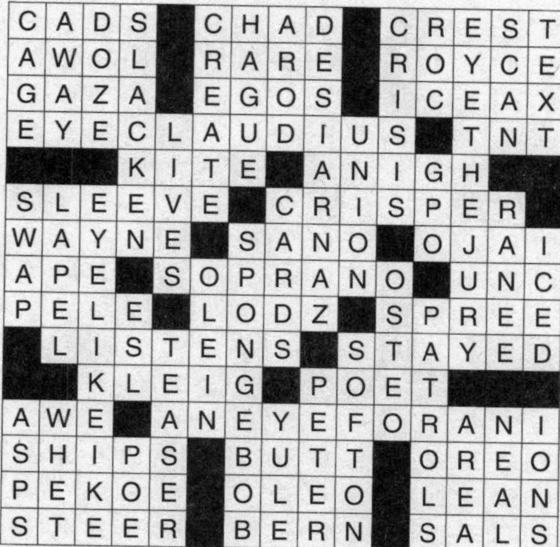

87

88

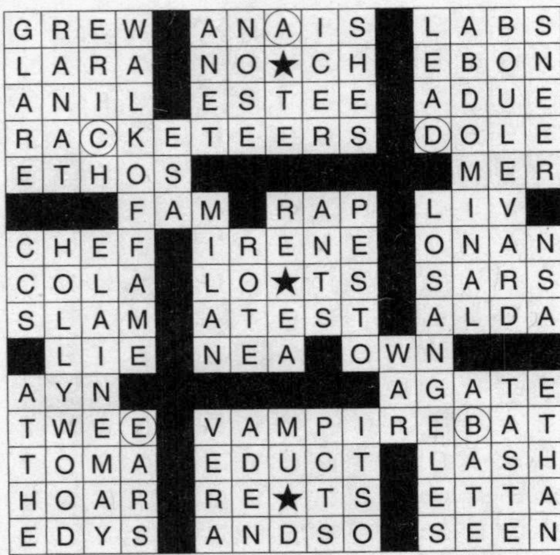

## 89

DEBRA FARSI OAF
AREED ICEIN DRJ
WINDOWSHADE ETO
GQTYPE ELEVATOR
ETDS BEGOOD
LAX ESQ RARE
ILIVE USER NOSE
ATNO LAPPS DAWN
REGT OTRA DARIN
IPOS INN STE
SLOVAK ROAM
SINEWAVE ALCOVE
TEC STOCKMARKET
ABU AMTOO BAIRN
RYE TEENS SEEYA

## 90

PUTT RIP POLISH
ESAI IDA OPENTO
RECEIPTS STEFAN
GREASE ILENE
TOGAE GETSCARDS
ALUMNUS HEA SST
CAREER HEEL
ONUS STIRS ABBE
LUIS ARTERY
SAC ALE SWATTER
PULLSAGUN IRATE
UBOAT SPARTA
RUSHIN SKETCHES
GRETNA EEG TIVO
ENSIGN TDS SPED

## 91

## 92

## 93

ENJOY HADABLAST
DOONE URALRIVER
EPEES HOTPOTATO
REPAIR NEHI SHY
ALDER DALE
FUL ODES BEGINS
ONOR SCAREDYCAT
OHOH OUGHT PESO
TAKESXRAYS TSAR
STATEN SMOG CLE
TRAC EULER
SHE ATAD PINATA
CONSPIRED TUPAC
ARGUEOVER CREPT
MARESNEST HERES

## 94

SHORELEAVE ELIA
HULADANCER RADS
INDIANCORN NCOS
ETAS KERSEE RUE
SEGEL NOSEJOBS
TREASON TRUSTS
STROHS OSSIE
THAT ONEUP TETE
HELIX ONFOOT
EMINEM IDAHOAN
PACKRATS FERMI
ATA SKATED SAPS
PINY ENUMERATES
ETTA MINICAMERA
REEK EASTOFEDEN

## 95

## 96

## 97

JASMINETEA SGTS
SQUAREDEAL WAWA
BUCKROGERS AMOR
AIRE NASL STEIG
CLERK ROYAL BRA
HASSLE FMRADIOS
ARAFAT URNS
CABANAS SOANDSO
ADIA SITSIN
DEBRIEFS SUGARS
ILL DRIED TOLET
LAIRS CLII ULNA
LICE MAINSTREAM
ADAM TROGLODYTE
CELS SETSEYESON

## 98

REEKOF DESC PRO
ILLINI OLIO AEC
TASTINGMENU REA
ELEC ANIMALPELT
ASLAN IDENT
SCARECROW ASTOR
UAE PULSES THRU
STRETTI LASSOED
AHOT SELLTO OED
NOMAD REPUTEDLY
DETER TARSI
SETSFOOTIN SIVA
ORE COMEDIENNES
BAR ONOR NIECES
SYS NEON ENRAPT

## 99

## 100

# 101

EPICFAIL NEEDBE
LAQUINTA ANDREA
ANTENNAS STILES
TEES ALOHASTATE
ITS SPORE SURD
OTTAWA DATE REB
NASDAQ AVONLADY
DRUG YODA
COWSMILK TRIALS
ENA SNOW SUNLIT
NERD BASIN KOA
TITOPUENTE PANG
ROOTON ZEPPELIN
ATREST AMORTIZE
LANDHO ASPERSES


# 102

CUBEFARM AGHAST
ONENIGHT BEAVER
ASHTRAYS BIKINI
SHARERS ROSEATE
TOVAH FATHERED
DEPARTED AMINO
STOOLIES ECU
COG TUTOR SET
ANY DICTATOR
SCREE HIDESOUT
HEATLAMP MOPED
SOTHERE TROTTER
AVIATE MAINLINE
LEONES ACADEMES
ERNEST HOLSTERS

## 103

## 104

## 105

## 106

## 107

## 108

# 109

| B | R | A | S | S | ■ | S | T | S | ■ | ■ | P | L | E | A |
|---|---|---|---|---|---|---|---|---|---|---|---|---|---|---|
| E | A | R | T | H | Q | U | A | K | E | A | L | A | R | M |
| A | R | E | Y | O | U | D | O | I | N | G | O | K | A | Y |
| K | E | A | ■ | P | E | A | S | ■ | C | A | D | E | T | S |
| ■ | ■ | ■ | O | W | E | N | ■ | Y | A | Z | ■ | ■ | ■ | ■ |
| A | V | A | L | O | N | ■ | H | E | R | E | G | O | E | S |
| R | I | S | E | R | ■ | K | I | T | T | ■ | A | C | N | E |
| E | X | P | O | N | E | N | T | I | A | L | R | A | T | E |
| N | E | I | L | ■ | T | A | M | S | ■ | A | I | L | E | Y |
| O | N | C | E | M | O | R | E | ■ | A | N | S | A | R | A |
| ■ | ■ | ■ | ■ | U | N | S | ■ | R | U | T | H | ■ | ■ | ■ |
| M | T | F | U | J | I | ■ | S | O | R | E | ■ | H | A | I |
| C | I | A | H | E | A | D | Q | U | A | R | T | E | R | S |
| A | T | T | O | R | N | E | Y | G | E | N | E | R | A | L |
| N | O | S | H | ■ | ■ | O | D | E | ■ | S | A | B | L | E |

# 110

| R | U | S | S | I | A | N | L | A | N | G | U | A | G | E |
|---|---|---|---|---|---|---|---|---|---|---|---|---|---|---|
| I | N | T | E | R | L | E | A | G | U | E | P | L | A | Y |
| A | S | A | N | A | L | T | E | R | N | A | T | I | V | E |
| T | H | R | O | N | E | S | ■ | E | N | R | I | C | O | S |
| A | U | E | R | ■ | R | A | G | E | S | ■ | M | A | T | H |
| S | T | R | A | G | G | L | E | D | ■ | S | E | N | T | A |
| ■ | ■ | ■ | S | L | E | E | T | ■ | V | E | S | T | E | D |
| R | I | C | ■ | U | N | S | A | F | E | R | ■ | E | S | E |
| E | M | O | T | E | S | ■ | T | I | N | T | O | ■ | ■ | ■ |
| P | A | L | O | S | ■ | M | A | R | E | S | N | E | S | T |
| I | G | O | R | ■ | C | E | N | T | R | ■ | E | N | T | O |
| P | I | S | T | O | L | A | ■ | R | A | D | I | O | E | R |
| I | N | S | U | R | A | N | C | E | B | R | O | K | E | R |
| N | E | A | R | E | S | T | R | E | L | A | T | I | V | E |
| G | R | E | E | N | H | O | U | S | E | G | A | S | E | S |

## 111

## 112

## 113

## 114

## 115

ATAVISM ITSOPEN
NOBELPEACEPRIZE
CIAHEADQUARTERS
ELBE WII PEERAT
MENA HAAG
BAKERS WARDANCE
ASONE SERT OHS
STATIONARYORBIT
TIL VARY WAIVE
ENABLERS GENDER
RARE TADS
HEROIC SIN HEED
AMANCALLEDHORSE
PIZZAMARGHERITA
STEELED SIXTEEN

## 116

DISHFITFORAKING
INTERNALREVENUE
ATOMICSUBMARINE
LIMA USES INT
EMPTOR SLEIGH
RESIN DROP LARA
CODEINE SLAM
JAR RUNATAB SSS
ARES ASTORIA
WINK NEAP BLISS
SATIRE PICNIC
APE PINA ONME
INCONSIDERATION
TOALESSEREXTENT
STREETADDRESSES

## 117

## 118

# 119

JULIACHILD SAKS
IRONMAIDEN AMAT
MICRONESIA TERR
ASKOUT SEARLE
ROBOT ANIMA
HESS REMITS CAM
OXLIP ANNIEHALL
THEBEST YOUANDI
TIESAKNOT PRMEN
ALP LAIDON MENE
MAEVE KATEY
ARREST WAFERS
LACS ONECALORIE
ETAT DEADRINGER
SERA STRIKEZONE


# 120

ADOPT WHOCARES
DAVIES HANDMADE
AMENRA AGELIMIT
MEREMORTAL ATO
WEBS ISR BADEN
EDO ISNT SALADS
SNO NOSH ARE
TAKEADEEPBREATH
ABA BARI SOU
NORRIS ISAO KIN
ACENT SGT MALT
CTN MORALFIBER
HONOLULU DENOTE
OPERATES STOUTS
SISSYISH ARTES

## 121

## 122

## 123

## 124

## 125

GINORMOUS EDNAS
ADAPTABLE NOOSE
LOSTSTEAM DOONE
ALAS LANATURNER
NIH NAPPERS
SPOTON STMARK
LEPER BUILTINTO
IDEM DACCA ZORN
PINPRICKS JEWEL
STOCKS FOSSEY
CREASES SAG
CASTASPELL WIMP
CRAIN AXISPOWER
LEMON CAMEOROLE
IRENA EMERGENCY

## 126

SLACKJAWED COED
TABULARASA AXLE
ONEFINEDAY DIAN
ROLFE NEUT EDIT
ALA GLAD ROTINI
GIRL OSIRIS ZEN
ENDUES NEPALESE
TATI TPKE
QUIETING IAMNOW
UND ENDRUN SERE
ASIANS ALGA WBA
SHAH PENT LEWIS
HAMM ANNIHILATE
EDIE CRIMENOVEL
DENT EYEOPENERS

# 127

PATSAJAK STOMPS
AQUACADE AERIES
DUTCHMAN FLAYER
DIE YIN DELMAR
ENES ROSE MAZES
DOSIDO PLIE ADA
BEQUIET SKIN
NOWYOURETALKING
OVAL ACDELCO
REX HIHO IDAHOS
DRWHO INGA LOUT
TOAMAN ANG ETO
HORDES FUJIFILM
INKJET EGOMANIA
DESICA WEBPAGES

# 128

MANMONTHS MADAM
ATEAWAYAT AMEBA
SETSONESOWNPACE
HAWKE ALINED
AMT ANSELADAMS
ATLEAST HIE
PUPPETRY REESE
CROSSED CRAVATS
LAKES ILOVEDIT
ANE COMESIN
BORSTALBOY ATL
FAIRER CAPRA
GOASKYOURMOTHER
NICHE LEMONRIND
PLEAS ESSAYISTS

# 129

| I | T | S | A | S | H | A | M | E |  | T | A | L | K | S |
|---|---|---|---|---|---|---|---|---|---|---|---|---|---|---|
| B | I | K | I | N | I | W | A | X |  | A | L | A | N | A |
| I | N | A | M | O | M | E | N | T |  | C | O | Z | E | N |
| Z | E | L | I | G |  |  | H | A | W | K | E | Y | E | D |
| A | D | D | N |  | S | T | O | N | E | Y |  | B | B | B |
|  |  |  | G | A | L | O | O | T | S |  | J | O | E | L |
| J | U | G |  | M | I | N | D |  |  | G | O | N | N | A |
| A | N | A | T | O | M | Y |  | S | E | A | B | E | D | S |
| M | I | M | E | S |  |  | H | E | L | L |  | S | S | T |
| P | T | E | R |  | A | S | O | C | I | A | L |  |  |  |
| A | P | T |  | O | P | T | S | T | O |  | O | L | E | N |
| C | R | A | B | M | E | A | T |  |  | U | T | E | R | O |
| K | I | B | E | I |  | F | I | R | E | S | T | O | R | M |
| E | C | L | A | T |  | F | L | U | M | M | O | X | E | D |
| D | E | E | M | S |  | S | E | T | S | A | S | I | D | E |

# 130

| E | M | P | T | Y | S | U | I | T |  | A | A | M | C | O |
|---|---|---|---|---|---|---|---|---|---|---|---|---|---|---|
| G | O | T | A | M | A | T | C | H |  | S | P | A | H | N |
| G | U | A | R | A | N | T | E | E |  | I | O | N | I | A |
| S | E | S | S |  | D | E | C | O |  | A | L | B | E | N |
|  |  |  |  | P | E | R | O | N | S |  | O | R | F | E |
| W | A | S | T | E |  | S | L | I | C | E |  | E | W | R |
| O | M | E | R | T | A |  | D | O | R | A | M | A | A | R |
| R | E | N | O | I | R | S |  | N | A | T | A | S | H | A |
| K | N | I | T | T | I | N | G |  | M | E | R | T | O | N |
| S | T | O |  | E | L | I | O | T |  | R | E | S | O | D |
| F | O | R | K |  | S | P | O | R | T | Y |  |  |  |  |
| O | T | H | E | R |  | E | D | I | E |  | S | P | U | D |
| R | H | I | N | E |  | S | O | U | N | D | W | A | V | E |
| M | A | G | N | A |  | A | N | N | O | T | A | T | E | S |
| E | T | H | Y | L |  | T | E | E | N | S | P | E | A | K |

## 131

CLAMBED WWIIACE
RAVIOLI RALSTON
AHEADOF ICELAND
WARTY FAT SATIE
LITA BEETS MICA
ENE SURREAL MAR
RADIATIONLEVELS
TRANSMUTE
HOLDINGPATTERNS
ANO NOTATES COT
NEAP LACED MAMA
DINES SER HADIT
DROPLET IFORONE
YOUTUBE ABYSMAL
ENTOMBS LITHELY


## 132

DUPLICATORS AWE
ONLINEMEDIA PEA
STAGFLATION PET
TENNESSEETITANS
STIR TALIA
STETSONS VARLET
PERE VIEWERS
ADS PEPPERY BET
TONSILS BASE
BLOATS ALOUETTE
RANCH NAPE
AUTHORPUBLISHER
IRA LEAVEITTOME
DIP ENTERTAINED
SEE SESAMESEEDS

## 133

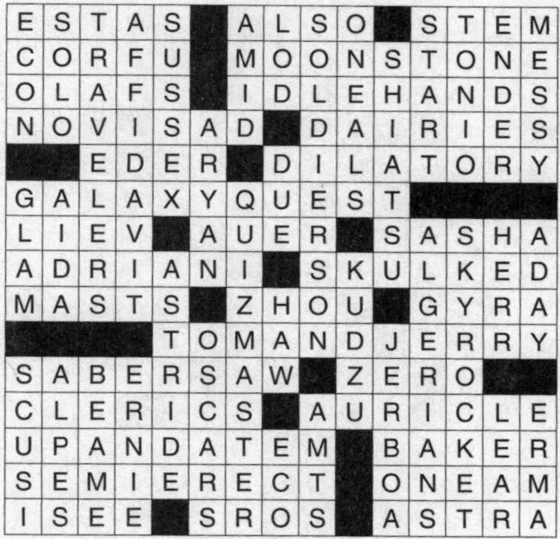

## 134

## 135

## 136

## 137

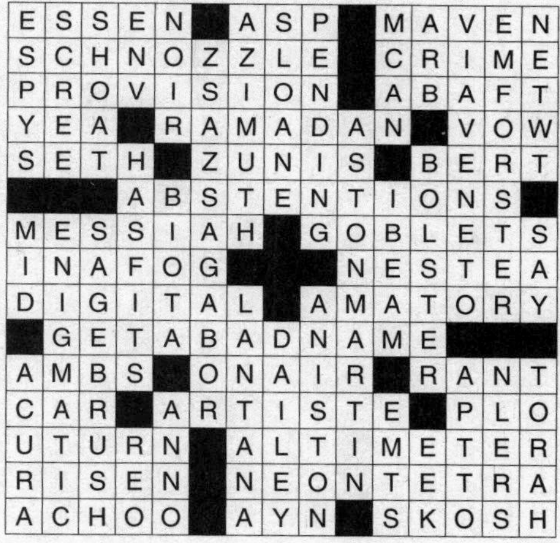

## 138

# 139

SHOTCLOCK MSNBC
TENURABLE ALERO
GRABASEAT RESIN
EBSEN ROCKETTE
RATS STENO PLOY
ARI STATEN SENS
RICHARDS APO
DAKOTAS ONAFAST
LET SKIPARKA
ASHY TACOMA KYL
GOES OSAKA YAWL
HARMONIC MUNRO
ARMOR MCPHERSON
STAKE OHIOSTATE
TONES VIPPASSES

# 140

PLASTICINE IRAQ
HAVEANIDEA VERB
OBITUARIES YAMS
BOATS CODES SON
ORTO DUMBLEDORE
SSE TOI ESTONIA
RITE TWEAK
SAM ITSLATE RLS
LIRAS SURE
ARMLETS TIS JAM
SWITCHEROO LOCO
HOY TENAM SOLOS
EMAG WHYAMIHERE
RAGE HOOTENANNY
SNIT ORNATENESS

# 141

# 142

## 143

## 144

# 145

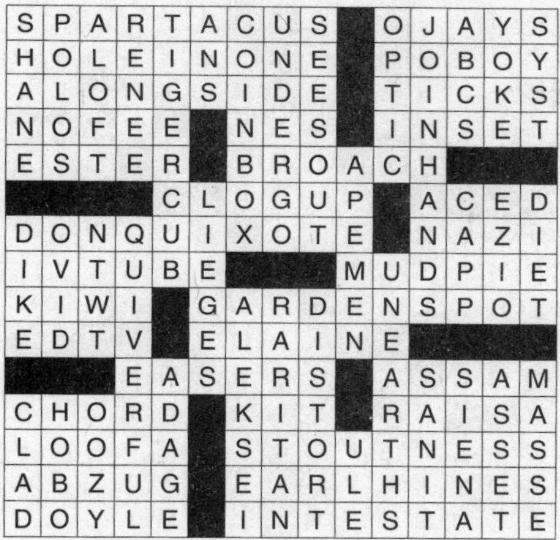

SPARTACUS OJAYS
HOLEINONE POBOY
ALONGSIDE TICKS
NOFEE NES INSET
ESTER BROACH
CLOGUP ACED
DONQUIXOTE NAZI
IVTUBE MUDPIE
KIWI GARDENSPOT
EDTV ELAINE
EASERS ASSAM
CHORD KIT RAISA
LOOFA STOUTNESS
ABZUG EARLHINES
DOYLE INTESTATE


# 146

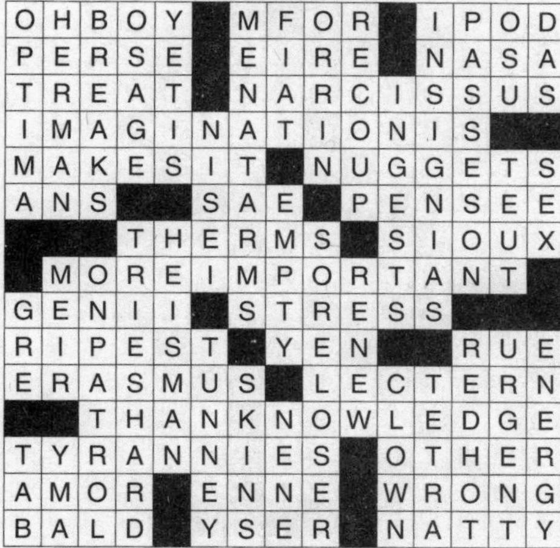

OHBOY MFOR IPOD
PERSE EIRE NASA
TREAT NARCISSUS
IMAGINATIONIS
MAKESIT NUGGETS
ANS SAE PENSEE
THERMS SIOUX
MOREIMPORTANT
GENII STRESS
RIPEST YEN RUE
ERASMUS LECTERN
THANKNOWLEDGE
TYRANNIES OTHER
AMOR ENNE WRONG
BALD YSER NATTY

## 147

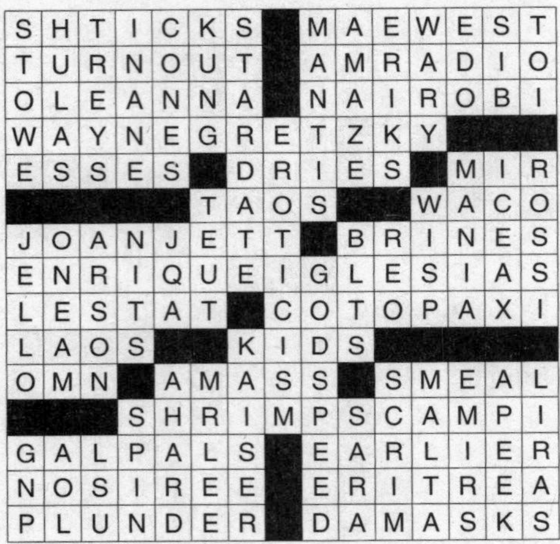

## 148

## 149

## 150